T0284869

Griffith Evans

SCIENTISTS OF WALES

Series Editors
Gareth Ffowc Roberts
Bangor University

John V. Tucker
Swansea University

Iwan Rhys Morus
Aberystwyth University

SCIENTISTS OF WALES

Griffith Evans

1835–1935

VETERINARIAN, PIONEER
PARASITOLOGIST AND
ADVENTURER

GAVIN GATEHOUSE

UNIVERSITY OF WALES PRESS
2024

www.uwp.co.uk

British Library Cataloguing-in-Publication Data
A catalogue record for this book is available from the British Library.

ISBN   978-1-83772-123-8
eISBN   978-1-83772-124-5

The right of Gavin Gatehouse to be identified as author of this work has been asserted in accordance with sections 77, 78 and 79 of the Copyright, Designs and Patents Act 1988.

The University of Wales Press gratefully acknowledges the support of the Books Council of Wales in publishing this title.

THE LEARNED SOCIETY OF WALES
CYMDEITHAS DDYSGEDIG CYMRU

MIX
Paper | Supporting
responsible forestry
FSC® C013604

Typeset by Marie Doherty
Printed by CPI Antony Rowe, Melksham, United Kingdom

For Gail and Liz

'There is also in my nature … the element of continued perseverance – if I have any object in view to attain to – and I take real pleasure in overcoming difficulties. That is my instinct. I am not in any way "brilliant" and never was – but a plodding tortoise that sometimes passed the sleeping hare.'

Griffith Evans in a letter to his wife from
Simla, 11 December 1879

CONTENTS

SERIES EDITORS' FOREWORD

Wales has a long and important history of contributions to scientific and technological discovery and innovation stretching from the Middle Ages to the present day. From medieval scholars to contemporary scientists and engineers, Welsh individuals have been at the forefront of efforts to understand and control the world around us. For much of Welsh history, science has played a key role in Welsh culture: bards drew on scientific ideas in their poetry; renaissance gentlemen devoted themselves to natural history; the leaders of early Welsh Methodism filled their hymns with scientific references. During the nineteenth century, scientific societies flourished and Wales was transformed by engineering and technology. In the twentieth century the work of Welsh scientists continued to influence developments in their fields.

Much of this exciting and vibrant Welsh scientific history has now disappeared from historical memory. The aim of the Scientists of Wales series is to resurrect the role of science and technology in Welsh history. Its volumes trace the careers and achievements of Welsh investigators, setting their work within their cultural contexts. They demonstrate how scientists and engineers have contributed to the making of modern Wales as well as showing the ways in which Wales has played a crucial role in the emergence of modern science and engineering.

RHAGAIR GOLYGYDDION
Y GYFRES

O'r Oesoedd Canol hyd heddiw, mae gan Gymru hanes hir a
phwysig o gyfrannu at ddarganfyddiadau a menter gwyddonol
a thechnolegol. O'r ysgolheigion cynharaf i wyddonwyr a pheirianwyr
cyfoes, mae Cymry wedi bod yn flaenllaw yn yr ymdrech i ddeall a
rheoli'r byd o'n cwmpas. Mae gwyddoniaeth wedi chwarae rôl allweddol
o fewn diwylliant Cymreig am ran helaeth o hanes Cymru: arferai'r
beirdd llys dynnu ar syniadau gwyddonol yn eu barddoniaeth; roedd
gan wŷr y Dadeni ddiddordeb brwd yn y gwyddorau naturiol; ac
roedd emynau arweinwyr cynnar Methodistiaeth Gymreig yn llawn
cyfeiriadau gwyddonol. Blodeuodd cymdeithasau gwyddonol yn ystod y
bedwaredd ganrif ar bymtheg, a thrawsffurfiwyd Cymru gan beirianneg
a thechnoleg. Ac, yn ogystal, bu gwyddonwyr Cymreig yn ddylanwadol
mewn sawl maes gwyddonol a thechnolegol yn yr ugeinfed ganrif.

Mae llawer o'r hanes gwyddonol Cymreig cyffrous yma wedi hen
ddiflannu. Amcan cyfres Gwyddonwyr Cymru yw i danlinellu cyfraniad
gwyddoniaeth a thechnoleg yn hanes Cymru, â'i chyfrolau'n olrhain
gyrfaoedd a champau gwyddonwyr Cymreig gan osod eu gwaith yn ei
gyd-destun diwylliannol. Trwy ddangos sut y cyfrannodd gwyddonwyr
a pheirianwyr at greu'r Gymru fodern, dadlennir hefyd sut y mae Cymru
wedi chwarae rhan hanfodol yn natblygiad gwyddoniaeth a pheirianneg
fodern.

ACKNOWLEDGEMENTS
AND PREFACE

My interest in Griffith Evans was ignited by a talk given by his granddaughter, Jean Ware, many years ago in the Zoology Department of what was then the University College of North Wales. I am most grateful to her for introducing me to this remarkable man. Sadly, Jean died in 2009. Evans's great granddaughter and Jean's niece, Gail Kincaid, has been a close friend of ours since 1972 and she, her brother Tony Craven Walker and sister Debbie Storch have supported and encouraged me throughout the preparation of the book. They have responded unhesitatingly to my many requests for information about the family and for access to family photographs and documents. Their contribution has been invaluable and I am most grateful to them all.

I am grateful to the editor of this series, Gareth Ffowc Roberts, for inviting me to write this biography and he and Llion Wigley of the University of Wales Press have been encouraging and supportive throughout.

The staff of the National Library of Wales, the British Library, the Wellcome Library, the Bangor University and Gwynedd Archives and the Osler Library of the History of Medicine at McGill University, Montreal, have been unfailingly courteous and helpful in response to the many demands I have made on them, both by email and during my visits. My thanks to them all. Lily Szczygiel of the Osler Library deserves special mention for her prompt and efficient responses to my many requests for her assistance.

I would like to thank my cousin Gillie Yanow and her husband Joe for their hospitality during my stay in Montreal. My thanks also to Bruce Bolton who took me on a tour of military sites in Montreal associated with Griffith Evans and the Royal Artillery.

I thank Hywel Thomas for his help with the genealogy of the Evans family and Dr David Roberts for tracing the fate of proposals for a memorial to Griffith Evans in the Minutes of the University's School of Agriculture Committee. Tom Jupp, Robin Davies and Professor Mike Lehane have read all or part of various drafts of the book and their constructive comments and suggestions have greatly improved the text. The same is true of Professor Deri Tomos who acted as referee for the University of Wales Press. I am grateful to them all. Any shortcomings or errors are, of course, my own.

Finally, I would like to thank my wife, Liz, for her encouragement and support and for tolerating my neglect of her and of my domestic responsibilities during the long periods spent closeted in my study or away from home.

The book was, for the most part, written during the Covid-19 pandemic of 2020–2 during which access to libraries and archives, including the National Library of Wales (NLW) whose archives hold the Griffith Evans Papers, was suspended or strictly limited. However, in addition to a limited number of other sources, I was fortunate to have access to the unpublished MA thesis, *The Life and Letters of Griffith Evans 1835–1935*, submitted to the University of Wales by Griffith Evans's granddaughter, Jean Ware (née Jones), in 1966. This was followed by a book, *The Several Lives of a Victorian Vet* by Jean and her husband Hugh Hunt, published in 1976. Jean Ware knew her grandfather (he died when she was eighteen) and her thesis is well referenced to the Griffith Evans Papers with which she was extremely familiar; the book is unfortunately not referenced. When they were first lodged with the NLW, the items in the Griffith Evans Papers archive were catalogued under a now redundant system which was used by Jean Ware in her thesis. They have since been re-catalogued under the current NLW system but no record has been kept of the original item identifiers. The result is that there is, I have been assured by the NLW archivists, now no way of matching the former system to the latter. The Griffith Evans Papers comprise nearly 600 items. Where the current item identifier makes the content clear, I have used the primary sources. Where it does not, I have generally cited secondary sources; although access to the NLW is now unrestricted, to trace the primary sources in all these cases would be impractical within any reasonable timeframe. Since Covid restrictions have been lifted, I have, of course, had full access to all the sources I have needed.

LIST OF ILLUSTRATIONS

ABBREVIATIONS

AVCTA	Arvon and Vale of Conway Temperance Association
CMG	Companion of the Order of St Michael and St George
FRCVS	Fellow of the Royal College of Veterinary Surgeons
FRSE	Fellow of the Royal Society of Edinburgh
LSTM	Liverpool School of Tropical Medicine
MRCVS	Member of the Royal College of Veterinary Surgeons
NWTA	North Wales Temperance Association
RAVC	Royal Army Veterinary Corps
RCVS	Royal College of Veterinary Surgeons

PROLOGUE

Veterinary medicine was a young, rapidly evolving profession in the mid-nineteenth century.[1] The earliest records of the treatment of animals in China in the first and second millennia BC focused on the horse as the animal most useful to man. In seventeenth- and eighteenth-century Britain, treatment of wounds and diseases in horses was in the hands of farriers or self-styled 'horse doctors' with no formal training. Their bizarre remedies were often gruesome and cruel, justifying Robert Burton's epithet for England as 'a Hell for Horses'.[2]

In France in 1762, veterinary medicine was placed on a more rational and scientific footing with the foundation, by Claude Bourgelat, of a veterinary school in Lyon followed, in 1765, by another at Alfort near Paris. These were soon followed by schools in Italy, Germany, Austria, Hungary and Denmark. The more *laissez faire* tradition in Britain, the less consistent demand for military farriers and the relative rarity of epidemic disease in livestock, made for less impetus for a more scientific approach than was felt in continental Europe.

In 1788, a Professor at Alfort, Charles Benoît Vial,[3] arrived in England and published proposals for a veterinary school in London. Receiving little support, he returned to France with his English wife but troubled by the turmoil leading up to the French Revolution, the couple were back in London in February 1789. In October, Vial announced a series of lectures on the 'veterinary art' following this up with the publication, in March 1790, of a pamphlet entitled 'Plan for establishing an Institution to cultivate and teach Veterinary Medicine'.[4]

Later that year, a committee was convened to promote the foundation of a school on the lines of those on the continent. It adopted Vial's plans and established a fund by subscription to provide 'a hospital for disease in horses, cows and sheep and [to promote] the science of Farriery by the regular education in it, on medical and anatomical principles'. The fund attracted influential subscribers setting the scene for the foundation of the Veterinary College, London. Vial was appointed Professor, statutes for its constitution and governance were adopted and the first four pupils were enrolled in November 1791.

The College still had no land or buildings. In September 1791, Vial presented a memorandum on the selection of a suitable site which laid down that a 'healthy situation' was required away from 'marshy and low Ground [which] exhales unwholesome and putrid vapours'. He also suggested that the site should be at a distance from London so 'the resident pupils being distant from places of dissipation, it will protect their morals and they will employ their time in study'.

After an approach by agents for Lord Camden, leases were taken on a house close to St Pancras Church and a substantial area of ground nearby. The site was in fact low lying and bounded by the Fleet River which was subject to flash flooding so its choice has remained a mystery. Nevertheless, the decision was taken, Vial moved into the house and plans were drawn up for buildings. With funds from subscriptions and low-interest loans, work to provide stabling, lecture and dissecting rooms and enclosing walls commenced in the summer of 1792.

Vial's course was intended to last three years, the first year covering 'anatomy, physiology, conformation and external diseases', the second 'surgery, *materia medica*, pharmacy and botany' and the third 'pathology, epizootic diseases, treatment and disease prevention, hospital practice and shoeing'. This curriculum was clearly beyond the capacity of one man and the appointment of a second Professor was discussed. However, in July 1793 before any appointment could be made, Vial died. The blow was followed by a short interregnum when the premises were left in the hands of the pupils until in 1794, Edward Coleman was confirmed as sole Professor and Principal of the College, a post he held until his death in 1839.

Coleman's long tenure as Principal was controversial.[5] Trained as a surgeon, he had no previous veterinary knowledge but there is little doubt of his commitment and determination to learn and contemporary reports suggest that he was a talented lecturer. Despite the failure to appoint a second Professor and chronic underfunding throughout his tenure, with the support of assistants the annual intake of pupils rose from fourteen to about fifty. Coleman was criticised for reducing the length of the course from the three years stipulated by Vial. However, students on the four-year course at Alfort usually qualified after one or two years while most students in London were examined after nine to eighteenth months. Longer courses were introduced progressively from 1844, culminating in the present five-year course in 1932. For all his limitations, Coleman successfully guided the College through its early years leaving, on his death, a serviceable institution.

The College made little progress under Coleman's successor, William Sewell, although it was awarded its Royal Charter by Queen Victoria in 1844. It was not until the appointment, in June 1853, of Charles Spooner that the College again moved forward.

When Griffith Evans arrived to take his place on a December morning in 1853, he will have passed through the pedestrian entrance, a wicket gate in large doors under an archway. In 1846, the College buildings were described as low, plain and bleak and it is unlikely that the layout was much changed from that described by James Beart Simmonds, Spooner's successor as Principal, when he was a student in 1828–9:

> The institution was built in quadrangle form, having now in the centre a large lawn or grass plot surrounded by posts and chains, and ... between the Buildings and these a broad pathway had been left, partly paved with stones ... used chiefly for testing the freedom from lameness of Horses.

Making up the sides of the quadrangle, Simmonds described lines of stables and loose boxes, the forge and a covered way used for exercising infirmary patients. Beyond were three paddocks, 'infirmary sheds', loose boxes for horses with infectious diseases and a dissecting room. Across the Fleet Ditch was the Principal's House, the house leased for Vial in 1791.

1

FAMILY, CHILDHOOD AND EDUCATION

Griffith Evans's forebears had farmed outside Tywyn (Towyn),[1] Meirionnydd, Wales, since his great, great grandfather, Ifan ap Siencyn, arrived in the town in about 1730.[2] Ap Siencyn leased a group of small farms nearby to form a single unit of 319 acres. He then bought and fenced an additional twenty-three acres, the only land owned by the family, on which he built a substantial farmhouse, Tŷ Mawr (The Big House). He and three generations of his descendants were to farm these acres for almost a century.

In his mid-forties, ap Siencyn was hard-working and in his prime and the farm prospered. He married Catherine Owen of Mallwyd,[3]

Figure 1 Tywyn and its surroundings in 1834.
(Llyfrgell Genedlaethol Cymru – The National Library of Wales)

daughter of Jane Vaughan of the Vaughans of Hengwrt who claimed descent from the Princes of Powys. Although his descendants were only tenant farmers, the family was accepted locally as gentry on the strength of his wife's ancestry.

Ap Siencyn was a poet and is still remembered locally as the bard of Tŷ Mawr. His grandson, Griffith Evan (he had dropped the 'ap' and adopted the patronymic Evan) married Mary Jones of Llanbrynmair, Montgomeryshire (Sir Drefaldwyn). She was a woman of strong character who had been influenced by a Nonconformist preacher, John Roberts, and her agreement to marry Griffith was conditional on being allowed to found the first Congregationalist chapel in Tywyn. The couple had two daughters and three sons.

The eldest son, Griffith, emigrated to Australia where his three children died without issue. The second, Evan, remained at Tŷ Mawr with his father on whose death in 1831, the sturdy, forthright, thirty-year-old, took over as master. The third son, John,[4] married Elizabeth Pugh of Abermâd near Aberystwyth. In this generation, the family patronymic 'Evan' became 'Evans'.

Mary Evan raised her five children as Nonconformists although they went to Tywyn church with their father. Evan was sent to Shrewsbury Grammar School with a view to enter the Established Church although, even if his elder brother had taken over the farm, it seems unlikely that Evan would have followed that path. His mother's influence had sown the seeds of independent religious thinking and an incident at Tŷ Mawr when he was fifteen soured his view of the Church. When his maternal grandfather, John Jones, was taken ill on a visit to Tŷ Mawr, the vicar of Tywyn, summoned to administer the last sacraments, arrived too drunk to do so and Mary had to watch her father die unshriven. Evan did not have his children baptised.

In 1830, Evan married another Mary Jones from Tyddyn-y-Berllan near Tywyn.[5] With her chestnut hair, she was 'an emotional and possessive woman and a zealous housewife' who spoke only Welsh and read only the Welsh Bible. Mary was to spend the first fifteen years of her marriage sharing the farmhouse with her formidable mother-in-law with whom, perhaps surprisingly given the personalities of the two women, she seems to have developed a rapport.

Evan and Mary Evans's first child, a daughter, Eliza, was born on 1 July 1831, nine months after their marriage. She was followed by a second daughter, Maria, born on 17 January 1833 and finally by a son, Griffith, born at one o'clock on the morning of 7 August 1835.

Griffith was born into a family of strongminded women with his grandmother, his mother and his two older sisters, Eliza and Maria, in the house and his father's two married sisters, Ann and Mary, nearby. With the maidservants, the ménage was overwhelmingly female and the only boy could do no wrong. Maria was a gentle child who seems rarely to have transgressed but her older sister, Eliza, had inherited her grandmother's strong character and was often chastised for defying her mother.

Religion played a central part in the lives of the three children. There was family worship in the kitchen every morning and evening attended by the servants and twelve farm labourers. Evan would read the Bible and the senior servants led the prayers; this was a time when servants would only have attended Sunday school where they learned, more or less, to read the Bible. On Sundays, the children were sent to Sunday school at the chapel founded by their grandmother whose dissenting, Congregationalist views dominated their religious experience. However, although Evan attended chapel and even sometimes took Sunday school there, he remained a member of the Anglican Church. His natural tolerance was consolidated in discussions with his friend, Captain Edward Scott, landlord of Tŷ Mawr, who lived in Kent but spent much of his time at his nearby country house, Bodtalog. As well as fostering Evan's open-minded attitude to religion, Scott encouraged him in his independent, rationalist approach to political and social affairs and he became an enthusiastic follower of William Cobbett.[6]

Although his mother regarded alcoholic drink as irredeemably sinful, Evan enjoyed the occasional glass of port at the Raven Hotel in Tywyn. He was 'temperance' rather than an abstainer and was responsible for founding the Towyn Temperance Society, the first in the area. When Griffith was two, Evan became a teetotaller and chairman of the Tywyn lodge of the Independent Order of Rechabites, a Christian movement promoting total abstinence. It was a portent of Griffith's life-long commitment to abstinence that, still in his homespun smock which boys wore till they were five or six, he was invited to become 'honorary treasurer' of the children's section of the Tywyn Rechabites, collecting farthing and penny subscriptions to pass on to the adult Treasurer.

Young Griffith idolised his father. The two were drawn together in the predominately female household and Evan came to treat the child as a companion as much as a son. Griffith in turn was drawn to his father for company; there were few children to play with near Tŷ Mawr and he was a serious child who preferred the company of adults. Although he loved his mother, Griffith's childhood memories were dominated by his relationship with Evan. An early memory was of asking his father at bedtime: 'Fy Nhad, gwelwch sut mae dim llai o oleu yn fy nghanwyll i ar ôl roi goleu i'ch canwyll chwi' (Father, look how my candle does not dim when it has given light to your candle) when Evan had re-lit his candle from Griffith's. Evan smiled without replying but over the

FIGURE 2 Evan Evans in the 1860s. (Llyfrgell Genedlaethol Cymru – The National Library of Wales)

years, Griffith was struck by the implication that he might convey good things to others at no loss to himself.

Evan took every opportunity to guard his children against the superstition and mysticism that then prevailed in rural communities. When the Vicar of Tywyn died, their nursemaid told them that an effigy in St Cadfan's Church had wept. Griffith mentioned this to Evan who took the children to the church on a wet day to show them moisture in the effigy's eye, the result of condensation in the humid weather, telling them: 'You must always look for a rational reason for silly stories.'

In later life, Griffith identified the event in his early childhood that he claimed had made the deepest impression on him. He was taken to the Congregational chapel by his father to hear an old farm servant, Sion Humphreys, preach.

> He took as his text Exodus XX, verse 8, 'Remember the Sabbath Day, to keep it holy' and he explained with great emotion how 'y meistr annwyl acw' [the dear master there] had sinned, and put his soul in danger of eternal damnation.

Evan's sin had been to bring in the harvest on a Sunday when bad weather threatened the crop. On the walk home from chapel,

> it made a never-to-be-forgotten impression on my mind to hear [Father] say: 'Rhydd i bawb ei farn, ac i bob barn ei llafar' [To everyone his freedom of opinion, and to every opinion a voice]. All my life this has coloured my attitude to those with whom I have disagreed. It has made me ... more tolerant ... while I have been even more outspoken arguing with them. Looking back over the way I have come, I think of this early impression, of the importance of freedom of opinion and speech, as the key to my relations with people.

As soon as he was old enough, Evan would take Griffith around the farm on horseback and to market in Machynlleth in the gig. He talked to the boy as an equal, discussing his concerns, telling him stories, composing poetry and above all instilling in him a love of the landscape.

Although Griffith learned a great deal from his father on these outings which he remembered with pleasure all his life, the time came for a more structured education. Evan had employed a well-educated young Welsh woman, Miss Mair Pugh, as governess to his daughters and she was now asked to turn her attention to Griffith. As well as giving him a sound grounding in English, Welsh and arithmetic, Miss Pugh was responsible for his robust and legible handwriting which remained largely unchanged into extreme old age.

The death of his grandmother, Mary, in 1846 marked the end of an era for Griffith and his sisters. Evan and their mother decided to send their daughters, then fifteen and thirteen, to a boarding establishment in Hereford. In the same year, a British School[7] was opened in the hamlet of Bryncrug (Bryn Crug) three miles from Tŷ Mawr and Griffith, aged eleven, was enrolled in its first intake. Miss Pugh, now redundant, left to take up a new post. Her departure distressed Griffith more than the death of his grandmother; she had provided the children with a sound basic education and he was never to forget the debt he owed her for his love of reading, his ability to express himself clearly in English and his thorough grounding in elementary mathematics.

Griffith respected the strong-willed Eliza but he loved the gentle, kind Maria. He later described his feelings at the breakup of the household: 'I felt lonely after my sisters had gone ... I missed Maria very much and was delighted when her letters began to arrive'. A crude portrait painted in this, his eleventh, year portrayed him as 'a fair-haired boy with a Byronic open collar. His nose is big, his mouth small. His best features are his determined chin and his honest, searching blue eyes, having in them a suggestion of loneliness.'[8]

Griffith was not used to the rough and tumble of play with boys of his own age and he appears to have remained aloof from the other pupils at Bryncrug. His status as the son of the doyen of the local farming community must have set him apart and his partial deafness – a consequence of childhood scarlet fever and the cause of his life-long habit of cupping his hand round his better ear – cannot have helped. Furthermore, Griffith's relationship with Evan had accustomed him to being treated as an equal by adults. His relative maturity and command of English soon led the schoolmaster to recruit him as a monitor to teach the language to the younger children. Aware of his son's distance from his contemporaries, his father gave the boy two Welsh terriers to which Griffith became devoted.

Evan was determined to instil in his son a sense of responsibility. He had opened an account at the new bank in Machynlleth and handing Griffith a purse of gold coins, told the boy to ride there and deposit the money in the bank, a journey of fifteen miles each way. As he was saddling up, Robin the farm foreman warned Griffith to keep a careful eye out for robbers and told him a cautionary tale from the story of Twm Siôn Cati.[9] The ride was uneventful.

Griffith was 13 in 1848, a year of great political ferment in Europe. He claimed later in life that his conversations with Evan had 'fixed [him] in rationalism and democracy' which later led him to become a follower of the radical Liberal thinkers, Richard Cobden and John Bright.[10] The following year, he was sent to a school in Pennal, a village ten miles from Tywyn. This was too far to travel every day so he lodged in the village, returning home every weekend. We know little of his experiences there but his most vivid memories were of the Hungry Forties[11] when he was often brought face-to-face with starvation and destitution on his rides to and from school and around Tŷ Mawr.

Griffith left school in the summer of his seventeenth year to work on the farm. It had been assumed that he would succeed Evan as master of Tŷ Mawr but he soon became impatient to experience more of what life and the world had to offer. Aware of his son's growing restlessness, Evan sent him to Shrewsbury for a few days to buy supplies. On this, his second excursion across the border into England – he had ridden there some years earlier with his father – he took a train which he found 'less exciting than a good gallop' but he was excited by the sensation of being in a foreign country. Far from curbing his longing for wider horizons, the trip excited it and he began to think seriously about an alternative career.

Griffith had been befriended by John Pughe, the young doctor in Aberdovey (Aberdyfi), who told him of his training at St Thomas's Hospital in London and his life as a country physician.[12] The boy began to spend more and more time with Pughe sometimes helping him by delivering medicines to remote farms. Evan must have realised that he was contemplating a career in medicine long before Griffith told him and raised no objection when asked if he might apprentice himself informally to the doctor. Pughe inspired in him an interest in anatomy and physiology and encouraged him to carry out his own experiments: allowed to study the heart of a dying donkey, Griffith stunned the animal and dissected it to observe the beating heart, shooting it before it regained consciousness. This early experiment may have kindled his lifelong interest in blood and its circulation.

Before Griffith could begin applying to medical school, Evan's circumstances changed dramatically for the worse. His brother, John, lived on his wife's estate at Abermâd near Aberystwyth where he had embarked on a series of over-ambitious improvements. Evan had unwisely agreed to guarantee loans John had raised to finance his plans but he had overreached himself and was now bankrupt. His creditors lost no time in calling in the guarantees and Evan was ruined. His resources were insufficient to cover the debt and he was forced to ask Griffith and his sisters to surrender the inheritance of £3,000 they had each received from their grandmother.

> Father looked white and ill. He explained to me and my sisters …
> what had happened. He asked us … to sign away the inheritance
> we had each received from Nain [Grandmother] Evans … [but]
> this was not enough. Father had to sustain a debt for the rest of
> his life.

It was a bitter blow. There was now no hope of realising his ambition to buy the leased land to secure Tŷ Mawr for the future. Nor was there any prospect of supporting Griffith through a medical degree. With his chosen career now out of reach, Griffith turned to John Pughe who suggested he enrol on the two-year diploma course to study veterinary medicine at the Royal Veterinary College in London.

The idea appealed to Griffith. It was now the late autumn of 1853 and Evan agreed to write immediately to the Principal, Professor Spooner, to ask whether he would be best advised to gain practical experience before attending college. The reply came that he should attend college first and that although he had missed the first term of the current course, he would be accepted if he could present himself for registration by a specified date in December. If he missed this deadline which was now only a few days away, he would have to wait until the following year.

Griffith hurried to prepare for his first prolonged absence from Tŷ Mawr and the longest journey of his young life.

> On a bitterly cold December night in 1853, I packed my bags in the little room where I had slept since I was two. I was to ride off with my father before daybreak [to] catch the stagecoach from Machynlleth to Shrewsbury ... When Mother bent over me with a candle at four in the morning, she said that a blizzard was blowing and the snow was already deep.

Father and son rode out of the farmyard and struggled through the snow as day broke and through the morning. They arrived in Machynlleth soaked to the skin and with only minutes to spare before the departure of the Shrewsbury stage.

> As the coach headed eastward, Griffith thought of home and his father.
> The horses moved to a rhythm ... of a verse my father wrote, which has been my favourite quotation all my life ... It was his idea of life and death, and to me, leaving home for the first time to plough my own furrow, it had the ring of truth.

> > Pob un rêd, pawb yn ei rwn – ar risiau
> > Yr oesoedd cyflymwn;
> > I fedi yr ymfudwn,
> > Byd o hau, yw'r bywyd hwn.[13]

> > [Everyone runs, each in his furrow – on the steps
> > Of the ages we speed.
> > To reap, we emigrate.
> > A life for sowing, this life.]

The coach arrived in Shrewsbury just in time to catch the last train to Stafford for a week as the blizzard closed in. A family friend, who was to accompany him to London declined to board the train in the conditions but Griffith was determined. From Stafford, he would have caught the London train to arrive at Euston station late the same evening, no doubt exhausted by his long journey.

2

THE ROYAL VETERINARY COLLEGE AND BRIDGNORTH

Evans must have been awed as he walked through the Great Hall of the newly rebuilt Euston Station and out onto Drummond Street. Swept along by the crowds, he reported only that he was astonished to see so many horses on the crowded streets.

Arrangements had been made for him to be met by the family with whom he was to lodge; confident that he would never have set out in the conditions, they had decided not to meet the train and were surprised when he presented himself at their door. The next morning, he made his way to the Royal Veterinary College in nearby Camden Town.

> [In] the quadrangle, I saw a handsome stallion being walked up and down the flagstones. A friendly student … explained that they were testing for lameness. When I said I had come to register, he told me his name was Meyrick.[1]

Meyrick led the way to the office where Evans registered and was taken to meet the new Principal, Charles Spooner. The formalities complete, his new acquaintance showed him round the college.

The encounter was to lead to a friendship that lasted until James Meyrick's death in 1925 and they were to remain in touch throughout their closely parallel careers. Each was to support and encourage the other through their long lives and after marriage, the families remained close friends. It was a relationship between two very different characters.

Born in London, Meyrick was reticent, sensitive, diplomatic and subtly humorous, attributes Evans decidedly lacked.

The curriculum for the diploma course covered 'the anatomy, physiology and pathology of the horse, ox, sheep, pig and dog and of the domestic animals generally', veterinary medicine and the law relating to the veterinary profession. Practical skills expected of the students included diagnosis and treatment of diseases and injury, dissection and farriery. To cover the scope of this curriculum in two years would have seemed daunting for any new student but Evans had already missed a whole term.

The staff at the time consisted of Spooner, two other Professors, an Assistant Professor and a demonstrator. The chair of cattle pathology was held by James Simmonds and that of Chemistry by William Morton. The Assistant Professor of Anatomy was George Varnell. Although all appeared to be talented lecturers, William Pritchard, who was to succeed Varnell, said of his student days in the later 1850s:

> when we think of the amount of matter … in the … curriculum … one conclusion only can be arrived at – that, however good and great the ability, the energy, the labour, and the desire of these men to fully and completely accomplish the task … it must of necessity have been beyond them.[2]

It soon became apparent that although the curriculum would be covered in outline in lectures, students were expected to acquire the depth of knowledge that would be required of them by independent study. The daily routine allowed time for this: lectures or formal dissection classes took place between 9 a.m. and 4 p.m. but the library and dissecting rooms remained open into the evening for unsupervised study.

Evans knuckled down immediately to follow the second term's work and catch up what he had missed. He was fortunate to find in James Meyrick a likeminded companion who was also determined to make the most of the opportunities the course offered. It was exceptional for either of them to miss a class, unlike the more frivolous majority. 'They called us "sweats", but having missed a term, I was anxious to catch up.

Every week I spent in lodgings was at the expense of my father who was also paying a substantial sum in fees.'

Evans enjoyed his time at the college and retained fond memories of the personalities and idiosyncrasies of the staff who taught him. During an outbreak of equine influenza, Professor Spooner, a habitual user of snuff with a sense of humour, asked the class what they thought influenza was.

> A student said it was an influence. 'But what is influence?' [Spooner] asked. When the class looked baffled he repeated the question: 'Gentlemen, what is influence?' Then, taking another pinch of snuff, he said 'God knows. I don't.'

Spooner specialised in equine medicine and believed that sick animals have a tendency to recover provided they are kept in well ventilated accommodation and given access to plentiful fresh water.

Evans had particular respect for Professor James Simonds and told him of his interest in the structure and properties of blood. At the time, no microscopes were provided for student use so, at Simonds's suggestion, he bought a second-hand instrument with a book of instructions for £5.[3] 'It will be your best friend', Simonds told him, 'but be careful of the lenses and don't let any spittle fall on them.'

> A new world opened up for me. I started with simple things noting the difference in the blood of various animal species, observing in healthy animals the changes in blood before and after feeding. I discovered the difference in ratio between red and white corpuscles.

This introduction to microscopy was to lead ultimately to his outstanding contributions to veterinary and medical science.

Evans must have been seen as an outsider by his peers. When they teased him by imitating his Welsh accent, he was perplexed rather than annoyed: 'I did not imitate their accent; why should they imitate mine?' He seems to have shown no interest in girls and shunned alcohol and when Meyrick suggested they might go to the music hall, he declined on the grounds that his poor hearing would mar his enjoyment.

Camden Town in the mid-nineteenth century was a pleasant, largely middle-class, outer suburb. Evans would spend the limited leisure time he allowed himself walking in the neighbourhood or in nearby country-side, alone or with Meyrick. The pair avoided horse trams and omnibuses to save money and at weekends, would sometimes walk the three miles into London and down to the Thames 'which stank like the sewer it then was'. Although he had seen extreme poverty in Wales during the Hungry Forties, the deprivation and depravity in the poorer areas of London shocked him. Returning late one evening from Westminster, a pale, skinny girl of no more than fourteen accosted him in Tottenham Court Road, asked for sixpence and pointed to a nearby alley. 'I did not understand what she meant ... I gave her the sixpence and told her to get herself a meal.' Other excursions were related to their veterinary studies. Students were encouraged to visit the Zoological Gardens in Regents Park which Meyrick and Evans did frequently. They also paid regular visits to the new Metropolitan Cattle Market on Caledonian Road to observe the treatment of livestock brought into the capital.

As the evenings lengthened, Evans and Meyrick would walk further afield to enjoy the heathland and lanes of Highgate and Hampstead. As they walked, the two young men discussed every aspect of life and the events and preoccupations of the time. British politics were dom-inated by the Crimean War but the first half of the nineteenth century had seen a booming economy and a general optimism engendered by the inventiveness and industrial self-confidence expressed in the Great Exhibition in 1851. Advances in science and technology were creating tensions with orthodox religion leading to the open conflict precipi-tated by the publication in 1859 of Darwin's *On The Origin of Species* and culminating in the great Oxford evolution debate between Thomas Huxley and Bishop Wilberforce. Religion was a frequent topic of their discussions; a year older than Evans, the more sophisticated Londoner was outspokenly agnostic while Evans, with his Nonconformist Welsh background, was sympathetic but less forthright in his views. These con-versations were to be the foundation of a lifelong interest in religion and religious practices although Evans's own convictions were to evolve into a firm agnosticism.[4] Having arrived in London as a naive eighteen-year-old country boy, he was maturing rapidly and expanding his horizons; it was an exciting time to be making the transition to manhood.

In the summer of 1854, an outbreak of cholera in the City of Westminster caused widespread panic in the capital.[5] Evans's hard work during the year had taken its toll; tired and fearful of the disease, he longed to see his family in Wales. Evan urged him to come home for the last week of the summer vacation and sent him money for the journey. After eight months away, Evans was delighted to be back although Tŷ Mawr seemed smaller, his parents looked older and Maria thinner. Eliza had married a merchant seaman, Griffith Dedwydd, and now lived in Barmouth (Abermaw).

The visit was soon over and Evans returned to London for his final year. The winter of 1854–5 was harsh and he worked harder than ever. There was no respite over Christmas which he spent in Camden but in the final examinations in May 1855, his application was rewarded when he graduated and was elected a Fellow of the Royal College.[6] His dissertation on 'The diseases of the Alimentary Canal of the Horse' submitted to the Veterinary Medical Association was singled out for special commendation. His achievement was impressive: he was still nineteen and had been at the college for only eighteen months of the two-year course.[7]

Evans now returned to Wales to take stock. Apart from a desire to see more of the world and an ambition to engage in research, he had little idea of his next step. His parents' health had suffered during the hard winter and his mother implored him to find employment near home. Evans felt obliged to accede to her wish and applied successfully for a post as assistant in a veterinary practice in the Shropshire market town of Bridgnorth which he took up in September.

There are few records of this period of Evans's life but his employer would seem to have been James Atcherley who had recently taken over the principal practice in the town after his father was killed in a carriage accident.[8] He was soon put to the test: while his employer was ill, there was an outbreak of disease in cattle. Working round the clock, he appears to have gained the respect of the local farming community and at the end of his first year, Evan on a visit to Bridgnorth was pleased to hear farmers speak well of his son.

Two months after he started work, James Meyrick was appointed assistant in a practice across the Welsh border in Newtown (Y Drenewydd). The two friends arranged to meet whenever they could and began a correspondence comparing notes on their cases. In one exchange, the two young vets bemoaned the meanness of farmers. Meyrick wrote of a case of blindness in a colt caused by a worm between the pupil and cornea which he proposed to treat for nothing as the farmer would not pay. Evans replied that he too had treated a heifer without charge to relieve its suffering when the owner refused to pay and been reprimanded for doing so. In his letter, Meyrick also complained about a farmer with a horse suffering from the poll evil[9] who had taken his horse to the local blacksmith for treatment. 'The horse with poll evil of which I told you, was cured by the old blacksmith. I cannot find his mode of treatment. It is I believe a secret in his family.'[10] Evans quickly came to respect the best traditional treatments employed by farriers; they were often based on common sense and an understanding that sick animals tended to recover spontaneously if kept under the right conditions.

They also resumed their discussion of their other interests and preoccupations, foremost among them religion. Although Meyrick held fast to his agnosticism, both were interested in comparative religion and attended services of the different denominations in their respective towns, discussing their impressions. Evans was evolving his stance as a freethinker which he was to retain throughout his long life. His philosophy was centred on a belief in the teachings of Christ as expounded in the Sermon on the Mount together with scepticism as to his divinity. He had a particular aversion to the institution of the priesthood in all religions; for him, faith was a matter of the individual's direct relationship with God.

During nearly five years in Bridgnorth, Evans resisted efforts to involve him in local society. He appears to have shown no interest in women and there is no mention of close friendships other than with

Meyrick. He spent his spare time pursuing a new interest in entomology. His notebooks at the time are full of drawings of insects and arachnids but he was dissatisfied with his skills: 'I took lessons in drawing because my attempts to draw insects were so poor … This was a pleasant and useful experience.'

Meyrick enjoyed the company of women and in 1859, confided that he had become involved with a Miss Bickersteth in Newtown whose parents were strict Methodists. They were scandalised by Meyrick's agnosticism and with their daughter's support, insisted that he accept the Christian faith if he was to continue to see her. Evans's advice was to stand by his principles and break off the relationship. Not wanting to hurt the girl's feelings, Meyrick decided that his only option was to leave Newtown and he wrote to Evans suggesting an urgent meeting in Ludlow.

The meeting was to transform the course of both men's lives. Evans had seen a notice in the *Times* announcing that the British Army was in urgent need of veterinary surgeons and inviting applicants to London to sit an examination. Successful candidates were to be awarded commissions, a procedure radically different from the usual practice of purchase of commissions in the British Forces. Evans and Meyrick decided then and there to seize the opportunity. In due course, the day of the examination arrived and on their results, both men were accepted as commissioned Veterinary Officers, among the first to enter the Forces by this meritocratic route.[11]

3

WOOLWICH – THE ROYAL ARTILLERY

Evans, now twenty-four, and Meyrick, twenty-five, were mature, well-built young men impressive in their new uniforms as they reported for duty as Acting Veterinary Officers at the Royal Artillery's Woolwich Barracks on 30 January 1860. They were taken to meet John Wilkinson, the Queen's Principal Veterinary Surgeon in command of the army veterinary service at the Royal Horse Artillery Infirmary. Wilkinson was an unimaginative, unpopular figure although, since his appointment in 1854, he had improved the performance and standing of the service. For this, Evans respected him.

Evans's strong sense of direction, decisiveness and self-discipline resonated with the demands of military life and he quickly found his feet. However, he was disturbed by a pathetic letter from his mother soon after his arrival in Woolwich. She was convinced her son would be corrupted by the licentiousness she believed characterised army life and had been scarcely able to eat or sleep since hearing of his commission. Writing in illiterate Welsh, Mary Evans begged him to reconsider his decision.

The day he received the letter, Evans was waiting for a train at Woolwich Arsenal station when he saw on the platform an elderly and seemingly friendly clergyman. On the spur of the moment, he approached him, explained his dilemma and asked for his advice. The clergyman replied that he believed a young man could lead a clean life in the Army provided he had sufficient character and was willing to face the music and live it down.[1] Evans recounted the incident in his reply to his mother written that evening. He promised her that he would always abide by the principles she had instilled in him and that nothing would persuade him to touch alcohol. Nor, he reassured her, would he ever associate with loose women. He went on to describe his friend, a fellow Welshman Major Phillips, who was, Evans wrote, deeply religious with a comprehensive knowledge of the Bible. These reassurances were apparently enough; a letter from his father told him that his mother now appeared reconciled to her son's new profession.

Although he enjoyed army life, Evans never felt comfortable in the opulent surroundings of the officers' mess where rigid protocols of dress and behaviour were strictly enforced and where his abstinence soon led him to fall foul of tradition at a regimental dinner. When the port was passed to him by the officer to his right, Evans pushed it back with a curt 'No thank you'. He was unimpressed when Meyrick, sitting to his left, explained that tradition demanded the decanter be passed to the left, clockwise round the table. Nor was he interested in participating in the informal social life of the mess, finding the drinking and rowdy

FIGURE 3 Griffith Evans at the Royal Artillery
Barracks, Woolwich. (Tony Craven Walker)

parties inane and offensive. Nevertheless, his diaries show that Evans made many friends at Woolwich.

Prince George Duke of Cambridge, a cousin of Queen Victoria, had been appointed Commander-in-chief of the British Army in July 1856, a position he held for 39 years. He was known to be deeply conservative and had the reputation of being irascible and unreasonable. Evans's friend, Major Phillips told him of an encounter during an inspection at the Woolwich Barracks. The Duke made some bad tempered and unjustified criticism of a junior officer.

> When I remonstrated with him … he fired a volley of abuse and blasphemy at me which I found intolerable. 'Sir', I said, 'I am responsible to you but I am also responsible to God and His orders are that His name is not to be taken in vain.' Turning to the Colonel the Duke demanded: 'Who is this lunatic?' The Colonel replied: 'Your Royal Highness, Major Phillips is one of my best officers.' The Duke left without completing the inspection.

A few months later, on Whit Sunday 1860, Evans had his own encounter with the Duke as he accompanied a Royal Artillery troop marching from Woolwich to the new Army camp at Aldershot.[2] Just beyond Kensington, he noticed 'an old gentleman' in civilian clothes and mounted on a magnificent horse watching them pass (the 'old gentleman' was only forty at the time). The gentleman beckoned to him to approach and demanded to know why Evans had not saluted him.

> 'I don't know why I should salute you,' replied Evans taking him to be a civilian, 'I don't know who you are.' 'I am the general commanding-in-chief,' spluttered the Duke, 'Go and tell your commanding officer he will have to answer for not calling the troop to attention while meeting me.'

No one had recognised the Duke and when they arrived at Aldershot, the commanding officer showed Evans a War Office order demanding an explanation of his failure to salute the Commander-in-Chief.

'Tell his Royal Highness that I did not recognise him in mufti, and that he expressed himself in such bad language, cursing and swearing, that I thought he was a lunatic ... I have no other apology.' The C.O. 'had a wigging' but Evans heard no more about it.

Evans remained at Aldershot for several days. During his stay, he wrote to his father describing the Camp set in what he described as 'expanses of dreary moor'. With the arrival of the army, the village had expanded rapidly with a proliferation of public houses and brothels. Drunkenness was a perennial problem and Evans describes coming across a party of soldiers on punishment detail in the summer heat. 'I wished I could have shouted to them to use their common sense and abstain from alcohol.'

Back in Woolwich a few weeks after his twenty-fifth birthday in August 1860, Evans received his formal commission dated 31 January 1860.[3]

The remainder of the summer and early autumn seems to have passed uneventfully but in October, Evans was granted leave and returned home to Wales. His parents were concerned at the poor health of Evan's second cousin, Dr John Jones[4] and his wife, Catherine, in Llanfaircaereinion, Montgomeryshire and suggested that he break his journey to pay them a visit. They knew that John Jones's poor health was a consequence of alcoholism while his wife's was caused by anxiety at his health and the decline of the practice.

Evans arrived at the doctor's house after dark and the door was opened by his third cousin, Katie Jones, whom he had last seen as a little girl. Katie, now nearly seventeen, was an attractive young woman with dark brown hair and smiling eyes.

She was scarcely more than five feet tall and her eyes were level with the top button of [Evans's] uniform. She said:
'Griff Evans, Tŷ Mawr!'
She led him into the parlour and they talked for a while in their native tongue. She told him her mother was ... a little better but still quite poorly. Her father was asleep in his surgery. He had

been too unwell to see the evening patients: she had had to send them away.

Katie led him upstairs to see her mother who invited him to stay the night.

In extreme old age, Evans recalled the pleasant evening he spent with Katie that October night seventy-five years earlier:

> She made no fuss. She told me she had no proper dinner for me but if I was hungry she would give me some food or else I must go to the village inn. I preferred staying with her and take what pot luck she might give, and she gave me a basinful of gruel with an egg beaten into it. I never relished food better than then.

Next morning, as Katie accompanied him to the village to catch his coach, he asked if he might write to her. She replied that she would be pleased if he did and they exchanged letters through the winter. Discovering that her birthday was in December, Evans sent her a shoulder wrap 'to keep you warm while you are sitting up with your mother at nights'. He was clearly smitten.

The following spring, 1861, Evans was again given leave and hurried back to Llanfaircaereinion to be warmly greeted by Katie. They talked and went for long walks and before he left, sitting on a log on the banks of the river Banwy, Evans proposed marriage. Katie hesitated. This was only their second encounter as adults and she told him that she was too young and that they would need to know each other better before she considered such a step. However, she raised no objection to Evans telling her father of his intentions. Dr Jones was blunt. He was not prepared to contemplate marriage for his daughter at such a young age, least of all to a soldier. In any case, he went on, both he and his wife needed her at home. Evans had no alternative but to accept but asked if he might write to her. Dr Jones assented but again made it plain that marriage was out of the question for many years.

4

THE GREAT EASTERN

The British Government saw the outbreak of the American Civil War in April 1861 as a threat to the Province of Canada. Although Queen Victoria had proclaimed neutrality in May that year, the perception in the United States Government was that the British ruling elite favoured the Confederacy; the strong trading relationship with the southern states based on cotton, as well as covert military and other support in Britain for the South, reinforced American suspicions. In early 1861, Canada's defence capability consisted of a locally recruited volunteer militia of cavalry, infantry and artillery units comprising a little over 10,000 men. Concerned that worsening relations might lead to an American attack on Canada which this force could not hope to repulse, the British Government set about reinforcing Canada's defences by sending 11,000 regular troops across the Atlantic.[1]

At 8 a.m. on Sunday 9 June 1861, Griffith Evans was summoned to call urgently on John Wilkinson. Wilkinson informed him that he had received instructions that the Fourth Battery of the Fourth Brigade, Royal Artillery,[2] was to be deployed to Canada immediately and that he had chosen Evans as their veterinary surgeon. He was to make ready at once; the main body of the battery had already left for Aldershot to prepare to travel to Liverpool for embarkation.[3]

Evans carried on with his plans for the day, going first to the Welsh Cymanfa (Congregation) in Poplar and then to call on a friend, an experienced soldier, in Greenwich who gave him advice on the practicalities of embarking a force of men and horses overseas. On his return to Woolwich, Evans was told the Battery was to march north from

Aldershot that Thursday 13 June leaving him little time to make his preparations.

The following morning, Monday 10 June, Evans was at the Royal Horse Infirmary early to see his cases and to arrange for medicines and instruments to be made ready. Reporting to the Colonel, he found that his orders to travel to Aldershot had not yet been received. After some confusion, which was only resolved by Evans's personal intervention at the War Office, he was assured that he would receive them the following morning. Returning to Woolwich, he spent the evening writing letters. These included a hurried note to Katie Jones explaining that he was to embark for Canada almost immediately and expected to be away for several years. He then turned to packing his papers, books, clothes and other necessities which took him until after midnight. Up early the next morning and receiving his orders at last, he caught the noon train for Aldershot.

The Battery remained at Aldershot for five days before marching to Birmingham from where it was to travel by train to Liverpool. The interval allowed Evans to ensure the horses were fit for the march and to organise supplies of forage for the journey. His preparations complete by Saturday evening, he spent Sunday in nearby Farnham visiting the birthplace and grave of William Cobbett. Describing the visit to his father, he reminded him that Cobbett, too, had served in the army in Canada.

On Monday morning, 17 June, the battery marched out of Aldershot. The first day took them the twenty miles to Reading. On Tuesday they reached Abingdon and on Wednesday marched fourteen miles to Woodstock. Skirting Oxford, 'we came to the top of a hill, where all at once we saw that city of palatial colleges and churches beneath … it was uncommonly hot.' On Thursday and Friday, they continued northwards reaching Warwick on Friday afternoon. The following day, Saturday 22 June, the last day's march of twenty miles took them into Birmingham.

After resting on Sunday, the battery marched through Birmingham to the railway station on Monday evening 24 June led by the band of the Royal Irish Dragoon Guards and cheered by 'an immense crowd'.

There they boarded an overnight train for Liverpool reaching Edge Hill Railway Station early the following morning. The weather was wet and blustery and men and horses had to wait at the station until 10 a.m. before marching through the city to the Landing Place on the River Mersey. There they were to be transferred by steam tender to the *Great Eastern* moored mid-river but the river was so rough that embarkation was delayed until 3 p.m. Then the horses were walked onto the tender to be hoisted one after another to the ship's deck where stables had been prepared for them.

Evans was impressed by the scale of the ship. Launched in 1858, she must have been an impressive sight as the tender approached; displacing 32,000 tons, she was over twice the size of contemporary steamships.[4] She had been chartered to transport troops from Liverpool to Québec and on this voyage carried 2,144 officers and men with 200 horses (including Evans's battery), accompanied by 473 women and children. When he had seen to the horses and settled in himself, Evans explored the ship, marvelling at its 'wonderful construction' and the spacious, comfortable cabins and saloons. The ship rolled and pitched in the

Figure 4 The *Great Eastern*.
(Ann Ronan Picture Library/Heritage-Images)

choppy waters of the Mersey for almost three days before it became calm enough to weigh anchor at noon on 27 June. Steaming down-river, they were seen off by crowds on both banks and accompanied by small boats.

Evans claimed to have discovered early in the voyage that he was the only teetotaller on board. He had never been to sea before and his journal is full of notes on the ship and the progress of the voyage. That evening he wrote:

> Going at the rate of 12½ knots ... Consumes about 300 tons of coal daily. Weather foggy. Ship answers to helm ... much better at night ... because people are all below ... her steering varies considerably during the day because men move about.

Every day, the horses were taken out of their stables and exercised on deck, impossible before as no previous transport had been large enough.

On the first Sunday at sea there were church services on deck morning and afternoon conducted by the Chaplain, the Rev. Williams, 'a stickler for church regulation of religion'. However, at 6 p.m., an American pastor, Mr Hammond, was given permission by the Colonel to address the men on deck. His relaxed, informal manner proved popular with the men and he interspersed his words with religious songs sung to popular tunes, the men joining in. They continued singing after he had finished only to be ordered to stop and disperse by two infantry officers who objected to the informal conduct of the meeting. Evans who was watching, saw that 'the men felt indignant ... they had to obey though the officers had no right to interfere. I told them so, what the men could not'.

The following morning, Evans was on deck early to find the sea smooth and what seemed to be a range of mountains on the horizon. Told they were fog hills, he was reminded of accounts of Columbus's voyage to the New World when sightings of land turned out to be mere fog banks. The day after, he described a close encounter with the Cunard Mail boat, *S.S. Arabia*, en route from Boston to Liverpool. One of the bigger passenger liners, she was dwarfed by the *Great Eastern* and was pitching and rolling in the heavy swell which seemed hardly to affect the larger ship.

After several encounters with fog and an alarming passage through a field of icebergs, the Cape Race lighthouse on the south-eastern point of Newfoundland was sighted on the evening of Wednesday 3 July. The following day the *Great Eastern* steamed into the sound between Newfoundland and St Paul Island to the south. There were now ships of all sizes around them, among them a three-masted American sailing ship, a magnificent sight under full sail. The 5 July saw them off the thickly wooded coast of New Brunswick where a pilot boarded to take the ship into the St Lawrence. Evans describes the banks of the great river as beautiful: 'thick forest except the clearings near the river. We are able to see much farther inland ... because we are so high above water.' As she approached Québec, the ship was met by crowds of excited sightseers.

> The cheering was tremendous. Fireworks in the evening, all the ships and houses specially lighted. We dropped anchor at 7 p.m. having made the quickest passage ever.
>
> I saw more ... pretty girls today than I did in the whole of our march in England.

The battery remained on board for two more days. On the morning of Wednesday 10 July, Evans went ashore to look round Québec. He found the streets narrow and the houses and pavements of wood, all very different from English towns and 'not nearly so comfortable'. Evans was also disparaging about the inhabitants and wondered where the pretty girls he had seen from the ship had gone, concluding sadly that 'distance lends enchantment'. The battery disembarked the same evening to travel overnight by train to Montreal. There they formed up to march through the city to the Old Cavalry Barracks. In contrast to Québec, Evans found Montreal to be 'a large well-built city, many good stone buildings ... stone pavements, roofs of wood or tinned iron plates'.

The battery had lost one horse during the journey: an animal suffering from hydrothorax[5] shot by Evans on the last day of the voyage.

5

MONTREAL

Accommodation at the Old Cavalry Barracks just outside the city was meagre: the officers were allocated an empty house but the men were to live in tents.[1] The following days were spent settling in and exploring. The Brigade Major, Captain Waller, had been in Montreal for some months and showed Evans around the city, inviting him to his house.

Once settled to a routine, Evans and his fellow officers found that military duties filled only part of the day. With time on their hands, the majority spent it amusing themselves but Evans cast around for a more constructive way to occupy himself. He realised that such a large deployment of forces to Canada implied a long stay which might provide an opportunity to fulfil his old ambition to read medicine. Presenting himself at the McGill Medical School, he managed to persuade them that his limited military duties would leave him time to study and was offered a place. He had then to seek permission from his commanding officer: 'I explained that I should not let it interfere with my military duties. On this condition, and on the understanding that I might have to terminate my studies suddenly, he agreed.'

Evans embarked on the three-year course in the fall term of 1861. To meet the demands of his new dual life, he adopted a rigid daily regime. Getting up in uniform, he made his rounds of the stables to check that all was well with the men and the battery's horses. After dealing with his limited administrative duties, he changed into civilian clothes and spent the rest of the day as a medical student.

Much of the first year was spent in the dissecting rooms under instruction from the young demonstrator in anatomy, Horace Nelson M.D., who was intrigued by Evans's background and his obvious intelligence and dedication. With little difference in their ages, the two soon became friends, Nelson treating Evans more as a colleague than a student. With his veterinary training, he made rapid progress.

Subjects for dissection at the McGill Medical School were generally obtained from dealers in the United States who acquired the bodies of slaves from their owners or by grave-robbing, packed them in casks and smuggled them across the border. According to Evans, students at the other medical school in Montreal, at the French Catholic University, could not afford corpses from this source and relied entirely on theft from local graveyards to supply their needs.[2] Being practiced in grave robbing and careful how they went about it, they were seldom discovered but when the mainly English students at McGill robbed graves, their motive was mischievous amusement rather than necessity. Generally in need of Dutch courage before they set out, they did their work carelessly and were often caught. Evans describes the gruesome *modus operandi*:

> The safest way to do it is, after obtaining information of a recent interment, go to the grave when it is snowing, dig down to the coffin, place the lifted earth in as compact a heap as possible to minimise the mark, cut the lid off ... place a loop of cord round the neck of the corpse, pull it up out of the coffin, replace the lid and the lifted earth, cover all with snow, the descending snow will obliterate the footmarks if the last of the party will sweep about evenly, carry the corpse to a provided sleigh nearby and off.

The practice could have macabre consequences. Evans was in the dissecting room one day when the corpse of a woman, clearly the victim of a local grave robbery, was placed on the next table.

> Presently a student came up to her, gazed, then exclaimed with horror: 'Good God! That is my aunt; my cousin is down below at

the chemical lecture and will be up here soon' … There was consternation, most of us saying 'What shall we do?' One said 'Dissect the skin of the face off quickly!' Agreed. Two students commenced doing so immediately and fortunately did enough to make recognition impossible before her son came in. I watched him, he went to see the new white subject, cheerfully joked with the dissectors, congratulated them on their successful adventure, etc.

The students found it repugnant to continue with the dissection but had no alternative as there was no other means of disposing of the body without arousing suspicion.

Some weeks after this incident, Dr Nelson took Evans aside to tell him he had been informed by the police that 'the boys' had exhumed two bodies from a graveyard. The police had searched the Medical School without success but the sleigh driver on the night had divulged the name of one of the students. Nelson explained that he had received a letter from a lawyer representing relatives of the deceased that threatened prosecution but made an offer: if the bodies were returned immediately to their families unmutilated, no further action would be taken. When told of the offer, the five culprits confessed immediately and accepted.

The bodies were to be handed over that evening and at Nelson's request, Evans agreed to witness the transaction. The students led the way to a shed where the frozen bodies were hidden and carried them to a waiting sleigh. It was a clear moonlit night so they propped the bodies up, Nelson beside one and Evans beside the other, drawing up the buffalo-hide mantles so that passers-by would suspect nothing. Reaching their destination, they handed the bodies over to the lawyer who gave Nelson a written assurance that there would be no further repercussions. Nelson expressed his regret and promised to take steps to prevent further exhumations: at his instigation, the Governors of the Medical School approved a regulation stipulating that only corpses obtained through approved channels were to be brought into the dissecting room on pain of immediate expulsion. It was only later that the magnitude of the risk he had run occurred to Evans; discovery would almost certainly have cost him his commission even if he had avoided prosecution.

Such distractions aside, Evans applied himself diligently to his studies. He was particularly enthusiastic about the new approach to pathology advocated by Professor Brunt in Edinburgh and promoted by Professor George Campbell, Dean of the McGill Medical School. Its simple message chimed with Evans's own view that bodily systems were designed to function with 'ease' and that symptoms of any 'dis-ease' should be treated promptly to prevent complications. This principle of prompt intervention coupled with a preventative approach to illness formed the core of Evans's medical philosophy.

With his dual preoccupations, Evans seemed in no danger of bore-dom which was a hazard in any large garrison. To fill their abundant leisure time, members of the garrison engaged prominently in the social life of Montreal, as they did in theatrical and musical entertainments and sporting events.[3] Evans makes no mention of involvement in these activities in his journals and is likely to have steered clear of many of them because of his abstinence.

As always, he took a keen interest in religion. Although an agnostic himself, he respected the religious beliefs of others and defended their need for a formal framework in which to express them. Always ready to attend church services and other religious gatherings, he was also willing to take an active part in Bible study classes and Sunday schools as he describes in a letter to Evan in June 1863:

> There are several Welsh vessels in port now. I had about an hour's chat last evening with two captains in the cabin of a vessel from Aberystwyth: the brig 'Hannah' Capt Humphreys – he says he knows Dr Pughe well. He seems fond of talking and discussing religious subjects. I hope that we shall have a profitable 'Ysgol Sul' [Sunday School] next Sunday out of 3 or 4 Welsh crews, each being 10 or 12 in number.

Despite his prejudice against Roman Catholicism and priesthood, Evans had befriended a Catholic chaplain to the army. The two men met every week to discuss the New Testament, the authority claimed by the Catholic church and the value of tradition. The priest reported these talks to his bishop who, sensing that the meetings were threatening to undermine the priest's faith, decided that he should be transferred to protect him from Evans's subversive influence. At their farewell meeting, the priest confessed to thoughts that justified the bishop's concern.

> When I went to the convent to bid him farewell … he told me … he often felt during and after our weekly discussions that if he allowed himself to reason on religious subjects as I did, he would not remain in the Church another day … But he could not now cease trusting his faith … It was not possible for one like me to imagine the power of all that [was] preventing him to reasoning continually upon religious subjects. In parting he took my hand in both his, sobbed, and wiped tears flowing over it. I felt deeply affected. He was a good man. I am sure our fatherly God accepted him as a son.[4]

Raised as a Congregationalist, Evans continued all his life to regard the denomination as the one closest to his convictions, attending its services when he could and taking part in its assemblies and conferences. Nonetheless, he was prepared to be sharply critical of its ministers if he thought they merited it. In a letter to his father in 1863, he wrote:

> During the past week or nine days the Congregational Union was held in … Montreal. There were ministers delegated from several of the Northern [American] states … every one of them [was] so full of the 'war spirit'[5] that they had nothing else to speak about … instead of informing the assembly of the state of the churches in the states, which they represented, they all spoke … to justify the Northern cause, etc. They said that peace with the Southerners is now out of the question, it must be fought out until the whole population of the South [is] exterminated, and the Northern soldiers are to be remunerated by the Southern states being divided

among them! Moreover these evangelical (?) ministers said that they rejoiced to think that the united (Northern) states made no objection to the enlistment of clergymen and ministers as active soldiers, so that if necessary they would take up arms and lead their congregations to war and victory, or die in such a glorious effort!! So much for Yankee Christendom![6]

Other Nonconformist movements and sects also interested Evans. Among his friends, he counted several Irvinites, a group he had already encountered in Bridgnorth. 'What fascinated me about these people was that they really believed Jesus would return in person any day. They had to be constantly expectant. Some of my friends … had a spare place, plate, chair etc. at every meal.'[7]

Outings into the surrounding countryside to picnic or explore in both summer and winter were a popular pastime among soldiers and civilians in Montreal. Evans took every opportunity to take part in these excursions although, typically, his expeditions tended to be more adventurous and ambitious than most.

In August, a few weeks after his arrival in Canada, he and an Irish officer, Captain Barton, found themselves in the village of Lacolle while patrolling the nearby border with New York State.[8] On a farm outside the village, they met the Peters family, who invited them into their simple, log house where they were 'most hospitably entertained'. The old farmer had been expelled from his Scottish croft during the Highland Clearances[9] and regaled the young officers with accounts of his forced emigration and early days in Canada. Now comfortably settled, he and his wife longed to return to Scotland unlike their children who had no wish to leave Canada. Evans and Barton took their leave to pressing invitations to return.

In winter, travel was by sleigh and the narrow tracks soon became elevated by accumulation of compacted snow and ice. Each fall of snow concealed the trails which were marked by poles but even in good weather, there was a danger of tipping over the edge into the deep drifts of soft snow on either side. Evans soon acquired a healthy respect for the hazards of winter travel.

Towards the end of January 1862, he and Barton decided to pay a return visit to the Peters. In the bitter cold of early morning, they set off by sleigh to cross the St Lawrence by the ice bridge making their way between huge blocks of ice thrown up by the force of the current. From the south bank, they took the train to Lacolle and after struggling through heavy snowfall on foot and by sleigh guided by Peters's son, they reached the farm where they received 'as warm a Highland welcome as they could have expected had they been fellow clansmen'. An excellent supper of apparently fresh beef and pork was served and Evans expressed surprise that such meat could be served in the depths of winter. The animals were killed months before as soon as the hard frosts set in, Peters explained, and the meat, dipped in icy water, was allowed to freeze solid and packed in clean snow in casks where it remained fresh all winter. Gathered round the stove after supper, they listened to the couple talking wistfully of life in Scotland while Mrs Peters puffed contentedly on her pipe.

After a comfortable night in a shared bed, Evans and Barton awoke to a clear, windless morning which revealed a spectacular snowscape. The day was spent exploring the area with the young Peters. When Evans asked him how the farmers passed the time during the nine months of the year when cultivation was impossible, he replied 'they fell and log wood and feed their cattle'. This, Evans suggested, could take only a fraction of the time to which Peters replied: 'Well, we have concerts, balls, etc., parties for enjoyment.'

The following morning was wet and cold and was spent visiting nearby farms – at one, Evans bought a 'splendid' fox skin for six shillings – before the young Peters took them to the station for the afternoon train to Montreal. While they were waiting, a young French Canadian with badly frost-bitten hands and feet was brought in. His inadequate clothing showed him to be poor and he told them he had come from Montreal the previous day on his way to visit relatives just across the border. Before he left Lacolle, he had called at a friend's house to warm himself and take a drink of 'liquor' before resuming his journey on foot. Overtaken by nightfall, he had sheltered in a ruined house. The following morning with his hands and feet frozen hard, he managed to crawl outside where he was seen and carried to a nearby house. His rescuers applied the local remedy for frostbite, covering his swollen limbs with soft snow which, as it melted, slowly thawed them but his extremities were still black and as he was by then very weak, a priest was called. After hearing his confession and giving absolution, the priest suggested he seek help at the Hôtel Dieu, the Grey Nunnery Hospital, in Montreal and gave him a note of introduction. His rescuers then carried him to the station where they hoped he would be helped. As the stationmaster was unwilling to do anything for the man, Evans took charge, wrapped him well in his railway rug and when the train came in, had him carried to a first-class compartment.

During the journey, they were told that the sleigh track across the St Lawrence was now dangerous. The ice had cracked in fierce winds and two days earlier, a sleigh had fallen through into the freezing water; fortunately, the occupants survived and the horse and sleigh were recovered. Despite the warning, Evans and Barton had no alternative but to attempt the crossing. 'The sleigh was shaken about fearfully ... and we were upset once but ... the patient was not thrown out ... we got on fairly well considering the state of the track.'

Safely across, the sleigh driver offered to take the frozen man and Evans to the Hôtel Dieu without charge.

The hospital and convent were housed in a forbidding building surrounded by a high wall which Evans likened to a prison 'which it is for the nuns'.

> We were for a long time knocking ... the great door was opened, we drove in to the antecourt, the door closed behind us with a great bang and [was] bolted or locked. I cannot forget what I saw and felt then, shut within this prison.

They were led inside,

> where I see six or eight nuns, one of them holding a large lamp ... I told them all I knew ... of the patient [showing them his] letter of introduction ... There were two or three particularly good looking

girls among them, pure and sweet countenance ... I wished they
were somewhere else, and thought I would willingly risk my life
to help them out of this prison to freedom if they wished it ...
Having assisted to undress [the patient], and put him in a good
bed, I felt gladly relieved in leaving him in the tender care of the
nuns. In driving to my quarters my thought was of the 'dark ages'.

Evans heard later that the man had recovered fully after 'minor
amputations'.

Exposure to extreme low temperatures was a constant hazard during the Canadian winter and it was common for patches of exposed
skin to become frozen. If ignored, these could expand rapidly and it was
considered polite to draw attention to the characteristic white spots on
another's face. The remedy was to rub the area gently with dry snow or
fur to thaw it and Evans made a habit of rubbing his face with his fur
mitten until he felt a glow, particularly before entering or leaving a warm
house; he claimed never to have suffered frozen skin or frostbite which
he attributed to this precaution, to his good circulation and especially
to his abstinence. He remembered that the frostbitten French Canadian
had taken liquor to warm him in Lacolle and he recalled that during
his first winter in Canada, many sentries given a rum ration before
taking up their posts suffered severe frostbite, often after falling asleep.
When, on medical advice, the rum was replaced with strong coffee,
Evans claimed that no sentry suffered frostbite or was found asleep.

Another eventful expedition took place in March of 1863 when
Evans and his good friend, Major Waller, set off for the small country
town of Huntingdon south-west of Montreal. Crossing the St Lawrence
by steamer, they hired a sleigh to take them and a French Canadian,
Monsieur Ste Marie, twenty-eight miles up the Chateauguay River to
Durham where they were to spend the night. Although they encountered some drifting snow, the first few miles were uneventful but from
then on, the only passable track was along the frozen river. While the
passengers were dozing, the sleigh overturned without warning and
they and the driver were thrown out. Waller remained dry but the
others found themselves knee-deep in icy water. When the sleigh was

righted, Evans encouraged Waller to stay aboard but the others got out to lighten the load and they and the pony struggled through deep slush covering the river ice as the track continued to deteriorate. When the exhausted pony could go no further, they found another driver at a hamlet to take them the remaining eight miles. Ste Marie drove the sleigh while its owner rode ahead to find the track. Evans started in the sleigh but fearful that his wet legs would freeze, decided to walk to keep his muscles active. Their guide soon became alarmed at the state of the track and begged them to turn back but Waller was warm and dry and Evans was keeping warm with exercise and they insisted on continuing. The night was now fine and clear and the two of them, exhilarated by the experience, roared with laughter at the least excuse and were greatly enjoying themselves, their high spirits contrasting with the dejection of the French Canadians. They reached their hotel in Durham just before midnight and paid off their guide. In the warmth of his room, Evans removed his frozen trousers which stood 'like two cylinders of glass' but he had kept his legs and feet from freezing by walking and running beside the sleigh. Warm and in borrowed dry clothes, he and Waller settled down to a supper of hot milk, eggs and buttered bread before falling into bed exhausted.

They awoke to a fine morning and thoroughly refreshed, spent that and the next day exploring Huntingdon and the surrounding country-side with its well-tended farms and thick cedar and pine forest. On the third day, the two officers caught the early Mail sleigh to return to Montreal. The weather was again clear and still and they made good progress on the river track without once upsetting. Passing through a village, Evans noticed that a new Roman Catholic church was being built and was told that the construction was financed by a system of obligatory tithes payable by all Catholics. His journal records with dis-approval the draconian reaction of the clergy if these tithes remained unpaid: property was seized and one priest imprisoned a debtor in his church until his debt was paid. This same priest had been known to horsewhip members of his flock for religious misdemeanours but the victims never complained for fear of excommunication, preferring to be 'whipped in this world to being sent to hell by their bishop'. Crossing the St Lawrence by ferry, Evans and Waller arrived back in Montreal in the late afternoon. Some days later, Evans heard their companion, Ste Marie, had died from the hypothermia he had suffered on the outward journey. Somewhat heartlessly given that Ste Marie had driven the sleigh on the last leg to Durham, Evans remarked that he was sorry to hear it but 'I think it was his fault in keeping in the sleigh after wetting his feet and legs instead of exercising like I did'.

Later that year, Evans himself suffered an accident which had a curious sequel. Thrown from his horse in a Montreal street, he sprained his right wrist badly and the next day, the pain was so severe that he 'could hardly hold a feather between finger and thumb'. He was nonetheless determined to attend a lecture that evening on the Old Testament Prophets. With his wrist bound and his arm in a sling, he chose a seat near the exit in case the pain became too great to bear. Waiting for the lecture to begin, he was stunned to see a man he took to be Mr Wilkinson, the Queen's Principal Veterinary Surgeon from Woolwich, come in through the door.

> I was so surprised and astonished to see him that I felt thoroughly electrified, as I had felt ... handling an electric machine ... [I] felt a strong aura or gush of something flow steadily from my spine down my right arm to the tip of my fingers ... After it passed through the sprained wrist ... the pain stopped instantly and never renewed. Before the lecture ended I could press and pinch hard with my right hand and finger ... The man so like Mr Wilkinson ... [passed] my seat and ... I recognised him.

During the spring and summer of 1863, Evans concentrated on his medical studies. However, in late summer, he conceived an ambitious plan to pay a visit to a Native American settlement in Wisconsin.[10]

> I am informed that the station master at Milwaukee has ways of getting in touch with Indians who travel from there to New York to take part in Barnum's Circus. I shall pay one of these to guide me to an Indian settlement. They will see I am unarmed and

they will trust me. I have been advised to travel looking obviously Canadian so that I am not mistaken for an American and to take with me some tobacco.

He had chosen an inauspicious time for the adventure. Treaty violations by the US Government had led to resentment among the Dakota or eastern Sioux in neighbouring Minnesota which was exacerbated by deprivation and hunger caused by corruption among agents of the Bureau of Indian Affairs. In August 1862, a faction of the tribe attacked settlements south-west of Minneapolis killing the inhabitants. Despite the distraction of the Civil War, the US army responded swiftly and crushed the uprising. The murders had caused fury in the community and summary trials of prisoners by a military commission condemned 370 of them to death. Most were reprieved by President Lincoln but thirty-eight ring leaders were hanged in public in the largest mass execution in the history of the United States. Although the Dakota had been subdued, it seemed likely that any visiting white man would meet with suspicion and hostility.

Evans, undeterred, was granted a week's leave. When his attempts to find a fellow officer to accompany him failed, he wrote to James Meyrick who was serving in a different sector. Meyrick's reply enclosed a newspaper cutting from December 1862 describing the mass public execution.[11] He reminded Evans that Minnesota still offered a bounty for Amerindian scalps, pointing out that a white stranger in their territory was very likely to be taken for a bounty hunter. Still undaunted, Evans wrote back to Meyrick that he would go alone and set off on the 750-mile journey by carriage, Mississippi river steamer and train to Milwaukee on the western shore of Lake Michigan.[12]

He had been told the Milwaukee stationmaster could 'walk to the end of the platform and whistle up a couple of Indians from the woods'. At Evans's request he did so and two Amerindians emerged from the trees. In rudimentary English acquired in the circus they agreed to guide Evans to a Dakota settlement in the forest. Evans hired horses and they set off. Over the next two days they rode some fifty miles through woodland without encountering a single

Amerindian. When they emerged into settled country, Evans noticed several scalps drying in the sun on the fence of a homestead which, the guides explained, would have been taken from Indians murdered for the official bounty.

We stayed only to replenish our water bottles, and I undertook to see that no white man caused them any trouble. We plunged back into the forest, and [next morning] came across a settlement of Indians in a clearing. The women were squatting on the ground, listening to a boy playing the flute.

The guides went ahead and beckoned to me to follow. As I rode nearer I saw the boy was European. The guides said he had been stolen as a baby and brought up as a male Indian … Here they were all squaws except the boy. The men were out hunting …

I was taken to an empty wigwam and left there alone. I sat down … and said to myself 'at least I can say I have sat in a wig-wam' … But soon [at the start of a thunderstorm], a number of young women came silently in and, without a word, they rustled down into a semi-circle, squatting with their backs to my back, supporting me like an arm-chair. They made it clear I was to lean against them, and make myself rested and comfortable. I … wished my brother officers could see me now as I reclined against their pretty brown shoulders. The girls stayed until the thunderstorm was over. Then they stole away as silently as they had come.

Evans remained alone in the wigwam until, at dusk, one of his guides looked in to tell him that the hunting parties had returned and that the chief wanted to meet him. He led him to the chief's wigwam where,

I was entertained and fed, the guides acting as interpreters. I greatly admired some wooden spoons and bought some to take home. I tried to explain that in my country, young Welshmen carved spoons for the girls … and called them love-spoons. The evening was a great success. I told them about Wales and spoke a little Welsh and they seemed to be interested.

Waking early after a good night's sleep, Evans emerged to find the women cooking breakfast. He was greeted affably as he explored the village, joking with the small children who followed him everywhere. Near one wigwam, he noticed a decorated papoose slung from the branch of a tree and admired the baby it contained. The atmosphere everywhere seemed friendly and relaxed. When the time came to leave, the villagers gathered to bid him farewell. His admiration for the baby had been noticed and the guides told him the family were willing to sell him the papoose as a keepsake. Evans explained graciously that he had actually been admiring the baby but accepted their offer. The formalities completed, Evans and his two guides rode off into the forest to return to Milwaukee. They arrived back at the station without incident and after paying off the guides and returning the ponies, Evans retrieved his suitcase from the stationmaster.

Before he had set out, an acquaintance had given him the address in Milwaukee of a young Welsh woman born in Tywyn. Evans now called on her and she offered to show him the sights of the rapidly developing port. On their tour, they passed a professional photographer's studio and Evans suggested that they should have their photograph taken as a souvenir of this encounter between two natives of Tywyn far from home. The following morning, Evans took the train back to Montreal where he sent a copy of the photograph home to Tŷ Mawr.

Nearly two years earlier, Evans had written to Katie Jones to tell her that he was to read medicine at McGill. The letter was formal and made no mention of the understanding they had reached on his last visit to Llanfaircaereinion.

If the battery stays in Montreal for three years there is no reason why I should not be a doctor by 1864. A medical degree will be of great assistance in my career. I think it is right that I should make the most of my opportunities ... I shall always think of you warmly but you must not consider yourself in any way bound to me.

Katie's response was a cool note wishing him success. There had been no further communication between them and almost a year later, Katie called at Tŷ Mawr while staying with her aunt in Tywyn. On the dresser, she spotted the Milwaukee photograph of Evans and the young woman which convinced her that Evans's attentions were now focused elsewhere and that she should forget him.

With graduation only a few months away, Evans concentrated on his thesis. Characteristically, he had chosen a challenging and controversial subject: the pathology and histology of tuberculosis, at the time a deadly disease of young and middle-aged adults. Primarily associated with poor living conditions, it also afflicted the affluent and although its prevalence had been declining during the nineteenth century, it was still a major cause of mortality in 1900.[13]

Evans's thesis dealt with the causes, symptoms and treatment of tuberculosis and described the histology of the pulmonary lesions it caused. Even at this early stage in his career, he showed scant regard for orthodoxy and sought evidence to support his conclusions. Thus, contrary to contemporary opinion, he asserted that the disease was contagious, that consumptives should be isolated and that doctors and nurses treating them should take precautions to avoid infection. More controversial still was his insistence that patients should be exposed to fresh air and sunshine, contradicting the conventional view that sufferers should be protected from cold air and 'night humours'. These ideas were in advance of their time: it was not until 1865 that Jean Antoine Villemin proved that tuberculosis was contagious and another seventeen years passed before Robert Koch demonstrated that it was caused by an infectious bacillus, *Mycobacterium tuberculosis*.[14] It was therefore unsurprising that his thesis was greeted with scepticism but although his evidence was anecdotal and circumstantial, his arguments were cogent and the authorities recognised that they needed to be taken seriously.

When the thesis, *De Pathogenesi et Histologica Tuberculosis*, came before Convocation in the early summer of 1864, the examiners decided that it merited a 'challenge', customary when students put forward original hypotheses. The challenge was led by the chief examiner, Professor William Fraser, who subjected Evans to an intense interrogation on the question of infectivity. Evans's defence was spirited. He enumerated cases in which individuals with no family history of tuberculosis contracted the disease after marrying consumptives and others in which women became infected after nursing their sick husbands. He cited the case of a patient of Professor George Campbell, the one faculty member sympathetic to his views: on diagnosis, Campbell gave the patient three years to live and suggested that he make the best of the time left to him. The man's favourite pastimes were camping and hunting and he disposed of his business to devote his remaining time to these outdoor activities. Five years later, he called on Professor Campbell who was astonished to see him. 'I could hardly believe my eyes. The man was cured, and the only trace I could find of his old complaint was a slight depression in the chest where the mischief had been.' His examiners acknowledged that Evans's defence of his thesis had been masterly and he was awarded his M.D.[15] fulfilling an ambition he had harboured since boyhood. However, there is no evidence that his thesis had any influence on the medical establishment, a precedent for the fate of his trail-blazing report on another disease, this time of horses, sixteen years later in India. The thesis was never published and was later destroyed in a fire in the University library. No copies have survived.

When Katie heard from her aunt that Evans had qualified, she wrote him a formal note to congratulate him. Evans wrote back and receiving no reply, wrote again but Katie did not respond.

ABRAHAM LINCOLN AND
THE AMERICAN CIVIL WAR

Within a month of completing his medical degree, Evans succumbed to a severe bout of dysentery. Young and fit, he was soon on the way to recovery but the disease had taken its toll; he was judged unfit for active service and given two months convalescent leave. Never one to remain idle, he began casting around for something to do to fill this unexpected furlough.

It had become fashionable for young officers in Canada to try to reach the Union lines on the eastern front in the American Civil War. However, after the appalling slaughter of the Battle of the Wilderness in northern Virginia in early May 1864, passes had become almost impossible to obtain, not only for adventurous young officers but also for senior British officials in Canada. Undeterred and with six weeks of his leave remaining, Evans resolved to visit the front.[1]

The war was now in its third year and during the summer and fall of 1863, the tide had turned decisively in the Union's favour.[2] The Battle of Gettysburg in early July was considered a victory for the Union's Army of the Potomac under General George Meade although the losses on both sides were terrible.[3] Almost simultaneously in the western theatre, General Ulysses S. Grant had forced the surrender of Vicksburg which commanded a crucial stretch of the Mississippi. This was a severe blow to the Confederate cause: the Union now controlled the full length of the river threatening the Confederate heartlands of the Deep South.

In spite of these setbacks, the Confederate armies were far from defeated and continued to contest the conflict vigorously.

Evans was well aware of the US Government's hostility to Britain because of British political support for the Confederates and the supply of British arms and ammunition to their forces. Nevertheless, he set about making preparations with his characteristic enterprise and attention to detail. His first step was to seek a companion among his brother officers. One of them seemed enthusiastic until he heard that two senior British officials, General James Lindsay, commander of the Brigade of Guards in Canada and Dr William Muir, Principal Medical Officer, had been refused passes to visit the Northern Armies. When he also learned that attempts by several fellow officers to reach the front line had been thwarted – one had been turned back trying to get through dressed as an American civilian – Evans's prospective companion withdrew, judging the enterprise to be doomed to failure.

Despite this setback, Evans was determined to press on and set about seeking advice from friends, acquaintances and colleagues in Montreal. For the most part, their responses were discouraging; like his prospective companion, they were convinced he would fail. One piece of advice he did receive was that he should on no account draw attention to himself by wearing his British uniform in America. Evans rejected this out of hand, spurning any subterfuge and insisting he would make the trip in uniform as a member of the British forces in Canada or not at all.

A few people were, however, willing to help and Evans began to accumulate useful information and crucially, introductions to influential people in the United States. Among others, he called on members of the medical faculty at McGill University and intrigued by his audacity, several were ready to provide letters of introduction to colleagues and friends in New York and Washington.

The letters he managed to amass included introductions to several influential figures, among them Lord Lyons, British Ambassador in Washington, Professor Joseph Henry of the Smithsonian Institute, arguably the most distinguished American scientist of the nineteenth century and a personal friend of Abraham Lincoln, several generals in the Union Army and Dr Austin Flint, a leading figure in the American medical establishment who had excellent contacts in the Union military hierarchy.[4] Dr Flint was in New York and wishing to see the city, Evans decided to call on him on his way to Washington.

His preparations complete and wearing his uniform, Evans set out by train for New York in the afternoon of Monday 20 June 1864. Crossing the newly constructed Victoria Bridge over the St Lawrence, he took the ferry across Lake Champlain before entraining once more to travel overnight down the Hudson Valley to arrive in New York on the morning of 21 June. Early that afternoon, he called on Dr Flint who was friendly and helpful. After briefly discussing his medical work, Flint gave him some further introductions in Washington and suggested a brief sightseeing tour of New York should he be unable to leave for Washington that evening. Evans then set out on foot and by streetcar to see something of the city centre before catching the Washington train.

He arrived at the station in good time to be told that his portmanteau had gone astray so, forced to remain in New York for the night, he took a room at the Fifth Avenue Hotel. Exhausted by his long day, he slept well and after an early breakfast, set off on a day's sightseeing. He took a streetcar to Harlem 'quite in the country' and crossed the Harlem Bridge, to take 'the cars' into Chester County passing 'through pretty country with green fields, bushy hedges and villas with gardens and conservatories, etc'. On the way back, he took a river trip.

> On return to Harlem Bridge took the steamboat down the East River to Peck Slip about eight miles down the river, had an excellent view of that part of the city, the docks, Long Island and many public buildings including the hospitals, House of Correction, etc.

The next pages of his journal are missing but Evans appears to have caught the overnight train to Washington on the evening of 22 June. He lost no time in delivering his letters of introduction. His first call was at the British Legation where the Ambassador, Lord Lyons, received him kindly but said he was afraid he could do nothing to help him; he explained that he had recently failed to persuade the American authorities to grant passes to Dr Muir and Major General Lindsay. However, he was impressed by Evans's introduction to Professor Henry and suggested that this provided his best hope of success. Lord Lyons appears to have taken an immediate liking to the young Welshman and ended the interview by inviting him to dinner that evening.

The following morning, Evans called at the 'Castle', the Smithsonian Institution's building on Maryland Avenue, where Professor Henry also received him sympathetically and invited him to tea at his house that afternoon. There he introduced Evans to his wife and daughters who seem to have warmed to him immediately and invited him to make himself 'freely at home' with them during his stay. Henry then offered to take Evans to meet President Lincoln at the White House the following day.

FIGURE 5 The White House in 1860.
(Library of Congress, Prints and Photographs Division)

The pages of Evans's journal describing his first meeting with Lincoln are missing, possibly torn out by an American journalist who visited Evans in his retirement. However, in an interview with the *Manchester Guardian* seventy years later, he described the occasion:

Professor Henry was told to bring me to the White House at 10 a.m. After a formal introduction, I told Mr Lincoln of my wish. After a general conversation, the President said he would talk about me to the military authorities and asked me to call again the next morning. When I called the second time Mr Lincoln, whom I saw in his private room, said he would grant me a roving commission to visit the Northern Army and that he would direct all military authorities in the field to help me go where I wished. But it was on one condition, that I was to make myself medically useful to the troops and help the wounded. I readily agreed.[5]

During the last five years of his life, Evans dictated his recollections of this interview with Lincoln to his daughter, Erie:

I explained to Lincoln my purpose as a recently qualified medical student, to see all I could of medical work in the field, and how Lord Lyons could not help me on account of anti-British feeling. Lincoln looked at me and said in effect, 'You ought not to be surprised at our feeling, considering we have good reason to believe that British manufacturers are supplying our enemies with ammunition and the British Government is not as careful as it should be as a neutral.' I then looked at Lincoln and I said that although I was a British Officer in uniform, I was not there to represent the British Government; and although my personal sympathy was with the South, because I thought they were putting up a good fight for their freedom, yet I was there simply as a recently qualified medical student, wishing to see all I could and to be free to follow my own line of observation.[6] I said that armament makers were out simply to make money and that, if they could make as much by selling to Lincoln, they would do so. I said I supposed that business men in the Northern States would be equally ready to make money selling to countries at war in which America was neutral…

He told me to return next day. In that second interview, Lincoln gave me a permit signed by the Quarter-Master General [Brigadier General Montgomery Meigs] granting me every facility to go wherever I wished on condition I rendered medical help if called upon. He added that he would be obliged if I would call upon him on my way back through Washington to make a report. This I said I would be honoured to do.

On the day after his one-hundredth birthday, Evans was interviewed by a reporter on the *Detroit News* who asked him to recall his impressions of Lincoln at that first interview:

> Lincoln was a big man ... big frame and loose-jointed, and when he crossed his legs his knees made a sort of mountain peak ... I knew I was in the presence of a great man. His simplicity impressed me from the first. He was direct and natural: there was nothing formal or stiff about him. He welcomed me cordially and I felt at ease in his presence ...
>
> I think my youth appealed to him ... His face was careworn & deeply lined & in repose very sad; but he smiled occasionally, and he chuckled once, I recall. Still, I wouldn't say he was jovial. Nor was he hurried, though many were waiting to see him ... He expressed concern as to England's attitude toward the North. He was terribly burdened, you know ... He had many characteristics, but there was nothing singular in him. He was a unity. He appeared to be kind, gentle, patient, considerate and, I would say, easy to get along with. Still, I can believe he had a will that nobody could break when he knew he was right. I thought him capable of anger yet holding it well in hand. He gave me no reason to believe him to be vindictive.[7]

FIGURE 6 Abraham Lincoln in 1864, the year of Evans's visit. (Library of Congress, Prints and Photographs Division)

Evans's reception in Washington is instructive. The young man, still only twenty-nine years old and strikingly good-looking, must have had a charisma and charm that appealed to both men and women. The degree of trust he seems to have inspired was evident in his reception by the President and by the senior military officers he encountered, all of whom must have been pre-occupied with the Civil War.

Leaving the White House, Evans hurried back to the British Legation where Lyons congratulated him heartily on the outcome of his interview with the President. During their conversation, Lyons told Evans of the impact of the War on the Union side, telling Evans that the Federal Army had lost nearly 100,000 men in the less than two months since the beginning of May. He claimed that there were 15,000 sick and wounded in Washington's hospitals, about sixty of whom were buried every day. Lyons ended the conversation by inviting Evans to dine with him on the eve of his departure for the front. Later, Evans met General George Ramsay, US Army Chief of Ordnance, and asked him what troops were available to protect Washington. 'Only the invalids' he replied, 'Washington is one great hospital'. He asked whether it was safe to leave the city so exposed. Ramsay replied that he believed it to be safe as there would be enough warning of an impending attack to allow reinforcements to be sent from the nearby front line. He explained that every available man was needed at the front as more fighting was expected any day and the Army had been much weakened by their recent heavy losses.

On the evening before his departure, Evans presented himself at the Legation for dinner. Among Lord Lyons's other guests were the Second Officer and two others from HMS *Phaeton*, a frigate placed at the disposal of the Ambassador and anchored at Hampton Roads at the mouth of the St James River on Chesapeake Bay. They were returning to the ship next morning after shore leave and invited Evans to travel with them.

The next morning, in his British Army uniform and armed with his free pass from the President and introductions, Evans joined the *Phaeton* officers on the river steamer. That night, exhausted by his arduous few days in New York and Washington, he suffered a recurrence of his dysentery. The attack weakened him and in the morning, he asked to be put ashore to seek treatment at a field hospital. Fortunately, the officers persuaded him to accompany them to the *Phaeton* to be treated by the ship's surgeon; Evans later insisted that their intervention had probably saved his life as camp dysentery was rife on shore and the US army medical service overstretched.

He was well cared for and entertained aboard HMS *Phaeton* and was again strongly advised against wearing his British Army uniform; he was told his life would be worth nothing if he wore the uniform because of the strength of anti-British feeling in Union ranks. Evans was still adamant: '[I refused] to don the dress uniform of the Northern Army. I definitely told them that if I went to the front, I would go as a British officer in my own uniform, or not at all. Lord Lyons [had] told me I did quite right.' Thus far, wearing his uniform had helped rather than hindered him; President Lincoln had taken his insistence on wearing it as the mark of an honest man.

AT THE FRONT

His strength restored by the care he had received aboard the *Phaeton*, Evans was ready to resume his adventure. As a first step, he decided to leave the ship for a day to see something of nearby Fort Munro.[1]

General Benjamin F. Butler, who commanded the Army of the James on a nearby sector of the Front, had just arrived at the Fort on a visit. Butler was a controversial figure. He had commanded the force that occupied New Orleans for the Union in April 1862 and had acquired the nickname 'Beast Butler' for the harsh regime he had imposed on civilians, an epithet taken up by the British Press.[2] So it was no surprise that Evans was received coldly when he presented himself at the Fort and as the senior officer present, Butler only agreed to see him after he had explained that he had a pass to visit the Union lines. He then grudgingly arranged for him to be shown around.

At the end of his tour, Evans asked to see Butler to express his thanks and take his leave. At this second meeting, the General's manner seemed quite changed and he received Evans warmly. Maps were produced and Butler proceeded to describe the disposition of the armies in his sector and to discuss the current state of the conflict. To Evans's surprise, the General concluded the interview with an invitation to accompany him to the front the following morning which Evans accepted subject to the *Phaeton*'s doctor passing him fit; Butler even offered him the use of the tent normally occupied by Mrs Butler. They were to start their journey by river steamer and Evans was told to be present on the quay ready for embarkation early the following morning.

Evans described the events of the morning in a press interview a week before his one-hundredth birthday:[3]

> I was told [by the ship's doctor] that the risk was great, but so was the temptation, and I recognised the great kindness of the General. So next morning … I arrived at the spot where the steamer started before the appointed time, so I waited on the shore by the steamer. For two hours I waited, and the General came along with a flourish of trumpets. I stood up and gave him the military salute, of which neither he nor the officers with him took the slightest notice. They went by, treating me with the utmost contempt. I was rather surprised, because I had simply accepted his invitation – a kind invitation it was. They all went aboard the steamer, and the gangway was drawn in. The steamer moved away and left me on the shore. I came to the conclusion that some evil report had been spread about me, so I threw my blankets on the steamer and jumped towards it. I was left suspended for a time, but I managed to clamber aboard. The same aloofness was shown when I got to the deck. No one took any notice of me … [which] made me more determined than ever to find out what was wrong.

Evans sat on his bag on deck until at last an officer appeared to say that Butler had sent for him. Without a word, the General handed him a dispatch from the *Times* correspondent to the Confederate Army intercepted the previous night which made several references to 'Beast Butler'. He then complained angrily of sentiment in England in favour of the Confederacy: 'How can I or my officers be expected to hide our feelings against an Englishman?' Evans insisted vehemently that he was not English but a Welshman and reminded Butler that he was there as his guest. He went on to say that he would not, however, conceal his admiration for the Southern Armies for fighting so well. His reply placated Butler who, from that moment, did all he could to assist him. Elsewhere in his journal, Evans referred to the incident behind the nickname 'Beast' Butler: a woman who had insulted occupying Union soldiers in New Orleans had allegedly been mistreated.

He always maintained that the epithet was misplaced: '[Butler was] <u>not</u> a beast ... There was nothing beastly about his character ... [he was] a lawyer and a very fine soldier'.

Evans appears to have reached the front, presumably in Butler's company, late on the afternoon of 2 July and was allocated a marquee, a servant and a horse or carriage. The next morning at sunrise, he rode out with a Dr Woodhall for his first sight of the front line. The sector extended for about two miles across the peninsula between the James and Appomattox Rivers some fifteen miles south of Richmond, the Confederacy's capital, and north of the sector commanded by General Sherman. The country was thickly wooded so Butler had felled a belt of trees about 200 yards wide in front of the line. Immediately

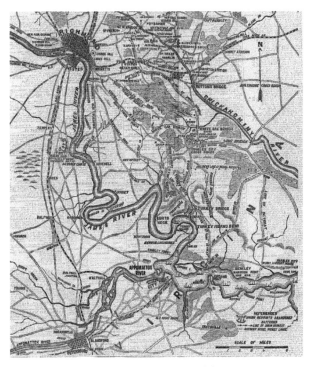

FIGURE 7 The northern front in 1864. The front line at the time of Evans's visit ran between the James and Appomattox Rivers. (Library of Congress, Geography and Map Division)

behind the cleared belt, an earth and timber wall 5ft high had been built on a zig-zag line. The wall was topped with sandbags with firing ports at intervals and batteries of four or five field guns every 2–300 yards. In front of this fortification, an abattis[4] was prepared from the felled trees with a trench behind it. This defensive position was considered to be strong and Evans was told that 5,000 men would be sufficient to hold it. The Regiment, some 20,000 men strong, was encamped in the woods to the rear of the line with earthworks thrown up in front of the tents to protect against shrapnel.

Evans and Dr Woodhall returned to camp for breakfast after which he was taken to visit hospitals on both sides of the Appomattox River. He was impressed by what he described as the 'sanitary condition' of the facilities and by the skill and commitment of the medical staff he met. He was then taken aboard a hospital boat packed with the more seriously wounded ready to be transferred downriver to the more sophisticated medical provision at Hampton Hospital. During the day, he met and conversed with many people, discussing, among other things, the merits and deficiencies of Afro-American soldiers. He heard claims that the Black soldiers fought well in a charge but less so in skirmishes or unexpected encounters. They were found less susceptible to malaria than whites but more at risk from severe pneumonia to which they often succumbed.

Since his arrival, there had been no firing on Butler's sector although Evans could occasionally hear the big guns from across the Appomattox in the direction of Petersburg whose church spires he could see plainly. He was, however, told of a cavalry raid just before his arrival to disrupt railway communications to Petersburg from the south. On their return, the raiders were accompanied by runaway slaves taking advantage of the protection of the Union troops to escape north to freedom. Before they could reach safety, they were intercepted by Confederate cavalry who killed several troopers and mercilessly cut down the runaways so that very few escaped. Evans met one of the survivors who told him that, before the war, he had been one of seventy slaves owned by a farmer near Richmond who, he claimed, had 'reared' him. He said his master had joined the Confederate army taking him along as a servant and

FIGURE 8 General Benjamin F. Butler and his staff in
1861. Butler is seated, front row, fourth from the left.
(Library of Congress, Prints and Photographs Division)

claimed that the officers were tired of the war and that women and
children were starving in Richmond. Later in the day, Evans went for a
walk in the woods behind the camp to collect beetles and on his return,
heard claims that an average of ten men a day were deserting from the
Confederate Army to the Union, a statistic he found hard to believe.

The following day was 4 July, Independence Day, but Evans saw
no sign of any commemoration. At about 8.30 a.m. he took his leave of
General Butler and left the sector with an escort to Bermuda Hundred
on the James River a few miles to the east. Here he was taken to visit
the Medical Purveyors's Department housed in a large boat moored on
the river where he was impressed by the stocks of medical supplies and
the 'medical comforts and luxuries' the Department held.

His next port of call was General Ulysses S. Grant's Headquarters at
City Point at the confluence of the Appomattox and James Rivers and a
special steamer was provided to take him downstream. Evans noted that
some boats on the river were dressed in celebration of Independence Day
which did not appear to be marked in any other way except by the firing
of a salute at midday at City Point. On arrival, he received a friendly

reception from a Dr Dalton who provided an escort to the Provost Marshal's[5] office where he was given a Pass to the Headquarters of General Meade. Evans called next on Brigadier General Rufus Ingalls, Quarter-Master to the Federal armies operating against Petersburg and Richmond, whose logistics base at City Point was soon to become the largest port operation in the Western Hemisphere. Presenting an introduction from the US Quarter-Master General, General Meigs whom he had met in Washington, Evans explained that he was recovering from a recent bout of dysentery and was anxious to make his way to the furthest point of General Meade's sector some fourteen miles to the south-west without delay, so that he could work his way back to City Point as his health and time would allow. As Evans felt too weak to manage the distance on horseback, General Ingalls provided him with a comfortable covered carriage drawn by four 'splendid' mules, with a mounted orderly to accompany him.

Evans declared that he would never forget the drive that day. The road was no more than a track made recently across country by the Army; the existing roads were ignored unless they provided a direct connection between destinations. The weather was sweltering hot with no wind and the constant movement of troops, ambulances and every kind of wagon had stirred up a persistent, choking cloud of dust. All around was desolation: fences had been pulled down for use as fuel, crops in the fields trodden down and houses either occupied by troops, deserted or burned. Thousands of graves of men dead from wounds or disease were everywhere, most so shallow that the stench was overpowering. Dead cattle and horses lay everywhere and abandoned equipment and all manner of detritus was strewn about. The scene was horrific and Evans was sickened and saddened by what he saw. Passing through the many camps along his route, he was struck by a remarkable stillness and reflected that this might be the calm before a storm.

> Everybody looks sober and sad, few smile … Officers and men talk in a subdued tone and, when asked, they speak of 'fearful slaughtering' of men that they were recently engaged in as if they wished to forget it and they heartily long for their field duties to be over.

Evans arrived at General Meade's Headquarters before 5 p.m. and presented his pass to Dr Farley, the Principal Medical Officer, who gave him a letter of introduction to a Dr Doghearty[6] of the Second Army Corps. He also called on General Humphries with an introduction from Professor Henry and was introduced by him to General Meade. Evans warmed to both men whom he recognised as 'West Pointers',[7] easily recognisable, he claimed, as they all 'had the manners of gentlemen'.

Later in the evening, Evans heard a little brief cheering and shouting in the camp, presumably in celebration of Independence Day. An engagement was expected at any time so the camps had been cleared of all unnecessary baggage and equipment and Dr Doghearty and the Assistant Surgeon shared a bell tent in which they made room for Evans. Making a pillow of his valise, trousers and coat, he wrapped himself in a 'railway wrapper' (blanket) and was soon asleep.

Rising early, Evans went for a stroll in nearby woods and listened to the birdsong to a backdrop of cannonading by heavy guns from the direction of Petersburg. After breakfast, he rode out with Dr Doghearty who was looking for a suitable place to establish a Divisional Corps Base Hospital to the rear of the line in readiness for the expected recurrence of fighting. Here again they found desolate country ravaged by war and several fine houses, some burnt, others deserted or occupied by troops. A few were still occupied by the women of the families that owned them; in general, women were left unmolested and if in need, supplied with provisions on condition that they took the oath of allegiance to the United States. Only a few old and sickly men remained, all able-bodied men having fled or joined the Confederate army. In most houses, some evidently the homes of well-off families, the fabric, furniture and carpets had been terribly damaged or destroyed by the troops. Carefully tended gardens had been ravaged and flowerbeds trodden down. The sight upset Evans as he recalled the care his mother had devoted to her garden in Wales and he expressed sadness at seeing 'happy homes thus broken up'.

The following day, 6 July, he decided to move on, concerned that sleeping on the ground in a malarial area was threatening his already compromised health. The hospitals in the sector were empty as all serious cases had been evacuated to City Point so there was nothing to be gained and much to be lost by staying on; the Union line was well within the range of an enemy battery which was expected to open fire at any time. If there was renewed fighting, the surrounding country was flat and so heavily wooded that he would see nothing unless he was in the thick of it and so at great risk of being shot: 'As I have no interest in the quarrel worth my while to run that risk I have determined not to do so.'

His decision made, Evans asked General Meade for transport back to City Point to be told that there were no troop horses to spare. However, General Humphries volunteered to lend Evans his own horse and a mounted orderly for the journey. While the horse was being readied, Evans had a pleasant conversation with the General who told him that he believed there were 120,000 men actively engaged on the front in the armies of General Meade and General Butler. His return was on a more shaded road than his outward journey but the countryside they passed through was as ravaged and desolate as before. Evans arrived back at City Point in time for lunch with Dr Dalton who introduced him to Dr Mitchell, Principal Medical Officer at the Cavalry Corps Hospital. This comprised large numbers of tents of all kinds, shapes and sizes pitched in a pleasant site on the banks of the Appomattox. Dr Mitchell received him kindly and arranged for a marquee to be pitched for him.

No more of Evans's journal survives until the entry for 20 July. Some has certainly been lost but it is also likely that Evans had little time during this period to record his experiences. What we know of that eventful period is limited to recollections in interviews with the press, many in old age, and memories recorded by his daughter, Erie. These, however, tell us nothing of his activities between 6 July when he arrived back at City Point and 11 July. The only document that survives is a stained and tattered pass issued by the Office of the Provost-Marshal General and dated 9 July 1864.[8] All that is legible on the pass is 'The Bearer Dr Evans, Royal Artillery, has permission to pass from these … Washington DC. This pass will expire on July 12, 1864. By Command Brigadier General Patrick, Provost Marshal General'. The pass is signed by a Captain and ADC and on the back is written: 'Permit to take a rifle and shield picked up on the field'.

Evans must have used this pass for a brief dash back to Washington, taking with him his souvenirs from the battlefield. He was certainly in Washington on 11 July when the capital was threatened by a Confederate force under Lt General Jubal Early. He was woken that night by intensive fire from heavy guns and when he was told that Fort Stevens in north-west Washington was under attack, he found a horse and rode off to see what was happening. Near the Fort he was told that the Confederate force was retreating, probably after receiving intelligence that Union reinforcements under Major General Horatio G. Wright had arrived in Washington that afternoon. Evans and a Union officer followed them for some miles to the country house of the Postmaster General which had been sacked and burned by the invaders. There, the retreating force had left behind a number of wounded and Evans spoke to the Confederate medical officers who had stayed behind to look after them.

He seems to have returned to the front on 12 or 13 July where he spent much of the following week as the guest of Ulysses S. Grant, Commanding General of the US Federal army at his City Point Headquarters. His stay with Grant coincided with something of a lull

FIGURE 9 General Ulysses S. Grant in 1864.
(Library of Congress, Prints and Photographs Division)

in the fighting before the Battle of the Crater which followed the mining of the Confederate line outside Petersburg on 30 July. However, minor encounters were taking place all the time and preparations for laying the mine must have been underway.

Evans brought with him two letters of introduction to Grant, one from Dr Flint in New York and the other from General Butler and received a friendly welcome from the Commander-in-Chief. All that is known of the visit comes from later interviews with the press and correspondence with a dramatist, John Drinkwater.[9] These suggest that Grant was a genial host, dining with Evans every day. In one conversation, Evans remarked that the Union forces appeared disorganised, a view that had been expressed to him by Lord Lyons in Washington. 'Yes, of course we are disorganised' Grant replied, 'but we shall win.' Evans also recalled that he had been with Grant when he sent a cavalry brigade to attack Confederate railway communications between Richmond and Petersburg and the South. Grant told him that interrogation of prisoners captured during the raid confirmed that the Confederate armies were suffering a severe manpower shortage 'whereas we', Grant claimed, 'are sure of getting recruits and can afford to lose ten to one so long as we can keep organised'. He agreed with Evans that this seemed cruel but said it was necessary if the Union was to win. When asked for his impressions of Grant, Evans's response was that they were 'all good'. He was particularly adamant that he saw no evidence of Grant's dependence on alcohol which was widely rumoured and stated emphatically that he was satisfied that Grant was, at the time, an abstainer.

Evans's health was still fragile and he suffered a recurrence of dysentery while staying with General Grant. The doctor's advice was that he should return to Washington before his condition deteriorated further. This he agreed to do but he insisted on one more visit to the front line before he left. On or about the 17 July, he set off on horseback to the headquarters of General Thomas.[10] On the way, he came across three Union officers observing an engagement through field glasses from a hilltop, 'a splendid target for snipers'. Two of them rode away as Evans approached in his British uniform but the third handed me the glasses so that I could see Robert E. Lee's head-quarters. As the American was describing the Southern General's positions, a bullet whizzed between us. I returned the glasses, we separated, and rode away … But I was glad to have seen the head-quarters of the great Confederate General who was such a hero to both sides.

Arriving at his destination, Evans found General Thomas in a trench about to launch an attack. He proffered his pass and a letter of intro-duction from Dr Flint. Glancing at these, Thomas handed them back, seemingly confounded at being confronted by a British officer. Evans recalled that he 'looked disagreeable' and 'rather sulky':

'Nobody wearing a British uniform should expect a welcome here. British sympathies are all with Lee. But I suppose I can't throw out a friend of a friend.' I thanked him and said that although the sympathy of any British officer might be with Lee because he was entitled to fight for his native state of Virginia, yet Britain was, after all, neutral.

'Neutral!' said Thomas. 'Take a look at that!' and he thrust a shell into my hands. 'That is what landed on my breakfast table this morning. Well, what is it? Tell me.'

I replied that it looked like a dud shell. 'Dud shell!' said the General. 'Yes, it's a dud shell. If it were not a dud I wouldn't be here now. Tell me who made it?'

I turned it over and saw that it was made by Whitworth and Co. 'Can you deny that it is a British shell and made by a British firm?' Thomas demanded.

'I cannot deny the evidence of my own eyes, sir!' I said. 'I sup-pose my country cannot prevent private firms from supplying the South with ammunition. I promise to report what I have seen to the British Ambassador in Washington.'

Evans then reminded Thomas that they were both Welshmen. The General responded disdainfully that he had no connection with, or interest in, Wales and that he was entirely ignorant of the Welsh language. Adding that he had no more time for Evans, he offered him the choice of remaining with him in the trench or of climbing onto a platform from which an officer was directing a barrage by the Union battery. Evans chose the latter, watching the action for a time before resuming his ride towards the James River where he hoped to find a steamer to take him to Hampton Roads. As he rode, Evans reflected that, during the entirety of his visit to the Union lines, he had heard nothing but praise for General Robert E. Lee from officers and men. All spoke of him as a valiant enemy and he was generally acknowledged to be 'a perfect gentleman and Christian' and 'the best General in the world except for our own General Grant'.

Reaching the river, Evans found a steamer to take him downstream and embarked. Weakened by another recurrence of his dysentery, he retired to a cabin where he soon fell into a fitful sleep.

I dreamt I could hear extraordinarily musical voices … I realised I was awake, that it was no dream, and I felt my way in the dark between the decks till I came upon a crowd of negroes singing hymns. They looked frightened. I told them I was their friend, and that I came from Canada. They looked relieved. They told me that they had been released by the Northerners and were on their way to employment. They had been warned by their Southern masters that if the Northerners got them, they would shut them up somewhere with snakes. 'Is that true?' they asked me. I assured them it was not.

Arriving at Hampton Roads the next day, Evans went aboard HMS *Phaeton* where he was welcomed and offered a bunk for the night. After dinner, he went ashore to make a brief visit to the oldest Protestant church in North America. He had a vague memory that his father had told him that the Welsh poet, Goronwy Owen, had served there as rector or curate. He found the church in ruins, burned by the Confederates two years earlier and could find no record of any incumbents.

On his way back to Washington up the Potomac, Evans considered the report he had undertaken to provide to the President on his return. With few exceptions, he had met with a warm welcome and generous hospitality wherever he went and had been offered every assistance in carrying out his mission. Although he had had little opportunity to intervene medically himself, he had visited medical outposts and field and base hospitals and spoken at length to doctors and staff. He had been allowed to examine patients and had discussed their medical histories. His copious notes included observations on how much better medical and surgical patients appeared to recover when housed in tented accommodation rather than in buildings, even in the best hospitals, observations which chimed well with his own prejudices and his experience in veterinary medicine. He had seen no evidence of indiscipline or insubordination among the troops and had been impressed by their resolve to defeat the enemy. On the other hand, nowhere did he find evidence of vindictiveness and cited the consistent respect with which General Lee was regarded.

On reaching Washington, Evans disembarked briefly on the west bank of the river opposite the capital to visit Arlington, Robert E. Lee's home confiscated by the Union.[11] The house was occupied by Brigadier De Russy, Commander of the southern defences of the capital but part of the grounds had already been designated a military cemetery. The estate also housed a Freemen's Village for freed slaves where he met an old man who claimed he could recite the whole of the Old Testament.

> He told me his former Massa's little boy had taught him to read as they played together. He said he had found an Old Testament on a rubbish heap and committed it to memory. He longed to have a New Testament, and on my return to Canada I posted him one.

Evans's request to visit the house itself was turned down.

Crossing the river, Evans made several visits in Washington. Among them was one to a military hospital which President Lincoln had inspected the day before and where a doctor told Evans of an encounter which he was often to quote to illustrate Lincoln's sharp wit.

Among the patients the President visited was a young soldier whose scrotum had been shot away. A wealthy lady patron of the hospital who was visiting at the same time asked him what injury he had suffered. The embarrassed patient and attending medical staff were evasive and exasperated, the lady turned to Lincoln to ask what was wrong with the young man. 'Perhaps he will tell me,' replied Lincoln and turned back to the patient's bedside. After a short exchange, the President returned to the lady: 'Well, ma'am, all I can tell you is that if you had been standing where he was at the precise moment he was hit, you would not have been hurt at all.'[12]

Evans's journal resumes with an entry for 20 July:

From the Capitol I went to Professor Henry. He had invited me to his house at five p.m. to take me to visit the President at his country residence, hoping to find him disengaged, and to spend the evening with him. On our way we saw the President in his carriage at a distance of about 200 yards returning home escorted by 20 mounted men. I am told that he is persuaded to take this escort because his life would be in danger otherwise from Southern sympathizers. Before calling on him we visited the 'Soldiers Homes' in the grounds ... Unfortunately, while we were thus loitering, the Secretary for War came to see the President on some urgent business and Mr Lincoln sent us word that he was extremely sorry in not being able to see us and requested us to call again tomorrow or any other evening.

Evans's leave had almost expired and he needed to leave Washington the next day. As he was determined to make his report to the President, Professor Henry agreed to try and arrange an interview at the White House early that morning. His journal continues:

About 9.30 a.m. we called on the President at the White House ... He received us very kindly, but as there were many people waiting before we arrived, to see him on official business, we only remained a few minutes. In appearance he is what is termed a tall lanky yanky, his upper eye-lids drop partly over his eyes, his lower lip is very prominent. He has a 'knowing' smile which however is not unpleasant. He shows marks of mental overwork, which reminded me of what Lord Lyons told me the other evening: 'Mr Lincoln is not the man to look at that he was four years ago.' It is very remarkable the absence of all formality or insignia of office in this country. There was nothing about the President or his official residence to show that he was different to an ordinary subject … There was no military guard at the office nor did I see any man about in Livery. The White House is not at all a grand place, very little of it appeared to be furnished. The 'Grand Reception Room' and some others I saw were very seedy looking.[13]

The subsequent pages of the entry have been lost. Much later, Evans remembered that he had told the President of his positive impressions of the morale and determination of the Union troops. As Jean Ware says:

One can imagine the smile … on Lincoln's expressive face at the ingenuousness of this young officer who imagined that on the strength of a few weeks at the front he could tell the President anything about his army's morale that he did not already know.

Evans recalled later that Lincoln had appeared to be pleased to see him but had had to end the interview before he could deliver his report which he left with a member of the President's staff. Later that day, 21 July, Evans left Washington for Montreal which he reached on the evening of 30 July after breaking his journey briefly in Philadelphia, West Point where he visited the Military Academy and Saratoga.

8

HOME, MARRIAGE
AND FAMILY

Evans's strenuous month in the United States would have taxed the constitution of a young man in full health but he had been convalescing from a sapping attack of dysentery when he set out. He was soon paying the price of ignoring the doctors' warnings of the probable consequences of his expedition when, further weakened by the recurrent attacks of dysentery while he was away, his lungs became seriously congested as he returned to Montreal. Pneumonia was diagnosed and he was ordered to the military hospital.

In the next few days, his condition deteriorated further and typhoid fever was diagnosed. By his twenty-ninth birthday in early August, Evans was fighting for his life. Gasping for breath, he drifted in and out of consciousness and the doctors feared the end was near. That night, the senior medical officer was called to see him and during one of his brief interludes of awareness, warned him that he was unlikely to recover. He had underestimated Evans's will to survive:

> During a brief return to consciousness I heard voices. One said, 'It was madness to attempt such a journey', and another said, 'If he lives it will be months before he can return'. At that moment I resolved to live.

Very slowly, his condition began to improve.

Before his convalescence was over, his battery was posted to Toronto where he joined it when he was well enough to travel, resuming his duties a few weeks later. Although no diaries from 1865–7 survive, Evans made it clear in later life that this was a challenging period. His spirits were low and he had lost his usual energy and zest for life but above all, he felt lonely and disconnected from his family in Wales whom he had now not seen for more than three years. Much of his leisure time was spent on long, solitary walks on the shores of Lake Ontario, in reading and in copying verses which reflected his low spirits in the commonplace book he kept during his time in Canada.[1]

As he slowly recovered his morale and intellectual curiosity, Evans rekindled his interest in religion. He was particularly admiring of the Plymouth Brethren. Dr John Pughe had been a member of the open branch of the movement and Evans was impressed by their simple piety and renunciation of worldly concerns as well as by their rejection of any kind of formal ministry. However, he disapproved of the action of John Nelson Darby, a barrister turned evangelist who broke away to found the closed or exclusive branch.

> Some of my best friends in Canada were Plymouth Brethren of the liberal (open) kind until Mr Darby came there to demand them to be more strictly narrow and exclusive … I conversed with him often. When I disagreed with him, he told me bluntly that it was because the Holy Ghost did not teach me.[2]

Among these friends was a prominent and devout Plymouth Brother, Lord Adelbert Cecil, fourth son of the second Marquis of Exeter and godson of Queen Victoria, who was a lieutenant in the Rifle Brigade. In 1868, Adelbert resigned his commission to become a lay evangelist and author.

New interests also attracted his attention. In Toronto, he met George Washington Stone, a hypnotist and 'electro-biologist' and recalling his bizarre experience in Montreal in 1862 (p. 45), he became interested in the possibilities of both techniques. He was awarded a 'Diploma' by Stone in 1869 stating that he was now qualified to practise 'electro-biology' and mesmerism and entitled to 'apply the power of animal magnetism to the relief of pain or in the cure of disease'.[3]

Early in 1868, Evans was introduced to a leading medical practitioner and lecturer at Toronto University, Dr James Bovell. The two men got on well and Evans was invited to join Bovell's laboratory and participate in his programme of medical research. Evans accepted immediately and was once again absorbed by his old passion, microscopy. Later that year, Bovell engaged an eighteen-year-old medical student, William Osler, as his assistant. The son of a 'saddleback' minister in rural Upper Canada, Osler had intended to follow in his father's footsteps but had developed an interest in medical science. At Bovell's prompting, he had enrolled at the Toronto School of Medicine. Osler possessed a formidable intellect and great personal charm and Evans took a particular interest in him, greeting him each morning with 'And how is the young man today?' and providing him with encouragement and support. This relationship was to become the foundation of a life-long friendship that lasted throughout Osler's distinguished career in medicine in North America and Britain.

In the spring of the following year, 1869, Evans returned to Wales on leave after eight years in Canada. As soon as he disembarked, he headed for Tŷ Mawr where he asked his parents about Katie Jones. The last he had heard had been her impersonal letter in 1861 wishing him well on his medical course; she had failed to respond to his two subsequent letters and had put him out of her thoughts after seeing the Milwaukee photograph (p. 48). When he heard that she was still unmarried, his old feelings for her revived.

Unsure whether his attentions would be welcome, he embarked on an extended walk in his beloved Eryri (Snowdonia) mountains to arrange his thoughts and decide whether, at thirty-four, marriage was the right way forward. From Caernarfon, he set off up the Nant Ffrancon Pass to Capel Curig and then headed south to Bala. At this point he must have decided on marriage because he continued south to walk the twenty odd miles to Llanfaircaereinion.

Evans knew that Katie's parents, Dr John and Catherine Jones, had died recently but he must have expected to find her at the family home.

He arrived at dusk to find the house apparently deserted but when he knocked, a light appeared, the door opened and there stood Katie. She seemed pleased to see him and led him through to the kitchen where she prepared a simple supper for him as she had done nine years before. She explained how the health of both her parents had deteriorated until her mother had died some months earlier. Her distraught father drank even more and died soon afterwards. Katie had then moved away to live with her aunt and uncle, William and Mary Rees, in Tywyn and was only in Llanfaircaereinion on a brief visit to arrange the sale of the house.

As the years had passed, each had assumed the other had lost interest but their old feelings for each other quickly reawakened. They spoke of all that had happened during their long separation, of their misunderstandings over the tone of Evans's early letters from Canada, of Katie's subsequent silence and of the inferences she had drawn from the Milwaukee photograph. Much later, Katie wrote of her feelings at the time: 'While you were in Canada, I made myself unhappy raising some ghosts; it was because I did not know you.' Evans spent the night in the village and next morning, they set off for a walk along the banks of the River Banwy where Evans again proposed marriage. His proposal seems to have been couched in characteristically matter-of-fact language; Katie later admitted that 'when you proposed I [wished] you had been more off your head, and not so cool and collected'.

Evans and Katie's relationship was the attraction of opposites. In appearance, he was far from the popular idea of a typical Welshman. He was fair with piercing blue eyes, erect in bearing and abrupt and unyielding in manner and speech. As Jean Ware suggested, the Scandinavian marauders who had harassed the coasts of Wales had probably contributed to his genetic makeup. Katie was dark with deep brown eyes and a compact, comfortable figure. While Evans's approach to people was rather distant, searching and judgemental, she exuded warmth and empathy; it was generally Katie who formed and maintained the couple's friendships. She was sensitive, artistic and perceptive while he, though appreciative of craftsmanship, was a philistine with no artistic taste or appreciation of music and generally impatient of sentiment and culture. Perhaps because of rather than despite their differences, they remained in love until Katie died in his arms at the age of eighty.

Evans still had a year to serve in Canada so there was no prospect of immediate marriage. They decided that Katie would remain in Tywyn and that they would marry as soon after his return as possible. Evans returned to Tŷ Mawr and when Katie was back from Llanfaircaereinion, they continued to see each other during the remainder of his leave. Before he left, Katie gave him a lock of her hair.

Entries in Evans's journal are sporadic during his last year in Canada which was spent in Montreal. In late 1869, he was photo-graphed on a visit to the Niagara Falls.[4] The sepia image shows him posing against the backdrop of the waterfall; in a letter to Erie in 1913, he wrote 'When looking at the water coming in great waves rushing to the Fall of Niagara in 1869 I thought it was an allegory of events in time.' Although the memory suggested time was passing quickly, he must have been impatient for the year to end.

In that year, Evans saw action for the second time against Fenian[5] raids across the border into Québec. Although the first occasion in 1866 is not mentioned in his journals, in 1870 he received the Canadian General Service Medal with bars for the 1866 and 1870 engagements.[6] The latter appears to have been for action in the repulsion of an incursion near Huntingdon just over a month before he left Canada for good.

At long last, the time came for the battery's return to Britain.

July 5 – Left Montreal with the Battery for England in the new river passenger boat, 'The Montreal' to Québec …
July 6 – Embarked at Québec on board the Indian troopship 'The Crocodile', sent especially because H.R.H. Prince Arthur[7] is returning with the Rifle Brigade.

Evans described the Prince as 'almost teetotal' and claimed to have been the only true abstainer on board as he had been on his outward journey nine years earlier.

The voyage was uneventful until they reached the Isle of Wight in the English Channel:

July 16 1870 – The Royal Yacht, 'Victoria and Albert', ... sent by the Queen, who is staying at Osbourne,[8] especially to take Prince Arthur to her ... The Captain of the yacht informed us that FRANCE HAD DECLARED WAR AGAINST PRUSSIA.[9]

The battery disembarked at Gravesend on 22 July, reaching the Woolwich barracks by train at 8.30 p.m. There Evans learned that he had been gazetted Veterinary Surgeon First Class during the voyage.

Hopes he might have had of a quick marriage were dashed by the political instability in Europe which kept the battery in London for the next two months but in September, they received orders to march to a new posting in Ipswich. As soon as they had settled in, he wrote to tell Katie she could prepare for the wedding and the two of them were eventually reunited in Tywyn on the 21 October.

Evans had told Katie that he would prefer to do without any religious ceremony – 'I should be happy with a gypsy wedding or a Red Indian one' – but Katie wanted a marriage service and he conceded that they should be married by the Calvinist minister at Bethel Chapel in Tywyn. However he was adamant that there should be no celebratory event after the ceremony. His diary entry for the day reads: 'October 26 1870 – Married at 8 a.m. left by the 9.10 a.m. train. We were alone at last in a first-class compartment. Arrived at Caernarvon for dinner, then visited the Castle'. Their precipitate departure led to rumours that Evans had abducted his bride.

The Welsh bard, Robyn Ddu Eryri[10] who had written an englyn for the marriage of Evans's parents, Evan and Mary, forty years earlier now wrote one for Evans and Katie.[11] Evan and Mary had also chosen Caernarfon for their honeymoon and had taken a trip to Bangor to admire Telford's new suspension bridge across the Menai Straits completed four years earlier. Now Evans took Katie to Bangor to see Stephenson's revolutionary, tubular Britannia Bridge which carried the London to Holyhead railway across the Straits. The outing was nearly ill-fated. The couple must have sauntered between the lines past the massive stone lions guarding the mainland entrance towards dark openings to the two huge cast iron tubes.

We were strolling between the rails when we heard a terrible roar and not one but two trains bore down upon us, one from the Island of Anglesey [Ynys Môn] and one from the mainland, so that we were trapped between the two. I clasped Katie to me and shouted into her ear 'Stay perfectly still!' We clung together, her head buried in my coat, in the narrow space between the up and down line. The two shrieking monsters rushed past us on either side like flaming dragons and the wind of their passing lifted my hair and blew out the ribbons of Katie's bonnet.[12]

Towards the end of their honeymoon, the couple visited a photographer. Katie appears as a pretty young woman in a bonnet with Evans a thin young man with a serious, pensive expression at her side. Their honeymoon over, they returned to Ipswich where they set up house in Waterloo Road. The auguries for a long and happy marriage did not appear to be good: they can have known very little of each other and their experience of life was very different. Evans had seen something of the world while Katie had hardly, if ever, left Wales.

There are few records of their life in Ipswich. It is safe to assume that Evans pursued his interests in comparative religion and in local and national social affairs and politics. As always, he was active in promoting abstinence and appeared as a speaker at a meeting of the National Temperance League on 'Temperance in the Army'. The meeting, held at Exeter Hall in the Strand in London on 28 November 1871, was attended by 400 soldiers and in his address, Evans discussed the greater ability of abstaining soldiers to withstand hardship, fatigue and extremes of climate.[13]

As he had done in Toronto, Evans sought to engage in science and medicine. His commanding officer granted him permission to undertake research at the Ipswich Infirmary which he attended every day. It was here that he became involved in treating a young boy, the son of a sergeant in his battery, who had been run down by a dog cart. The wheel had passed over his head and he was carried to the Infirmary unconscious where, a few days later, his distressed mother begged Evans to treat him.[14]

I found that the boy had tetanus, and I was invited by the other doctors to a consultation ... I said I regarded the disease as a fever due to some specific cause for which there was no known remedy.

Like other specific fevers it had to run its course. I said our duty was to keep the patient in the best possible position for self-recovery; that was, to favour as much easy rest as possible, to avoid anything that might excite the spasm, keep in a dark, silent room, no noise from without or within, give no food of any kind, nor any medicine, but let the patient drink water ad lib. No one should go to see him except a specially selected nurse and the house-surgeon.

His proposed treatment met strong opposition from the other doctors who took special exception to the suggestion that no medicine should be prescribed; there was no evidence that any was effective and Evans was adamant that no unproven treatment should be administered.[15] With the consent of the boy's parents, he agreed to take full responsibility for his decisions and the boy recovered. 'It is the only case of tetanus I ever had to treat in man, but I have treated a number of cases in horses on the same principle and all recovered.' This instance of Evans undertaking the treatment of a patient outside his immediate circle was unusual. Generally, he made no practical use of his medical knowledge and skills except on his family and friends.

The most significant event during their time in Ipswich was the birth of their first child, a daughter, on 1 September 1871. His first grandchild was greeted by Evan with an englyn written in his bardic name of Ap Ieuan, a practice he repeated for each of his grandchildren. The baby was named Myfanwy Wynona but always called by her second name, a reference to his visit to the American Indian encampment and meaning 'eldest daughter' in the Sioux language. This was the first example of Evans's penchant for burdening his children with outlandish names based on significant places or events in his life.

Evans was an earnestly devoted father. As soon as the baby was born, he started a whimsical diary to chart her progress which he wrote in the first person as if the entries were Wynona's.[16] All this amused Katie. She said later that his 'droll seriousness' in their early

years together often made her laugh 'till the tears ran down my face …
This caused him to be alarmed that there was something wrong with
my tear ducts and he said he must examine them – and this made me
laugh all the more.'

In the spring of 1872, Evans was transferred to the Army Service
Corps and posted back to Woolwich. Katie and the baby returned to
Wales while he looked for a suitable house near the barracks. On 1 June,
Evans met them at Euston Station to take them down to their new
home in West Plumstead. There the family was to remain for the next
five years.

Once again, his duties occupied only a proportion of Evans's daily
round leaving him plenty of time for his new preoccupation, his love
for, and duty to, his young family. He and Katie were indulgent parents.
When Wynona was a year old, Evans took the entire household on an
outing to the Crystal Palace. His entry in 'Wynona's Diary' describes the
baby's delight at the animals and birds and the servants' bewilderment
at all the 'strange things' they saw. By December, Katie was pregnant
again. Their second daughter, born on 12 July 1873, was named Erie
after the Great Lake between Canada and the United States.

There were occasions when the army demanded more of him as
when the battery left Woolwich on manoeuvres or route marches. On
one of these, in September 1873, Evans spent the night at The Bell in
Edmonton where he wrote to his father describing the 'only moderately
interesting' country they were marching through. 'I am too much of a
Welshman and too fond of mountains', he explained, 'to be charmed
with England … But the road we came by has been the highway from
London to Chester and Môn (Anglesey) ever since the Roman invasion.'[17] Wales was always in his thoughts.

In spite of the new demands on his time and attention, it can
be assumed that Evans found time to pursue his usual interests. The
couple would have attended a local chapel and Katie would have become
involved with the wider community, her warmth and gregariousness
expanding the family's social circle. But he needed other outlets for his
intellectual energies. Woolwich was within easy reach of central London
by train, a fast service taking thirty-five to forty-five minutes to Charing

Cross. Less than a kilometre from the station were King's College and King's College Hospital where he enrolled on postgraduate courses in histology and experimental physiology. The nearby Royal London Ophthalmic Hospital provided another opportunity for expanding his medical expertise and he registered for a course in ophthalmology.

Evans's enjoyment of life with his young family was marred by worries about his family back in Tywyn. Both Evan, now seventy-two and Mary, in her late sixties, were in poor health and losing their sight. The younger of his two sisters, Maria, had married a labourer on the farm, John Jones, who had taken over the management of Tŷ Mawr as Evan's health had deteriorated. With three young sons, responsibility for running the farmhouse now fell to her and her health too was beginning to fail. His older sister, Eliza, had married a seafarer, Griffith Dedwydd, and had moved into a cottage in Barmouth with their eight children where she struggled to manage while he was at sea. To make matters easier, Evans bought them a house in Borth-y-Gest just outside Porthmadog.

His parents' difficulties were compounded by the realisation of a fear which had hung over them for some time. All but twenty-three acres of the land Evan farmed was now leased from Charles Edwards of Dolgellau and in the autumn of 1873, Edwards decided to sell, offering free possession when the lease expired on 25 March 1874. The auctioneer's catalogue described the land as:

> 363 acres of excellent arable meadow, pasture and uplands. The farms are occupied by Evan Evans who has held the same upon leases which will expire by Lady Day next, when greatly increased rents may be obtained ... Views from every part of this fine estate over Cardigan Bay [Bae Ceredigion] and Caernarvonshire [Sir Gaernarfon].

Evan was heartbroken. His family had farmed the land for over a century and he had lived at Tŷ Mawr all his life. He flatly refused to contemplate leaving the farm, insisting that he would continue to farm the twenty-three acres that remained his own.

The sale went through and the new owner appointed Evan's son-in-law, John Jones, as his manager. Although life for Evan and Mary appeared to carry on much as before, seeing Jones take over must have been a humiliating reminder that he had been supplanted as proprietor of Tŷ Mawr. The new owner's decision to build a substantial house directly in front of the old farmhouse rubbed salt in the wound.

In the autumn of 1874, Evans received a new posting to Ireland where he was to be stationed at Curragh Camp just outside Kildare. Katie and the children went to stay with Eliza in Borth-y-Gest while Evans found suitable accommodation. In April 1875, a few months after the family was reunited in Dublin, Evans received a telegram with news of his sister Maria's death at the early age of forty-two. Never strong, she had eventually succumbed to the strain of managing the farmhouse and caring for her husband, her sons and her ailing parents. Katie wrote later that Evans had been inconsolable and had wept in her arms so that she had come to understand, for the first time, the depth of his feelings.

In the autumn following Maria's death, Evan became seriously ill and wrote to Evans in Ireland for medical advice. He expressed his question in doggerel in English which he used for trivial themes, reserving Welsh for the expression of higher thoughts and feelings. This illness and the blow of Maria's death persuaded Evan and Mary to leave Tŷ Mawr to live with Eliza. Deeply distressed at being uprooted from their family home, the old couple divided their furniture between their two surviving children and Maria's family. On 16 January the following year, 1876, Katie and Evans's third daughter was born at the Curragh Camp receiving the customary englyn from her grandfather.[18] At Evans's insistence, the child was named Towena after Towyn, the anglicised form of the name of his family's home town.

In the same year, James Collins, then serving in Ireland, was appointed Principal Veterinary Surgeon to the Army, succeeding John Wilkinson at the young age of forty-six. Before he left to take up his new post, he was visited by his brother, F. F. Collins, himself recently promoted to Principal Veterinary Surgeon to the Army in India.[19] During the visit, the brothers called on Evans in the Curragh Camp. It seems both men had been impressed by his wide experience of veterinary science and practice and were considering him for a role with the Army in India.

Katie had always understood that Evans's army career would involve another period of service overseas and in the summer of 1877, he received confirmation that he was to be posted to India. The news came as another blow to his mother who sank into a deep depression from which she never recovered, dying on 11 July. Evans had always been close to her and kept a lock of her hair in an envelope marked 'Dear Mother's hair, cut August 31st 1872' all his life.

On 14 September 1877, Evans was gazetted back to the Royal Artillery from the Army Service Corps in anticipation of his departure and given one month's leave to prepare. The following day he received his commission in the Royal Regiment of Artillery. Just before they left the Curragh Camp, he and Katie were visited by James Meyrick, himself on leave from India. This was the first time Katie had met him and they took to each other immediately as Meyrick talked of his experiences and explained what Evans should expect in his new posting. Before he left, he helped Evans make a list of the kit and equipment he should take to India which he headed 'Memo Troopship'.

On 26 September the family returned to Tywyn. As the climate and conditions in India were considered unsuitable for young children, Katie reconciled herself to a long separation and they took a furnished house near her aunt and uncle, Mr and Mrs Rees, where she and the three girls would remain while he was away. Having made the necessary arrangements for his family, Evans set about acquiring his tropical kit and equipment. His 'Memo Troopship' listed:

3 white trousers, 1 cloak and cape, 1 cardigan jacket (to go in box with ulster), 6 merino shirts, 2 undress trousers, 3 flannel, 3 silk vests, 3 merino drawers, 1 helmet, 1 forage cap, 1 veil, 7 dinner napkins, 2 bath towels, 2 toilet towels, 6 silk pocket handkerchiefs, 1 cane-seat deckchair (carpet seats get dirty), 2 pairs of boots, 1 pair of slippers, 2 spectacles, white and black, 6 pairs of cotton socks, 1 box of safety matches and a few small wax tapers to light in cabin in emergency.

However for him, the most important item of his equipment was his new, state-of-the-art microscope with several lenses and all the necessary accessories.

His preparations complete, he parted from Katie and his daughters on the platform of Tywyn Station on 30 October 1877. He was not to see Katie for another three years and his daughters for eight.

9

INDIA

After final preparations at Woolwich, Evans left for Portsmouth on 3 October to embark on H.M.I.T.S.[1] *Jumna* which sailed for Mumbai (Bombay) the next morning.[2] When the ship called at Alexandria in early November, Evans posted a long letter to Katie.

> Here I am, Katie bach, actually on the Mediterranean Sea, surrounded by all that is sacred in ancient history. Homer's Iliad and Odyssey, Virgil's Aeneas, the Phoenicians ... the ships of Tarsus ... the Holy Land ... Now these countries are the 'dark places of the earth' and we are the bearers of 'Light to them who sit in darkness'. England is the focus of all that is civilising and good to regenerate the world.[3]

Evans was clearly ready to play his part in what was then perceived to be Britain's imperial mission to bring enlightenment, progress and peace to its subjects.

As had happened on his voyage to Canada, he found himself taking issue with the padre on the *Jumna*. 'We have a very high clergyman on board ... I was so sickened by his nonsensical ways that I sat through the whole service after the first hymn'. After the service, Evans went up on deck where he found two officers smoking and discussing the service: 'I don't believe men worship God by mummery like that. Read the Sermon on the Mount. That's my religion – all my religion is contained in that.'[4] Evans must have approved.

The *Jumna* reached Mumbai on 7 December 1877. Evans was fortunate in arriving in India during the long period of relative stability that followed the suppression of the Indian Insurrection in 1858. The East India Company, dissolved that year, had been replaced by direct rule by the British Government which attempted to extend contemporary British standards of governance to India and improve the lot of its Indian subjects.[5]

Evans wrote a long letter to Katie almost every week. The letters express his love for her and their daughters and his longing for their reunion while regretting his shortcomings as a husband and father.[6] The letters also provide an account of his life in India and of his impressions of the country, its customs and its people. It is plain from his first letter that Evans's attitude was very different from that of the overwhelming majority of his fellow Europeans and especially of his army comrades.[7]

> Perhaps the most wonderful thing is how most English people stick to the ordinary humdrum of civilisation. The officers and ladies who came out with me … spent today in visiting each other, loitering about the verandas of the hotels, smoking and drinking soda water, going to the club … I tried my best to get a party to Elephanta,[8] and found five willing to join if it could be done early, before the fashionable calling hour. That failed. Then I tried to get some to visit the 'Towers of Silence' and the native town, and all said it was too nasty. So I took my own bent and went by myself … it was far better alone than in ill-assorted company.

Evans's account of his exploration of Mumbai reveals his capacity for intelligent engagement with his new surroundings and the Indians he encountered; during the outing, he saw only one other European.

> I did not see a single woman veiled … [they] go about commonly nearly naked. In the aristocratic part of the Native town I saw many ladies driving out in very expensive attire – some of them had really beautiful faces – all the women, to the very poorest, have good figures with perfect grace in all their movements.

... what clothing the poor had [was] very clean ... I know extensive districts in London ... where the majority of people are far more dirty than the poor Hindoos ... So I am very favourably impressed.

Returning from Elephanta Island, Evans made his way to the Towers of Silence where Parsis[9] exposed their dead to be devoured by vultures. Evans had obtained a letter of introduction to the priest who answered Evans's questions about Zoroastrian doctrine through an interpreter. Evans concluded: 'I suppose the <u>Faith</u> of one is as blind and unreasonable as the other and so far as there is any virtue in blind, unquestioning faith, a Parsi is as good as anybody.'

During the day, Evans also visited a Hindu cremation site where he 'saw three fires, a body in each in different states of consumption. One was just commencing to roast, another was nearly all in ashes.'

As soon as he had come ashore, Evans had received orders to proceed immediately to Sialkot in the Punjab some 1,650 miles to the north-west. He was to investigate an endemic and often fatal disease among the army horses in this strategically important northern region of the province.[10]

Before he left, Evans engaged a head servant:

I have engaged a head servant ... He is 20 years of age and can speak and <u>write</u> a little English, and appears to be unusually intelligent. He is a Hindoo. Many officers object to intelligent servants, especially those who can read and write, but I take it as a recommendation if a man's good otherwise. I like this man's expression. I am glad he is young that I may train him for myself.[11]

Departing on 14 December, he travelled north to Agra where he interrupted his journey for two days. There he visited the Taj Mahal by moonlight where he was entranced by the echo. Lying on the tomb, he describes a mystical episode in which he was transported by feelings of affinity with his dead mother and sister and with Katie and the children. 'While my wife and children live ... may God grant me life also, and pardon me if I sin in longing for the dead ... There can be no sorrow for me in life more than I can bear while you remain with me.' While in Agra, he met a Baptist missionary who had been with him on the *Great Eastern* and found time to attend chapel and a temperance meeting where he encountered several soldiers he had known in Canada. He continued his journey to Wazirabad by train and thence by cart the 27 miles to Sialkot, arriving on 22 December 1877.[12]

At the time of Evans's arrival at Sialkot, the understanding of disease transmission was on the cusp of a significant advance in which Griffith Evans was to play a part.[13] Until the mid-nineteenth century, ideas on the causes of disease had been dominated by the Miasma Theory which held that diseases are caused by 'miasma' or poisonous emanations – 'bad air' – principally from decaying organic matter.[14] The theory did lead to some improvements in public health as a result of better housing and sanitary measures designed to reduce 'miasma' around human habitation. The Germ Theory that disease was caused by micro-organisms has ancient origins and was articulated by Girolamo Fracastoro in the mid-sixteenth century.[15] However his work and that of other early proponents of the hypothesis, including Bassi, Henle and Snow,[16] was undermined by the prevailing acceptance of spontaneous generation as an explanation of the appearance of organisms causing putrefaction and disease. Belief in spontaneous generation had persisted in spite of being refuted experimentally by Francesco Redi in the seventeenth century and was not finally disproved until Pasteur's famous 'col de cygnet' flask experiments in 1859.[17]

In 1850, Davaine had found 'small filiform bodies having about twice the length of a blood corpuscle' in the blood of sheep infected with anthrax. At the time, neither he nor his collaborator, Rayer, suggested that these were of any significance. Others reported the presence of similar micro-organisms in other animals infected with anthrax and in 1855, Pollender considered that they resembled bacteria. In a series of papers on anthrax between 1863 and 1870, Davaine reported finding the organisms in all infected, but not in healthy, animals and showed that the disease could be induced in healthy recipients by inoculations of minute quantities of blood from infected animals or by feeding contaminated food. His conclusion that 'bacteridia' caused the disease was not accepted by many contemporaries on the grounds that other factors in infected blood could not be ruled out. This would require that the microoganisms could be isolated which was impossible at the time. However, in an 1871 paper, Ernst Tiegel reported experiments in which he filtered infected blood through clay to remove the bacteridia. He found that healthy subjects injected with the residue containing the micro-organisms developed the disease while those injected with the filtered blood did not. Although Tiegel's work was largely ignored, by the mid-1870s, anthrax was recognised as the disease in which the evidence of an association with a micro-organism or 'germ' was clearest.[18]

Robert Koch published his first paper on anthrax in 1876. In it, he described the life cycle of the anthrax bacillus, *Bacillus anthracis* (Cohn 1872), showing that it produced resistant spores. He went on to show that healthy animals injected with 'entirely pure' spore masses from cultures of *B. anthracis* in vitreous humour[19] developed the disease and claimed this proved causation. However, the only evidence of the purity of the spore masses came from microscopic examination which his contemporaries regarded as insufficient to prove the absence of contamination by other potential causative agents. Among these sceptical contemporaries was Louis Pasteur who had shown earlier that microbes associated with disease in silkworms produced resistant spores and were the probable cause of the disease. In 1877, he published the first two of a series of papers on anthrax in which he set out to prove that the bacillus was indeed the causative agent of the disease. Using both organic and inorganic sterile media, he transferred the bacillus through a sufficiently long series of successive cultures to ensure that none of the original micro-organisms or any other material derived from the original diseased animal remained. He then filtered out the resulting microorganisms and showed that the residue invariably induced anthrax in healthy animals. Pasteur's claim to have demonstrated causality was challenged by Koch and others but came to be accepted by most workers in the field. Evans had been following this recent research and had clearly seen or was aware of the contents of Koch's 1876 paper. Whether or not he was aware of Pasteur's two papers on anthrax published in the year just past is not known.

After his long and gruelling journey, Evans set to work. The sick horses presented a wide variety of symptoms ranging from fever, enteritis and bloody diarrhoea to respiratory distress and trembling.[20] With no laboratory except his army tent, no trained assistants and under challenging climatic conditions, he embarked on sampling and examining the blood of infected animals with his new, portable microstand. 'You cannot imagine how trying it was. The glare, the intense heat, the stench, the lack of any other pair of hands, certainly did not make for fruitful research.' Nevertheless, he was delighted at the opportunity to indulge his passion for microscopy in tackling an important disease in the field. After several weeks of intensive work, he concluded that the disease was caused by a 'parasite of the blood'. Neither fixatives nor stains[21] were available at the time making observation of microorganisms extremely difficult, even under laboratory conditions with the best microscopes. Evans, working in the field under difficult conditions, managed to detect the characteristic rod-like bacilli in fresh blood from infected horses and to diagnose anthrax, the first record of the disease on the sub-continent.

He also made another significant observation:

> what surprised me most [was] that the first change in the blood seen by the microscope was a great increase in the number of large, white corpuscles before I could see a bacillus ... I expressed my conviction that the large, granular corpuscles had a very important relation to the bacilli, but I could not think what it was. I repeatedly emphasised my belief that it deserved special investigation.[22]

Three years later, he was to observe a similar surge in the numbers of white blood cells in horses infected with the degenerative disease, surra. Convinced that the phenomenon was significant, he was unable to explain its function, a failure that was to irritate him for the rest of his life. His report on the cause of the outbreaks in northern Punjab was accepted although his diagnosis of anthrax was greeted with scepticism in some quarters. However, his plea that he be allowed to continue to investigate the significance of the white corpuscles was ignored.

Evans was to spend a year in Sialkot. As usual, he made constructive use of his leisure time. He worked hard to learn Hindustani, engaging a *Munshi* or teacher whom he described as 'a very godly man'.[23] As always, he took a keen interest in local religions, interrogating his Munshi and priests at the temples and comparing the Hinduism of the dominant group in Sialkot with the Muslim faith of the peasants. In their frequent discussions about religion, his Munshi explained that the image worship of Hinduism had been misunderstood and that it represents a route by which prayer and praises are directed to the one true God in which Hindus, Muslims and Christians all believe.[24] Evans engaged with local customs and social behaviour praising practices he regarded as admirable and being sharply critical of those he felt were reprehensible. He was, for example, horrified to find children being sold by their impoverished parents in local markets.[25]

In May 1878, Evans and other Europeans in Sialkot were invited to a durbar by the Maharajah of the neighbouring princely state of Kashmir to celebrate the wedding of his fourteen-year-old son to a nine-year-old bride.[26] The durbar was to be held in Jammu where a similar durbar had been held in 1876 in honour of the visit of the Prince of Wales. The party left at dawn in the same 'drag'[27] that had been provided for the Prince and on reaching the banks of the River Tawi opposite Jammu, the men were transferred to magnificently caparisoned elephants to take them across, with a boat provided for the ladies.

They were to stay in the Palace built for the Prince of Wales where

> [a] sumptuous breakfast awaited us and I may say here once for all that we were from first to last entertained in a manner worthy of a Royal Host. Our number consisted of 7 ladies, 25 officers and two civilians … besides four or five young children … One lady having no child brought her pet dog. The consequence was that she was excluded from the Durbar as she would not leave her dog in charge of anybody else and dogs are not allowed at Durbars

though children are … The lady … felt aggrieved but she was not
the only unreasonable humanity amongst us

Evans spent the afternoon exploring the palace and its surroundings.
During the afternoon, a delegation led by the son of the Prime Minister
of the Court, a general in the Maharajah's army, called on them to
explain the evening's proceedings.

> In the course of a conversation with three of us he said that the
> durbar was going to be unusually grand … One of us was a full
> colonel in the Bengal army and to my shame he asked the general
> what this entertainment would cost the Maharajah. The native
> general showed his better breeding by looking astonished at the
> question and then in a tone of rebuke replied, 'I don't know what it
> will cost. Whatever it is, his highness does it for the entertainment
> of his guests' & then turned and walked off.
>
> The colonel showed his idiocy by laughing loudly. I felt inclined
> to kick him, and I took care to let our own General know it … It
> does appear sometimes probable that the Hindoo notion of the
> transmigration of souls is not far wrong [and] that this Col had
> the soul of an ass in the body of a man.
>
> There were some among our number who went there purely for
> the sake of gluttony… & other luxuries … There were others …
> who thought it was their duty to find fault with everything … and
> revile the natives who did only according to the ancient custom
> of their country.
>
> At 7 p.m. we started a procession on elephants for the full dress
> durbar … I find the greatest difficulty in conveying to you a faint
> notion of the scene. I could not possibly have imagined it if I had
> not seen it.

The boorishness of some of his fellow guests aside, Evans clearly enjoyed
the magnificence of the occasion. He was particularly taken with the
nautch dancers:[28] 'I had often heard of the beauty of Kashmiri women
but never expected to find one nearly so beautiful as several I saw'. The

following day, the guests were shown round the Maharajah's Palace and Evans was spellbound by the view from a balcony overhanging a garden, 'one of the most beautiful landscapes I ever saw'.

The following evening, the celebrations reached a climax with the veneration of the young prince and the presentation of gifts of gold, silver and precious stones; 'the poor boy so weighted by a heavy velvet and gold-embroidered robe, a massive solid gold crown, and a thick gold wire chain work veil hanging from the crown over the face down to his chest, that he could hardly walk'. During the evening, Evans learned that the gifts included a compulsory donation of a month's pay from every officer and man in the Maharajah's army; 'if that is true it is very unjust'. The following morning, the party returned to Sialkot.

Evans's handling of his investigation of the outbreak of anthrax established his reputation in the service as a skilled diagnostician capable of working under difficult conditions. In early August 1878, he was informed by Collins that he was to be promoted to Inspecting Veterinary Surgeon with effect from the following February. In the meantime, he was summoned to Kolkata (Calcutta) to take up the duties in an acting capacity. The train journey across northern India took a gruelling two days and three nights in searing heat made worse by the fact that Evans was sickening. As soon as he arrived in Kolkata, he was struck down by a high fever and might have died had it not been for a cousin in the city who took him to his house and engaged a nurse to tend him.

Evans gave instructions that Katie was not to be told of his illness for fear of worrying her but the absence of letters made her anxious that he had been sent to the North-West Frontier. Increasing tension on the Afghan border in September and October 1878 gave her reason for concern so she was relieved to receive his letter of 9 October, by which time he was regaining his strength.[29]

> For several days I thought I would probably die and the prospect of leaving you and the children was terrible … I believe also that if I had not been removed to Cousin's house … with a good nurse, I could not have survived.[30]

During his convalescence, Evans exercised on the flat roof of his cousin's house observing the life of the city below.

> Temperature in my room in a good shade has been 88 [° F] every day this week … Hardly any Europeans go out walking here, they all take horse or carriage exercise … Calcutta is a very fashionable and dressy place, being the seat of the Indian Govt in winter months … I see all the men in tall hats and kid gloves and black frock coats as if they were in London … Nowhere else in India have I seen men wear frock coats and black chimney pot hats.
>
> … I am determined to keep out of society here, no satisfaction can be got out of it. I do not feel in the least lonely except for you and the children because I have plenty to divert my mind … reading rooms, a very good museum of Nat[ural] Hist[ory] and geology.[31]

By the end of November, Evans was strong enough to begin his rounds of inspection of military stations to check on the health of the horses and veterinary provision. His remit as Inspecting Veterinary Officer included the larger part of the Ganges basin from Delhi in the west to Kolkata in the east. Very few of the stations on his tours could be reached by rail so he was forced to endure the acute discomfort of an unsprung dak-gharry[32] which typically covered no more than fifty miles in eight hours over the rough tracks. Where there were no tracks he rode a horse or mule, was carried by teams of men in a *palki* or palanquin or travelled by river boat. In these often remote areas, he had also to contend with the constant risk of attack by robbers although, as he wrote to Katie, 'you need not be afraid on my account. They dare not kill me on the Queen's service, but they will try to rob me if they think they can succeed. I shall certainly not spare to shoot them if they try!'[33]

His letters between November 1878 and February 1879 were written from the widely scattered stations on his circuit of inspection. During the first tours when his strength was still not fully restored, he risked exposure to disease. Of his visit to Morar, reached by river boat and an overnight journey by dak-gharry, he wrote: 'This is the most detested station I have been to not only for its difficulty of access to it but for its unhealthiness. Bad fevers are constant here, and cholera frequent – about 50 men and seven officers died of cholera here last summer.'[34]

His exhaustion after a day's travelling often led to restless nights. In Lucknow after a particularly gruelling tour, he was troubled by vivid dreams:

> Maria appeared to me very distinctly ... and I was in my dream conscious that she was dead.
>
> I understood her to say that I had formerly promised to pay for the education of her boys, and I replied: 'I have no recollection of ever making any promise of that sort. She then looked exceedingly distressed and said very slowly, 'You do not understand what I mean' ... and she gradually desolved [sic] away ... I smelt the smell of a corpse strongly

Since her death three years earlier, he had felt guilty that he had not done more for her when she was struggling to cope at Tŷ Mawr farmhouse.

Looking back on his year in a letter in December 1878, Evans wondered how he had managed to weather the demands of those first months in his weakened state.

> There is also in my nature ... the element of continued perseverance – if I have any object in view to attain to – and I take real pleasure in overcoming difficulties. That is my instinct. I am not in any way 'brilliant' and never was – but a plodding tortoise that sometimes passed the sleeping hare.[35]

Just before Christmas, he stayed at the Railway Hotel in Kanpur (Cawnpore) where the proprietor was a Welshman from near Llanfaircaereinion named Lee who remembered Katie's father. Lee had been a sergeant in the 53rd Highland Regiment during the Indian Insurrection twenty-one years earlier and recounted his experiences. He had been in the first detachment to reach Kanpur after the massacre of British men, women and children who had surrendered to the rebel leader, Nana Sahib. Lee showed Evans around the town while he told his story which Evans relayed to Katie. He was unable to sleep that night, haunted by Lee's vivid descriptions of the scenes in Kanpur and of the atrocities committed against the defeated rebel sepoys Lee had witnessed in November 1857 while serving with the 93rd Highlanders after the second relief of Lucknow by General Sir Colin Campbell. Moving on to Lucknow, Evans spent a lonely Christmas there in a hotel. On the morning of Christmas Day, he visited sites and buildings in the town associated with the Insurrection.[36]

His first tour in the new year took him to Faizabad in a densely populated farming region. Describing the splendid trees full of birds and monkeys, Evans told Katie of his concern at the rapid growth in population, revealing a lapse in his usual compassion for his fellow man: 'I am coming to think that it is evil rather than good for us to supply food to them in famine times since they will not emigrate, and persist in multiplying their numbers to a greater extent than the land can feed them.'

In early January 1879, Evans received orders to proceed to Bonda, thence to Nowgong and on to Sagar Island (Sangor) at the mouth of the Hoogly River in Bengal.

> Colonel Cowper ... recommended Government to let me do the business of the [Annual Casting] Committee [at Nowgong and Sagar] alone and on my own responsibility, as I am obliged to go there already for my inspection. It was never done by one man in India before and in England it is always done by the General commanding the district. The reason why a committee is adopted in India is that officers too often bring forward good government horses to be cast in order that their friends may buy them cheaper. I am flattered therefore to find so much confidence placed in my judgement and integrity.[37]

The task of these casting committees, normally comprising three senior officers, was to decide which military horses were surplus to requirements and to make sure that no sound animals were fraudulently identified for disposal.

Nowgong was a remote station in wild country 'inhabited by jackals, wolves and panthers which feed on the beautiful deer.' The Colonel and senior officers there were surprised that Evans, not yet officially gazetted as Inspecting Veterinary Officer, had been instructed to carry out the duties of the Casting Committee alone.

> [T]hey said if it cost too much to send Col Cowper and Col. Lane [the other members of the committee] two of the senior combatant officers at Nowgong might have been appointed to act with me. I told them I saw no reason to depart from the instructions I have received from the Government of India and that I would commence my duties tomorrow morning. No doubt the Government of India knew what it was doing.[38]

Evans's letter describing his return from Nowgong may have explained why Colonels Cowper and Lane were reluctant to make the journey.[39]

> Here I am again just returned from a jolting in an almost springless Dak gharry for 28 hours 123 miles from Nowgong ... At one place we stuck deep in dust going up a little hill ... I got out of my blankets, my servant also dismounted from the roof and we put our shoulders to the two hind wheels ... I ... feel now very shaky.

The next stage of the journey, from Fatehpur (Futtehpore) to Sagar, was no easier:

> I ... shall proceed tomorrow by rail via Allahabad and Futtehpore to Sangor. Sangor is two days and two nights by Dhooli Dak from the railway – that is, a conveyance on the shoulders of men

In his next letter,[40] Evans continues:

> We travelled at night, 2 nights resting the intervening day... twelve men, three at each end at a time – changing often but hardly stopping – carried me with my bedding and small baggage 37 miles

at a stretch in 13 hours. They are all Hindoos, vegetarians and teetotallers – walk barefoot, with hardly any clothing, humming a song all the time ... The road is through a wild country – hilly and stony and for want of rain, very dusty so that by morning I felt choked with dust.

Sangor is by far the prettiest place naturally that I have seen in India ... From the top [of the steep, conical hill] there is a splendid view of the lake and all about – I thought at the top only one thing was wanted to make the place beautiful and lovely and that was the company of you and the children.

After he had completed his inspection and casting duties in Sagar, Evans returned to the railhead and thence by train to Lucknow via Fatehpur where he drove to the Marble Rocks – 'the prettiest drive I have had in India'.

[It] would be a place of great resort if it were in Europe or America ... [where] there would have been great improvements made by Art – here all is left to nature and I was never more convinced than today that nature in all her phases can be improved by man from cultivating the Garden of Eden to trimming a man's beard.

On the last leg of the journey, an Italian priest entered the compartment and they began to discuss Catholic doctrine; the priest's initial assumption that Evans was Catholic was soon dispelled. The priest asked him to what sect he belonged.

I told him I belonged to no sect but was in fellowship and communion with all who served God as Christ did ... Priestcraft in all its forms I protested against as being contrary to the gospel of Jesus Christ ... because priests kept others from God by constituting themselves ... between God and men. He was rather astonished but took it in good part and said he did not know how to argue with me because I recognised no published creed or common prayer book that he knew of.[41]

There followed a long discussion until, shaking hands as they parted on arrival at Lucknow, Evans said he hoped they might meet again in Heaven. The priest 'looked rather doubtful but smiled and said farewell'.

In January, Evans was troubled by a letter from his sister, Eliza, explaining that their father, Evan, was being pursued by creditors for £300, money still owed under the guarantee Evan had provided for his brother which had overwhelmed his finances. In his letter to Katie, he expressed his exasperation.

> Eliza says if she had £300 she would pay it for father 'to wipe off the disgrace' ... I can't see any disgrace to Father, it is his misfortune – an error of judgement not in principle ... I am truly grieved but I conscientiously do not see any reason for me to take up the burden which has crushed father. I as well as Eliza and Maria gave up all that Grandmother left us (£3,000) in order to pay father's debts – debts not contracted for anything on our account. I have always refused to go beyond that ... Moreover, I have no money to give.[42]

Katie's response was to remind Evans that his old father had only a few years left to him and to plead that they should do everything they could 'to make those years bearable'.

In February 1879, Evans was officially gazetted as Inspecting Veterinary Surgeon and was warmly congratulated by James Meyrick who was passing through Kolkata; he himself was still awaiting promotion after ten years in the Punjab. Evans told him of his father's predicament and Meyrick immediately offered to lend the £300 himself. When it was refused, Meyrick remitted the money to Katie. Hearing of this, Evans agreed that Katie could accept the money as a loan provided they paid interest.

Evans had already been informed by Collins that his promotion would require him to remain in India for a further five years and he had written to Katie to express his disappointment. 'Five years is more than I can bear to entertain now. The experience of the past year has

FIGURE 10 Griffith Evans in the formal uniform of an Inspecting Veterinary Surgeon in the Indian Army. (Wellcome Collection)

not tended to reconcile me to live apart from you.' However, he could console himself that there were now strong indications that he was being thought of as Collins's successor as Principal Veterinary Surgeon in India. 'I stand a very good chance of succeeding Collins in Simla; and, in that event, I am in hopes of bringing you there too, if we can manage the welfare of the little ones.'[43]

Evans resumed his circuit of inspections through the following months but his letters were beginning to suggest that the constant and arduous travelling was getting him down. They began to show clear signs of his worsening spirits and increased nostalgia for home. It appears that a crisis point was reached in June when Evans enclosed with his usual weekly letter to Katie a secret letter which she was to destroy. There is no indication of its contents but in it he presumably confided what was troubling him and asked for her advice.

> [It] is a great relief to submit [my difficulties] to you. A good woman's instinct is far better than reason to guide me out of such darkness as I have been in for some time past. 'Valley of the shadow of death' it may truly be called ... For years I have trusted to guide myself and you through it safely. Having failed, I resign myself completely to you for leadership to guide us both to light and freedom and assured safety again ...
>
> I make no reserve whatever in this case but rely upon you with that confidence which I wish you to place in me in other cases.

Katie's reply, which he destroyed, evidently provided him with the guidance he sought and he replied immediately to tell her that her response had made him very happy. There may have been a hint of what had been troubling Evans in advice Katie gave their youngest daughter, Mair, when, many years later, she was about to be separated from her husband on his return to India in 1922. Katie told her it was difficult for a man separated from his wife for long intervals to sublimate his physical desires, adding, 'The great thing is to be sure you keep his love.' Whether or not a photograph of a Miss Burton which Evans had sent to Katie some months before was relevant will never be known. Katie had reacted to the photograph light-heartedly: 'how beautiful she is. I believe you would have fallen in love with her, too, if your heart had not been already filled with the perfection of all human excellence in my person.'

His mood and morale restored, Evans resumed his duties while continuing to pursue his wider interests, particularly his interest in comparative religion. In Kolkata between tours of inspection in August and September, he embarked on a lengthy correspondence with Katie on the subject. He had become involved with the *Brahmo Samaj*,[44] a monotheistic reformist movement in Hinduism, describing its members as 'a good lot of men, honest truth seekers' and developed a friendship with the Bengali philosopher and social and religious reformer, Keshub Chandra Sen.[45] Sen was a controversial figure but his attempts to reconcile aspects of Christian doctrine and western spiritual tradition with Hinduism to found a universal belief system and his endorsement of British rule in India, attracted the attention of the British establishment. This resulted in an invitation, in 1870, to promote his ideas in England where he had campaigned against child marriage and in favour of the education of Indian women.

When Evans met him, Sen's influence had been severely undermined after he sanctioned the marriage of his young daughter to the boy Raja of Cooch Behar (Koch Bihar). His promotion of education for Indian women had also turned out to be qualified when he opposed their access to all but elementary schooling. Katie thought him a humbug but Evans defended him: 'he is a pure-minded man, Duwiol iawn (very Godly), without a shade of cant ...'

Evans also sympathised with Sen's concerns about education for Indian women.

> It seems cruel to advance them too soon ... [Educated girls are] looked upon as useless appendages – abnormal virgins ... One is ... Principal of the Ladies School ... I never saw anywhere such a timid hare of a woman ... Sen told me she is by far the most highly educated woman in India ... She wants a husband & yet there is no intelligent non idolater native of a suitable age who wants a wife! Keshab told me that the experience of these girls helped to make him more willing to accept the offer of the Government to marry his daughter to the Maharajah of Kuch Bihar.[46]

His friendship with Sen is a good example of Evans's ability to gain the confidence of Indians and to engage with them on equal terms, a rare phenomenon among his compatriots in India at the time.

The final phase of the Second Afghan War was precipitated by the murder in Kabul of the British Envoy, Sir Louis Cavagnari and his entourage on 3 September 1879. A British force in which cavalry units played a key role entered Afghanistan and Kabul was taken by the end of October.[47] Maintaining the health of the cavalry's mounts was of paramount importance and a fatal disease of horses known locally as 'surra'[48] was causing the Army concern. During September, Evans had written to Katie that he expected to receive orders to join the force then being prepared, news she had long dreaded.[49] Instead, he received orders to report to Collins in Shimla (Simla), the summer seat of the Indian Government. There, on 4 October, Collins told him that he himself would be joining the Afghan expedition to deal with the surra outbreak and that Evans was to take charge of the office of the Principal Veterinary Surgeon in Shimla in his absence. As he now had no prospect of returning home in the foreseeable future, Collins suggested that he begin making plans for Katie to join him. Evans wrote immediately to propose that she should come out the following October to avoid the heat of summer and allow time to make arrangements for the education and care of their children. Although it involved no formal promotion, Evans's appointment as acting Principal Veterinary Surgeon was further evidence of official confidence and encouraged him in his ambition to succeed Collins whose tour of duty ended in 1881. Taking his new responsibilities seriously, he learned that some of the veterinary surgeons in Shimla were shirking their duties and called them in to warn them. 'When they don't attend and improve after being admonished I hand them up sharp to the commander in chief for discipline ... The V.S. of the Thirteenth Hussars I fear will lose his commission. But it will be a gain to the service.'[50]

The magnificent surroundings of Shimla in the foothills of the Himalayas and above all, the prospect of seeing Katie again fortified Evans's morale and restored his health. He had taken a house on the town's outskirts from which, in his spare time, he roamed the hills reporting to Katie on the local customs like the marriage markets in hill villages where the women for sale were decked out in their finery with ornate gold marriage rings in their noses. Evans spent the Christmas of 1879 in Shimla and began to think about their life together in India. He contemplated Katie accompanying him on his tours and was particularly eager to show her the country around Sagar which had so captivated him. In the new year, he resumed his gruelling circuits around his vast area of responsibility and the unavoidable hardships of cross-country travel through remote districts gave him second thoughts on the wisdom of inviting Katie to accompany him

The months of the hot season of 1880 passed and in September, with Katie due to sail to join him in mid-month, Evans began to plan his programme of inspections so as to be free to travel to Kolkata to meet her in November. His plans were to be overtaken by events.

KATIE

While Evans's weekly letters to Katie provide a vivid picture of his work, his impressions of the country, the people he encountered and his thoughts and hopes, they also express his love for her and their daughters. They both believed that the incident of the secret letter had strengthened the bond between them and in June 1879, Evans sent Katie two gifts, the first to remember their wedding anniversary in October and the second in anticipation of the tenth anniversary of their engagement in April 1869. This last was an Indian necklace with an engraved locket into which Evans put a tiny note:

> 'In memory of Foundation day, April 1st 1869 to October 26th 1870.'

On 9 July 1879, Katie wrote to Evans to tell him that she had been banned from attending chapel meetings in Tywyn by the Minister, Mr Symonds.[1] Her offence had been to read the newly published auto-biography of Harriet Martineau[2] which he described as 'the most dangerous book of the age' and to lend it to her women friends.

> I told him all my doubts and difficulties, which of course horrified him … He told me I was in the grasp of Satan … and that my guilt was immeasurable after having had the advantage of being brought up with such a good man as Uncle Rees.

Evans was delighted: '[y]our last letter was the best tonic medicine I have had for a long while. The idea of your having been excommunicated from the [Chapel congregation] for heresy is very refreshing ... My greatest sorrow is for the pain it has given, I suppose, to good Uncle Rees.'[3] Katie replied on 1 September:

> I told Mr Symonds that I did not believe the infallibility of the Bible, nor in Eternal Punishment, and that I doubted the divinity of Christ ... When he told me I was entirely in the grip of Satan I replied that amongst other things I had given up a belief in a personal Devil and he said: 'I dare say, indeed, Mrs Evans.'[4]

The exchange emphasised how far the couple's independent thinking had evolved from the Nonconformist dogma of the time in north-west Wales.

Her Uncle Rees's health was deteriorating through late summer and early autumn and his death in October left Katie to cope with her bereaved aunt and the distress of the children. Erie in particular was affected: 'Erie told me last night when going to bed: "I don't think I can live. I am more unhappy now than I have ever been. Uncle dead, and Father in India."'

Worried also by the prospect of Evans being sent to Afghanistan, Katie felt depressed and run down and her doctor recommended a daily glass of port wine as a tonic. She was unwise enough to mention this in her next letter to Evans whose immediate and thoughtless response was a three-word telegram sent through Tywyn Post Office: 'DRINK NO ALCOHOL'. His rebuke quickly became public knowledge, further damaging her already tarnished reputation following her 'excommunication'. When his tactlessness was spelt out to him, he was contrite but adamant that she must not touch alcohol, even as a tonic; what she needed to restore her was 'fresh air, good steak and plenty of sleep'.

In the next few months, Evans's letters reflected his excitement at the prospect of their reunion while expressing his sadness at missing his daughters' childhood. He had been writing notes and letters to them

FIGURE 11 Katie in her late twenties.
(Tony Craven Walker)

since he had left but as the years passed and they matured, it became increasingly difficult for him to hit the right note. Now he tried to explain to them that they would have to accept their mother's absence when she came out to join him:

> Your dear mother will come to me next year ... And as I shall have borne three years without her for you, so you will bear years without her for me. You know I am more fond of, and love your Mother more than it is possible to imagine ... and when we all meet again, won't we be a happy family!

His words cannot have been much comfort to the little girls, then aged between four and eight.

With the coming of the New Year, it was time to begin serious preparations for Katie's departure. Like other wives whose husbands were away manning the Empire, she was torn between husband and children and the prospect of leaving her family and friends and most of all, of abandoning her young daughters must have been daunting. Although the couple discussed arrangements by letter, the task of actually making the decisions fell to Katie. She was helped by the wife of an Army friend in Woolwich, a Mrs Jones, who recommended a local boarding school, one of many catering for the children of Empire. There, Mrs Jones claimed – mistakenly as it turned out – the girls would receive a good education and be well cared for. The children's older cousin, Eliza's daughter Gwenddydd, was recruited to chaperone them on their journeys to and from Wales for the holidays which they were to spend in Borth-y-Gest.

When Katie told her Aunt Rees of her impending departure, her reaction was predictable. Since her husband's death, Katie, now her only close relative, had been her consolation and companion and she made no attempt to hide her anguish at the prospect of losing her. When Katie mentioned that Aunt Rees had asked why he could not come home, Evans wrote: 'My coming home is simply out of the question ... we are so short of men in India.'[5] Two days later, he wrote to her, hoping to reconcile her to Katie's absence.[6] She received his letter in silence and never spoke of it to Katie who continued to make her preparations as inconspicuously as possible.

Evans's growing excitement at the prospect of reunion is palpable. Reminding Katie that she had rebuked him for his unemotional proposal of marriage, he wrote:

> I often think I shall be stunned with joy inexpressible so that I won't be able to do more than look at you in admiration. You must not be disappointed if I appear at first as cool as you used to think me in 1868. You must not misinterpret me as you did then.

Katie gave a glimpse of her mischievous sense of humour when she told him of a visit to his sister Eliza: 'I felt quite tipsy after Eliza persuaded me to drink some home-made elder wine, because the breezes of Portmadoc had chilled me.' After his reaction to her 'tonic', she must have meant to be provocative and it prompted a predictably heavy-handed response:

> I am not sorry you got so tipsy on elder wine though I am vexed that Eliza gave it to you … I hope it will be a warning to you not to be tempted again. If you should feel cold like that, take a good draught of hot water and some lemon juice. And sit in a bath with hot water between your thighs.

He continued in red ink:

> You must make Eliza promise solemnly that she will not let one of our children taste her elder wine, or let them have other alcohol drink of any kind under any circumstances whatsoever when they are in her charge.

The couple's letters now began to deal with the practicalities of Katie's voyage out to India and of the life she would lead there.[7]

> Your passage to India from Southampton to Bombay or Madras will cost £68 besides the fee you will be expected to give the stewardess, ten shillings or a pound according to the trouble you give her...
> Don't ornament your under-linen too much because the native wash-men beat them against stones.

As her departure approached, he wrote of his physical longing for her: 'I have felt much more playful during the past week … with the expectation of the enjoyment of your society in a few months … I have been dreaming about you every night this week.' However, he clearly believed in moderating his physical needs. Katie had written to tell Evans that Mr Symonds, the minister who had barred her from the chapel, had lost his wife. Symonds must have had a large family because, instead of expressing sympathy, Evans declared that he regarded causing a wife to have too many children as a sin. 'Husbands are often morally guilty of murdering their wives by not denying themselves the pleasure of sexual passion.'

This was his last letter before Katie left home to join him.

SURRA ON
THE NORTH-WEST FRONTIER

Collins returned to Shimla at the end of August 1880 while the conduct of the Afghan War was still being hampered by the outbreak of surra. The disease was decimating the cavalry mounts and draught animals of the Punjab Frontier Force: the Third Punjab Cavalry had lost more than seventy-seven horses. Elsewhere, there were reports of entire studs being wiped out. Camels used widely as pack animals were also subject to high levels of mortality.[1]

Collins as Principal Veterinary Surgeon was now charged with providing a remedy, a tall order because although the disease and its symptoms were well documented, nothing was known of its cause or how the infection spread. Any investigation would therefore have to start virtually from scratch. As his deputy and the most experienced and competent member of his staff, Collins entrusted the task to Evans, instructing him to proceed to the North-West Frontier forthwith to conduct research into the causes of the disease and to recommend ways of combating it. He was to be based in Dera Ismail Khan, a small frontier town and military station on the west bank of the Indus near the Afghan border. Collins was, of course, aware that Katie was due in Kolkata in November and apologised to Evans for this disruption to his personal arrangements, expressing the hope that Evans might be able to complete his mission before her arrival.

Evans set about his preparations immediately. His first step was to seek access to all reports on surra in both veterinary and medical departments. These showed that the progress of the disease was slow. Typically, affected horses suffered a fluctuating high fever and became weak and lethargic. This was accompanied by a 'staring' coat and wasting leading to death although appetite was largely sustained. The mucus membranes, notably of the vulva and vagina, became pale and often yellowish with petechial (pinpoint) or larger sub-cutaneous haemorrhages. Oedemas of the udder or testicles and sheath were common and pregnant mares aborted. Similar symptoms were observed in camels although some individuals appeared to maintain a chronic infection and survive for several years.[2]

Studying the reports, Evans came to the preliminary and at that time radical conclusion that the disease was probably caused by a parasite in the blood. He put this suggestion to two senior colleagues, Dr David Douglas Cunningham, the Surgeon-General and Director-General of Hospitals and Dr Timothy Richards Lewis, Special Assistant to the Sanitary Commission for India, a fellow Welshman and personal friend. Both rejected it out of hand: Lewis had convinced himself and the scientific community that parasites found in mammalian blood were non-pathogenic and he was unwilling to countenance any suggestion to the contrary.[3]

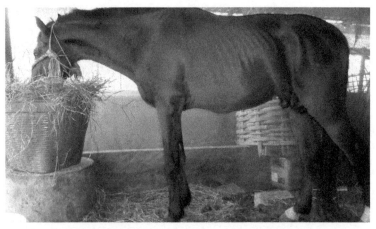

FIGURE 12(A) Feeding horse showing advanced symptoms of surra – note testicular oedema. (Desquesnes, M., Holzmuller, P., et al., 2013)

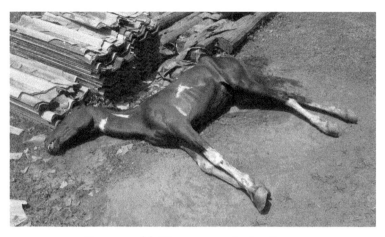

FIGURE 12(B) Horse succumbed to Surra.
(Desquesnes, M., Holzmuller, P., et al., 2013)

Undaunted by this blunt rejection of his working hypothesis, Evans informed Collins of his ideas and insisted that he could only undertake the commission if he was authorised to slaughter as many infected animals as he thought necessary to study the progression of the disease post-mortem. He further insisted that he would need to investigate its transmission to healthy animals and follow its development from the earliest stages. When Collins refused him permission to sacrifice healthy animals on the grounds that the shortage of mounts and draught animals was already causing the army difficulties, Evans asked leave to appeal to higher authority. The question was referred to the Lieutenant-Governor of the Punjab who, after what Evans described as 'some further cross-firing', decided in his favour.

His preparations complete, Evans set off to travel the 370 miles to Dera Ismail Khan, arriving on the evening of Saturday 18 September. He describes the journey in a letter to his children written the next day:[4]

> I arrived here all right but exceedingly tired after crossing this horrid desert from which I have not yet recovered – and I find this heat very great, day and night …

> I shall have to go about a great deal to out-of-the-way places
> on the frontier ... I have to be escorted from place to place by a
> troop of cavalry to protect me from the murderous Afghans who
> are always on the lookout for unprotected travellers.[5]

He was warmly welcomed by the Commanding Officer, Major Gowan, who offered him every assistance and told him that there were all too many victims of surra for his research. Gowan also identified a number of uninfected horses which were lame or otherwise unfit for service for the experiments.

Evans set to work immediately in atrocious conditions: 'The weather was exceedingly hot, and the temperature within a cool bungalow about 82° F[6] every day, but I had plenty of ice in large, felted baskets to preserve the organs while I examined them.' He had no alternative but to set up his microscope in the open air or in an open stable where, as well as the heat, he had to contend with windblown dust which penetrated his clothing and the mechanism of his instrument and settled on his specimens and slides. His discomfort was aggravated by swarms of flies attracted by the dead horses and carrion which were a constant irritation, clustering on his face and around his eyes and soiling the microscope stage and lenses. It was impossible to beat them off without shaking the instrument and disturbing the focus and the position of the specimens so their assaults had to be endured. To carry out critical microscopy for several hours a day in such circumstances required a remarkable exercise of will which Evans was able to muster.

The techniques Evans had at his disposal were relatively primitive. Before he left for India in 1877, he had equipped himself with a portable microstand with condenser, sub-stage and the necessary accessories together with the best lenses he could obtain. These included a set of Swift dry-objective lenses (1/5-inch and 1/8-inch) and a 1/12-inch immersion lens.[7] With no fixatives or stains, he could only examine fresh material which had some advantages as he later pointed out: early fixation techniques distorted cells and without stains, the close, careful observation required could reveal significant features of the living material that might otherwise be missed.[8]

In the report of his findings to the Governor of the Punjab, Evans described his observations and experiments over the next three weeks in great detail.[9]

Taking blood from an infected horse with advanced disease, Evans found it to be teeming with micro-organisms whose movements he described as 'undulatory, eel-like and as a rule wonderfully active'. There was no European veterinary surgeon on the station so Evans asked the surgeon, Dr Haig, to examine the sample. Haig was astonished at what he saw. He had no idea what the microbes were but suggested that they be named 'ferox' because they seemed to be attacking the red blood corpuscles. In his notes, Evans described the structure of these flagellated parasites which moved rapidly through the blood, propelled by waves along an undulating membrane attaching the flagellum[10] to the body of the parasite. The parasite was eventually named *Trypanosoma evansi*.[11]

Having established the presence of large numbers of these parasites in infected animals, Evans set about proving their causative association with the disease. He selected two uninfected horses which had been isolated from diseased animals and injected blood from an infected horse subcutaneously into one and poured the blood into the stomach of the other. The injected animal developed an intermittent pulse and fluctuating body temperature a few hours after inoculation which Evans considered to mark the transition from health to disease. The horse

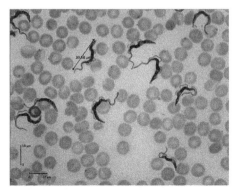

FIGURE 13(A) *Trypanosoma evansi* in blood (Giemsa stain)[12]

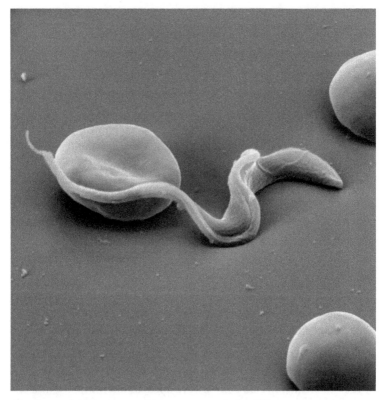

FIGURE 13(B) Scanning electron micrograph of *Trypanosoma brucei.* in blood. *T. brucei* is morphologically indistinguishable from and possibly synonymous with *T. evansi.* (Eye of Science/Science Photo Library)

infected by introduction of blood into the stomach showed similar but delayed changes in body temperature. The horses sickened over the next week and by the sixth day, every sample of blood from both animals contained high densities of the identical micro-organism. The experiment was repeated with the same result.

The yellowish tinge to all mucus membranes, usually with petechial subcutaneous haemorrhages, was evident in all infected horses, particularly in the membranes of the vulva and vagina in mares. Evans also found an abnormal amount of serum in the peritoneal cavity and enlarged, 'fluffy' lymph nodes in the infected animals. Both liver and kidneys appeared normal at post-mortem. As the disease advanced, progressive and often rapid weight loss was accompanied by general wasting and loss of condition and in the final stages before death, horses often lost the use of their hind legs. However, surprisingly, these symptoms were not associated with any loss of appetite and infected animals continued to eat well. Evans's description of the final stages of the disease is vivid:

> Some cases at last drop down, and die suddenly, perhaps when they are eating and enjoying food; others become delirious and struggle on the ground as if in pain; while other cases linger for days after they are down, too weak to rise or to stand, after they are helped up, but go on eating all the grass they get and much of the corn until at last they die, without pain, passing away like an English summer's day, no one can tell when the light ends or when the darkness sets in.

In all cases, the symptoms took longer to become apparent in horses infected through the stomach than in those injected with infected blood. Blood samples from one injected pony were shown to be swarming with parasites four and a half days later while samples from another receiving infected blood into its stomach were clear of parasites for seven and a half days before they became evident in numbers. As Evans points out, these 'experiments prove the common belief [that] seeds of the disease [lie] dormant in the system for many weeks [to be] entirely wrong'.

He observed that the level of parasitaemia[13] varied radically during the course of the infections he induced. At times, his blood samples were teeming with parasites but within a few days it became difficult to find any; Evans was confident that they did not disappear altogether as a persistent search generally picked up one or two. Thus, in one case:

> On the 26th September the parasites were swarming in each drop of blood. On the 29th, only one parasite was found in two drops of blood examined; on the 7th October great numbers were found in a drop – there were more than I could count on a slide. I was not

able to see this case again from the 9th until the 16th, when no parasite could be found in a drop of blood examined.

His conclusion was that 'ova or spores' remain in the blood 'for the development of another brood'.

> There is, therefore, some virus in the blood, which, when it is trans-
> ferred into a healthy animal, is as sure of growth and propagation
> as if we introduced seeds into a garden, or the roe of a fish into a
> suitable stream: the like reproducing its like, and no other.

Evans was not able to prove a definite relationship between the numbers of parasites and the expression of symptoms, a relationship that was later established by his young colleague, John Henry Steel, in studies of surra in mules in Myanmar (Burma) in 1884.[14] Steel found a clear association between the presence of large numbers of parasites in the blood and the cycles of the relapsing fever, particularly apparent in the disease in mules.

Recent research on the closely related and morphologically indistinguishable *Trypanosoma brucei*, which causes the trypanosomiases, sleeping sickness in man and *nagana* in cattle in Africa, has now shown the periodic parasitaemia observed by Evans and Steel and the associated relapsing symptoms to be due to Variable Surface Glycoproteins (VSGs) which coat the surface of the parasite and protect it from the host's immune response. Each trypanosome genome contains an archive of genes coding for different VSGs comprising as much as 30% of the genome and containing approximately 2,000 VSG genes. At any one time, allelic exclusion[15] ensures that only one gene coding for one specific VSG is active but, at intervals, the active VSG gene changes resulting in a change in the surface glycoprotein. Thus, as the host's immune system develops antibodies for the current specific antigen (the VSG) and eliminates the prevailing parasites, the parasitaemia declines. However, trypanosomes in which the active VSG gene has changed, so rendering them invisible to the current specific antibodies, are now able to multiply causing the new surge in parasite numbers. The host's immune system responds as before so the cycle is repeated until the host succumbs and dies.[16]

Although surra had never been reported in dogs, Evans tried infecting a dog and a bitch with the parasite by both subcutaneous injection of infected blood and its introduction into the stomach. In due course, both animals sickened and parasites appeared in their blood. The bitch had a young puppy which also became infected, Evans concluding tentatively that it must have been infected during suckling although he could not find the microbe in the bitch's milk; he had no time to confirm or disprove this hypothesis.

In his examination of the blood samples from horses and dogs, Evans noticed that the appearance of parasites was always accompanied by an increase in the number of 'large granular' white corpuscles or lymphocytes until they constituted one third to a half of all cells. In horses, this surge in lymphocyte frequency tended to occur simultaneously with, or slightly after, the appearance of parasites in the blood but in the dogs, he observed it before parasites were seen. He had already noted this phenomenon in animals infected with the anthrax bacterium in Sialkot in 1877 and was convinced that it was important. However, its significance escaped him.

Evans next looked for parasites in the dung and urine of infected horses. None were found although he did record albumin in the urine; in one horse this appeared to be associated with the cyclical disappearance of the parasites from the blood but, in others, it was present at all stages of the parasitaemia.

The disease followed a similar course in infected camels which presented with the same symptoms as horses. However, one animal thought to be infected with surra was different: petechiae were observed in the mucus membranes but there was no indication of the yellow tinge found in the others and in horses. This camel had dry eyes where the others 'wept'. Evans could find no trypanosomes in its blood but did observe ten to twelve microfilariae (larvae of a filarial worm) in every droplet. Post-mortem examination of this camel showed the right ventricle of the heart and the pulmonary arteries to contain 'tangled masses of adult filariae several inches long' which Evans assumed were the adult form of the microfilariae he had observed in the blood. They appeared almost identical to filariae described by Dr Timothy Lewis in his monograph on *Filaria sanguinis hominis*, a nematode parasite of humans,[17] although the adult worms appeared to be thicker. They were later described by Lewis and named *Filaria evansi*.[18]

After conducting his experiments on horses and camels, Evans turned his attention to transmission of the disease. Noting that the water provided for the horses at Dera Ismail Khan was 'very impure and obtained from shallow, narrow, winding irrigation channels choked with sedgy vegetation and slime, most favourable places for the breeding of all kinds of low organisms', he attempted to infect horses by giving them water contaminated with infected blood. No infections ensued. His earlier experiments showing that the parasites failed to survive even twenty hours in extracted, infected blood in either open or sealed containers and that horses infected with this blood failed to develop the disease, provided strong evidence against this mode of transmission. Nevertheless, he continued to speculate in his report that unspecified waterborne stages of the parasite's life cycle may have a part in the disease.

FIGURE 14 Vector of Surra – *Tabanus* sp. (Visavet)

Evans had heard that local people believed that the disease was caused by bites by a large, blood-sucking fly. As the flies were becoming scarce with the onset of autumn and he was approaching the end of his stay in Dera Ismail Khan, he was unable to test this hypothesis although he took the possibility sufficiently seriously to consider it in his Report:

> It is not improbable that these flies, so exceedingly troublesome at Jutta and other outposts, which bite horses so that the blood streams down the legs as if it had been squirted on, do convey the disease from one horse to another by inoculation. It is a fact that the disease does spread mostly at those posts where horses are closely packed and the flies are in greatest numbers, but these are the posts, also, where the drinking water is worst, so that it is exceedingly difficult to form a true opinion upon the subject without further experiments.
>
> However, the indications at present are that the horses affected with surra should be kept at a distance from other horses during the season when those flies are common. They were becoming scarce in the early part of October ... I do not know yet what is their scientific name. They are very large, of a brown colour, and common in many parts of India. The natives call them 'bhura dhang' which means 'great needle-like sting'.
>
> There is a common opinion prevailing among the natives of Dera Ismail Khan district, that this fly is the cause of the disease. I think the fly may sometimes propagate the disease by inoculation and thus be an item among the causes to account for the spread of the disease, more at some posts and in some years than others, though the disease would exist independently of them.
>
> When the horses stand close together, the fly is able to go from one horse to another before the blood about its mouth is dry; whereas if it had to travel some distance through the dry air in the hot sun, perhaps the virus of the blood would be destroyed.

Local tradition and Evans's hypothesis proved prescient but it was not until 1899, nineteen years after Evans's conjecture, that Leonard Rogers confirmed that *Trypanosoma evansi* is transmitted between hosts by biting flies. Flies of the genus *Tabanus* (family Tabanidae – horse flies)[19] are now known to be the principal vectors, with *Stomoxys calcitrans* (family Muscidae – the stable fly or biting house fly) also commonly involved. This transmission is referred to as *mechanical* as the fly picks up the parasites on the external surface of its proboscis as it bites an infected animal and then contaminates the blood of a new host through the wound made as it bites again. As parasites are generally unable to survive on the proboscis for more than a matter of minutes, successful mechanical transmission depends on the vector taking a meal from a second, uninfected host very rapidly.[20] As Evans anticipated, this is particularly likely to occur when hosts such as horses, camels or cattle are in close proximity. In these circumstances, the restlessness of the hosts when biting flies are present tends to interrupt their blood meals so that they seek to resume feeding, usually on a nearby animal, immediately.

Evans's conclusion that trypanosomes are unable to survive for long outside the mammalian host has now been repeatedly confirmed so *Trypanosoma evansi* must be transmitted to horses initially from a reservoir host. It is now known that its original hosts were camels[21] and that other host species (e.g. buffaloes, cattle, deer, dogs, rodents) may also harbour the parasite.[22] The parasite has also been reported in humans, in some cases causing mild symptoms.[23]

On or about 8 October with his time running short, Evans left Dera Ismail Khan to inspect eight other posts along the Afghan frontier. Travelling across rugged, mountainous country with a military escort, he observed the incidence of surra at each post, analysed the water and reported on the terrain, incorporating these data in his Report. In a letter to Erie,[24] he described the tour:

> I rode along the frontier on horses and camels with a strong escort
> of cavalry, and in one pass I had an infantry escort to guard the
> upper crest of the hills. There was no road anywhere.
>
> The people of the hills often make raids on the farmers and
> villagers below, stealing their cattle, their women and children ... I
> saw one town ... burnt down by them lately, and the people either

killed or driven away ruined. People in England never hear about these raids ... which are carried out by the independent tribes of Afghanistan and have no relation to the 'big war'[25] you have heard so much about lately.

Evans completed this whirlwind tour in eight days and returned to Dera Ismail Khan to collect his possessions and say his goodbyes before leaving for Shimla where he arrived on Tuesday 19 October. His baggage included his copious notes, several specimens including the 'bhura dhang' biting flies and most importantly, the infected puppy carrying the live parasites with which he hoped to conduct transmission experiments to other animals.

Although exhausted by the journey, Evans was keenly aware that time was short before Katie's arrival. He was determined to submit his official report before he left to meet her so settled down to the task immediately. Confident that his discoveries were highly significant and impatient to share them, Evans called on his friend Timothy Lewis and on Dr Cunningham, taking the puppy with him. Lewis was widely recognised as an expert on blood parasites having discovered and described the first trypanosome, *Trypanosoma lewisi*, in the blood of brown rats in India.[26] Examining the blood sample from the puppy, he concluded that the 'microbes are morphologically the same as those I found in rats; perhaps with some slight difference.' However, to Evans's consternation, he went on to declare 'I cannot accept that the similar parasites in the blood of horses are pathogenic. They couldn't possibly be the cause of surra.' The rats Lewis had examined, even those with a high parasitaemia, were, in his view, perfectly healthy.[27]

Evans was taken aback by this summary rejection of the conclusions of his careful observations and experiments and protested that Lewis was flouting the evidence:

If these parasites are not pathogenic, why is it that they do not exist in the healthy horses I examined? When the microbe is introduced into the blood of a healthy horse, that horse sickens and is plainly suffering from surra.

Lewis was unmoved, asserting that the microbe could be in the blood as a consequence of the horse contracting surra. Evans protested that the puppy had been infected with the same parasite and was now showing the distinctive symptoms of surra. Lewis's response was dismissive: 'That pup', he replied, 'is merely suffering from the common distemper of dogs.' Cunningham concurred. The rat parasite was the only trypanosome known to science at the time and generalising from Lewis's questionable assertion that it was benign, he and the wider scientific

FIGURE 15 Timothy Richard Lewis.
(Llyfrgell Genedlaethol Cymru – The National Library of Wales)

establishment were firmly of the view that 'no microbe found in the living blood of any animal was pathogenic'. In making this assertion, neither Lewis nor Cunningham challenged Evans's observations of bacilli and parasites in the blood of animals infected with anthrax and surra. Their claim was that these organisms were a consequence rather than the cause of the diseases, a conclusion which seems inconceivable in hindsight and even at the time, contradicted Pasteur's 1877 assertion that '*Le sang d'un animal en pleine santé ne renferme jamais d'organismes microscopiques ni leurs germes*' (The blood of a healthy animal never contains microscopic organisms or their germs).[28] Lewis argued that Pasteur was mistaken.[29]

During Evans's meeting with Lewis, he had also raised the question of the surge in numbers of lymphocytes he had observed in animals infected with surra and anthrax. He was convinced the change had significance and tried long and hard to understand what this might be. Lewis replied that he had not observed this change in rats infected with *Trypanosoma lewisi* and did not think it 'of any importance worth troubling about'. A few years later, the Russian microbiologist, Ilya Metchnikoff established that these white corpuscles or phagocytes were attracted to and ingested or engulfed bacteria, dead or dying cells and other harmful foreign bodies.[30] They thus play a central role in the immune response that protects higher animals from infection or invasion. Metchnikoff's work on the immune response earned him the 1908 Nobel Prize for Physiology and Medicine and Evans's failure to understand their significance irritated him for the rest of his life.

Evans's conviction that his conclusions were correct remained unshaken by these rebuffs. Leaving the encounter with Lewis which, in spite of their vigorous disagreement, had remained cordial, he resumed work on his 'Report on Surra Disease' which was submitted to the Governor of the Punjab on Saturday 13 November in time for him to meet Katie in Kolkata the following Friday.[31]

Before he submitted the report, Evans received orders to travel to Assam as soon as possible after Katie's arrival to investigate an outbreak of a fatal disease in horses. Collins realised that he needed a break after his arduous trip to the North-West Frontier District and in a generous gesture, suggested a tour of two or three months to provide the couple an opportunity to restore their relationship in relative peace and in a less oppressive climate.

The long-anticipated reunion took place at noon on Friday 19 November 1880 ending three painful years of separation since their parting at Tywyn station on 30 October 1877. Katie saw Evans from the deck well before the ship docked and her excitement is evident from her description in a letter to their daughter, Erie:

> I recognised his walk and knew him long before he knew me. We were obliged to look at each other from a distance a long time before the ship could be brought near enough for him to come aboard, which was very tantalising. I was more glad than I can tell you to see him again.

Evans too was delighted at being reunited with Katie. At thirty-six, she was still young and pretty while he now looked older than his forty-five years. His years in India had matured him and he had become more sure of himself.

Katie found Kolkata stifling but their week there passed quickly and they set off for Assam on Saturday 27 November. The journey took them northeast through the Khasi hills to the administrative capital, Shillong, where Evans received his posting to Silchar, the centre of the disease outbreak in Cachar (Kachar) District. There they were allocated the Circuit House as Katie described in a letter to Erie:[32]

> It is ... a building for Government officials ... there are 22 Europeans [here]. Four of them are married. Father and I went round to call on the four ladies as it is the custom in India for newcomers to make the first call.

Evans soon recognised the disease he had been sent to investigate as anthrax and quickly confirmed his diagnosis. Thereafter, his duties were light and he and Katie had time to revive their relationship and enjoy their surroundings and the cool climate. They made two expeditions to the forested Khasi Hills with Katie travelling in a joppa, a small sedan chair with a hood. She was excited by her first sightings of elephants, buffaloes and flying foxes but was startled by the nearby calls of jackals and by the vultures and eagles circling overhead. Between these excursions, they took part in the limited social life on offer:

> One day we [went] to meet our old Welsh friends, the Reverend and Mrs John Roberts. … [Father] called out in his most stentorian tones: 'A oes Cymro yma?' (Is there a Welshman here?) and out came our two friends, their arms outstretched in welcome.

This second honeymoon passed quickly and with Katie pregnant with their fourth child, they returned to Kolkata at the end of February 1881.

Before they left Assam, Evans was reminded of his clash with the authorities over his discoveries in Dera Ismail Khan. Given the dismissive reception his work had received from Lewis and Cunningham, he cannot have been surprised to receive the following brief communication from the office of the Governor of the Punjab: 'His Honour will not at present offer any remarks on this interesting report, but he extremely regrets to observe that no cure for surra has been discovered.' Any expectation that Evans might discover a cure for surra during his brief visit to Dera Ismail Khan was hardly realistic. In spite of the involvement of eminent figures such as Robert Koch and Paul Ehrlich in the search, thirty-six years passed before the discovery in 1916 of the first effective trypanocidal drug, suramin.[33] In his report, Evans had however made valid recommendations for limiting the spread of the disease by the isolation of infected horses and the avoidance of close confinement of animals to prevent mechanical transmission. These recommendations were largely ignored.

Back in Kolkata, Collins summoned Evans and informed him that the official view was that his conclusions were erroneous and that he had mistaken cause for effect. Many years later, in an autobiographical memoir published after the presentation to him of the Mary Kingsley Medal by the Liverpool School of Tropical Medicine in 1917,[34] he revisited this contention:

Both Dr Cunningham and Dr Lewis had in their official reports committed themselves positively to the opinion *that no microbe found in the living blood of any animal was pathogenic*. They did not doubt my reports of what I had observed in anthrax and surra, but they, as strongly as they could use words officially, negatived [my] conclusions ... We discussed the subject in private conversations, of course in the most friendly spirit.

This professional spat between the two Welshmen, Lewis from Pembroke and Evans from Meirioneth, was, as Jean Ware put it, 'a classic example of two professional men disagreeing violently in public and remaining the best of friends in private'. Evans continued

bear in mind it was some time before Koch published his classical postulates. I was groping in the dark with psychological rushlights only, impelled by a very strong scientific faith that the discovery of important pathological facts was imminent in the direction I was trying to go.

Evans's reference to Koch's postulates[35] is significant. Had they been known of at the time – they were not published until 1890 – there could have been no such misinterpretation of his findings. He went on:

The question ... is whether the presence of the parasite is the cause of the disease, or whether the disease is the cause of the appearance of the parasites ...

There are some eminent pathologists in India who deny *the parasitic origin of specific blood diseases*; they say the cause of all such diseases from smallpox to anthrax fever ... is some purely chemical agent which has never been discovered and that these organisms develop at once in blood which has been so chemically altered, each chemical virus developing its specific organism; the spores or ova of which are supposed to be in normal blood, ready to develop as soon as chemistry favours them. The organisms themselves ... are supposed, by these authorities, to be harmless.

Evans, however, alerted by Lewis's and Cunningham's dismissal of his working hypothesis that a blood parasite caused surra before he left for Dera Ismail Khan, had already addressed the issue in his Report: 'That is one of the most vexed questions of the present day in the pathological world, and it still strikes hard at the root of the science and practice of sanitation.' Evans goes on to rehearse his evidence that the parasite is the causative agent of the disease. With hindsight, his conclusions appear self-evident so there is no need to reiterate his arguments.

As Evans implies, the refusal of the veterinary and medical establishments in Kolkata to accept the evidence for the pathogenicity of blood parasites reflected the prevailing consensus farther afield. Even William Osler, by then an influential physician, was unconvinced on first reading his report: he could not believe that 'flagellating organisms should occur in the blood let alone that they should be pathogenic'. The considered view in India was that Evans's obstinate conviction that he was right did him no credit.

When he left Shimla for Kolkata to meet Katie, Evans had left the infected puppy with Lewis hoping that he might continue observations and even conduct transmission experiments. He had been particularly anxious to inoculate another bitch with blood from the pup to investigate, under properly controlled conditions, whether the parasite could 'pass via the lactal glands to sucking pups', a question that he considered important whether or not the microbe was pathogenic. On his return from Assam, Evans found that Lewis had returned to Kolkata, taking the puppy with him. He was shocked to find the animal 'in a wretchedly wasted condition' with a high parasitaemia. Even more galling was the fact that Lewis had done absolutely nothing with it. He merely reiterated his conviction that the puppy was suffering from 'the common distemper of dogs' and that the parasite was no more pathogenic to the dog than he believed his rat parasite was to its hosts. Evans asked him:

How do you know that the rats *were* healthy? How long did you keep them under observation? Did you take their temperature? A *casual* observer might not have thought that this pup was ill when I left him with you. But *I* knew because of my long experience of dogs and because of my close observations. Probably an expert in rat pathology would say that the rats that you thought were healthy were in truth not healthy at all.

Lewis's response is not recorded. However, it was enough to make Evans realise that any attempt to change his and Cunningham's minds was hopeless. 'It was useless to go on talking. He and Surgeon-General Cunningham remained obdurate. They seemed to think I had a bee in my bonnet.'

The authorities in Kolkata continued to maintain that all Evans had achieved in Dera Ismail Khan was the slaughter of several healthy horses and camels to no effect and the report of the Sanitary Commissioner to the Government of India on his work was couched in what Sir Frederick Smith later described as 'very unmeasured, in fact insulting language'.[36] Nonetheless, the Government of India published Evans's Report on Surra and circulated it locally. It appears that it was not totally ignored: almost forty years later, he wrote without further comment, 'I have been gratified by the assurance of some younger men that my statements spurred them to follow with much success the line I had indicated for further investigation'.[37]

The Report was then filed in the Indian Government archives where it remained until, shortly after the turn of the century, a team of German scientists studying trypanosomiasis in the sub-continent came across it and recognised its worth. One of them commented to William Roberts, a Welsh cotton planter in the Punjab, 'This man Evans seems to have done all our work for us thirty years ago.' Some years later, the remaining copies of the report and all associated documents in the archives (including Lewis's and Cunningham's responses) appear to have been destroyed, leaving just Evans's own and a few other copies that he had sent to friends and colleagues.

Fortunately, however, Evans had asked Collins to send the report to George Fleming, editor of the *Veterinary Journal* in London. Fleming agreed to publish but decided to do so in instalments distributed over six issues of volumes 13 and 14 in 1881 and 1882.[38] He clearly recognised it as significant to the study of disease: his editorial comment preceding the first instalment in the July issue stated '[the report] possesses much interest when read in connection with the description already published of *Filaria sanguinis* as producing disease in man and animals'. However, by publishing the work in instalments and as Evans complained, with deletions, Fleming significantly diminished its impact. 'Nobody will take any notice of it. I wish I had sent it to the British Medical Journal instead' was Evans's resigned comment. Nevertheless, he maintained his confidence in his conclusions. 'I knew I would be proved right' he commented much later, and he was prepared to wait until the veterinary and medical establishments caught up.

Back in Kolkata in early 1881, the authorities had decided that Evans was no longer an acceptable candidate to replace Collins as Principal Veterinary Surgeon for India on his retirement later that year. Although his succession had been implied by his appointment to the post in an acting capacity in 1879, Collins was under pressure from medical and veterinary establishments to remove this confrontational officer. He summoned Evans and informed him that he was to be appointed Senior Inspecting Veterinary Officer for the Madras Presidency in southern India with immediate effect, an effective banishment.[39] Accordingly, in March 1881, Evans and Katie left Kolkata to take up this post. He did not take the pup with them for fear of spreading the infection – the disease had been reported in the Madras Presidency – so it was put down.

Before they left, Evans received a letter from the Secretariat of the Government of India thanking him for 'his elaborate and interesting report'. It went on to 'express the hope that he will be induced as opportunity offers, to prosecute his researches in regard to the disease which has proved so destructive and baffling'.[40] This exhortation must have been galling to Evans; it was clear that his new post would leave him no opportunity for research of any kind.

BANISHMENT TO
THE MADRAS PRESIDENCY

On Thursday 17 March 1881, Evans reported for duty at Ooty, the short name for Udhagamandalam (Ootacamund), 270 miles west of Chennai (Madras) where he was to be based. Katie was delighted by Ooty, the summer capital of the Madras Presidency. The 'queen of the southern hill stations' and the healthy, sub-tropical climate in the Nilgiri hills was in stark contrast to the bustle and sweltering heat of Kolkata. Katie was astonished by the verdant landscape and familiar flowers, fruits and vegetables added to her sense of having arrived at a 'home from home'; 'there is even a mountain called Snowdon (Yr Wyddfa)!' she exclaimed. Over the next few weeks, the Evanses settled into rooms in Sylk's Hotel. As well as the climate and surroundings, Ooty offered a varied social life which revolved around St Stephen's Church and the Club with its sporting and recreational facilities. However, the couple's life is more likely to have been centred on the Zion Chapel,[1] then the only place of worship for Nonconformists in Ooty.

As before, Evans's duties involved visiting military stations to inspect and supervise veterinary provision for army horses. In the latter half of the nineteenth century, the Presidency governed an immense area including most of southern India. Evans's earlier postings had taken him all over northern India. Now he was to travel as extensively through the south acquiring a knowledge of the whole sub-continent which few natives or foreigners can have achieved before or since. Away on tour for much of the year, he was also required to spend significant periods in the military cantonment in Chennai but whenever the opportunity arose, he hurried back to Sylk's Hotel. It was there that their fourth child, a son, was born on 1 December 1881. He was named Ywain Goronwy ap Griffith Evans and was greeted by the usual englyn from Evan. Soon after Goronwy's arrival, the Evanses took the tenancy of the substantial Warley Lodge, where they remained for the remainder of Evans's posting.

As time passed, Evans became resigned to the fate of his Report on Surra which, as well as being side-lined in India, appeared to have attracted little attention when it was published in the *Veterinary Journal* in London. However, unknown to him at the time, some in the European scientific community had taken notice: the *Veterinary Journal* publication was seen by his old friend William Osler, by Robert Koch in Berlin and by Louis Pasteur in Paris. Moreover, news of the treatment Evans had received at the hands of the Indian Government filtered through to the profession in Britain and met with an angry response, as reported much later by Sir Frederick Smith. In his *History of the Royal Army Veterinary Corps* published in 1927,[2] he wrote:

> [c]onsiderable feeling was created in the veterinary service by the attitude of the Sanitary Commissioner, and the *Veterinary Journal* in its July issue for 1881 hit back very hard. The *Army and Navy Gazette* also took up the case and said that the Military Department of the Government of India had aggravated their offence by publishing a further criticism on Dr Evans's discovery, this time from the pen of the Editor of the *Indian Agriculturist*, a gentleman who admitted that he knew nothing of the subject!

James Meyrick had visited the Evanses before he left India in 1881 and was told how the authorities in Kolkata had received the Report and of its fate at the hands of the *Veterinary Journal* editor, George Fleming, in London. Back in Woolwich before his posting to the Anglo-Egyptian War as Principal Veterinary Officer in July 1882, Meyrick, with Evans's case as well as his own and colleagues' experience in mind, prompted the veterinary establishment to protest at the treatment meted out to its veterinary officers by the Indian Government. The protest began in a review of Meyrick's book in the *Veterinary Journal* in October 1881:

> Nothing can be more disgraceful than the neglect which allows such waste, unless it be the treatment to which the Indian Government subjects the officers of the Veterinary Department, nearly every one of whom is disgusted with service in that part of our Empire. Mr. Meyrick has done his best to diminish the loss, suffering, and cruelty prevailing in Hindustan but so far as recognition is concerned for what would have doubtless obtained for him honourable distinction had he been serving in a foreign army, he is more likely to be ignored, or snubbed and insulted through having his book submitted by the Government of India to some impertinent and ignorant doctor, or still more ignorant and presumptuous civilian hanger-on.[3]

Meyrick himself maintained the pressure in a letter to the *Veterinary Journal* published in March 1882: 'I have myself served nearly twelve years in India ... The prospect is of unremitting slavery in an exhausting climate ... very little leave ... and the conditions ensure certain loss of health to nine out of ten men'.[4]

The theme was then taken up in an editorial in the journal in May 1882:

> [The military authorities in India] seem from all accounts to be bent on inflicting every kind of indignity on veterinary surgeons ... The late campaign in Afghanistan has been the crowning indignity and has proved to be pretty well the last straw ... Those veterinary surgeons who were at last called in to rescue the army from disaster were worked night and day until at last some died, others were invalided, and the remainder were all but overwhelmed with the effects of the climate, hardship and fatigue.[5]

These criticisms and protests seem to have had some impact in Kolkata. The 1882 edition of 'Regulations for the Army Veterinary Department' contained some significant improvements in the treatment and status of its officers: promotions were accelerated and in 1883, Inspecting Veterinary Officers were accorded the rank of Lieutenant Colonel; Evans received his promotion that spring.[6]

At the end of September 1882, Evans and Katie had received a telegram with news of Evan's death. Evan and Mary had lived with Eliza in Borth-y-Gest since leaving Tŷ Mawr and he had continued to live there after Mary's death in July 1877. Evans was grief stricken; he had always expected to see Evan again when he returned home at the end of his tour. His anguish and sense of guilt were compounded by the fact that he had been away from Wales at the deaths of both Maria and his mother. The funeral was held in Tywyn where Evan was a well-known and respected figure. The local paper reported that shops had been closed and blinds drawn 'in tribute to a man universally admired for his sincerity and truthfulness, as well as his great powers in prose and song'.[7]

Evans continued with his arduous circuit of inspections throughout 1883 and 1884. As in northern India, many of the military stations and outposts were remote and roads, if they existed at all, were rough tracks. As in the north, where there were roads Evans travelled in dak gharries or, where there were none, in dandies or palkis (palanquins) carried by bearers; with a few days' notice, the Indian Post Office would arrange fresh teams of bearers at approximately ten mile intervals along the route.

Throughout his time in India, Evans enjoyed rummaging in shops and bazaars on the lookout for interesting artefacts and acquired some rare and interesting objects. Among these was a piece of carved crystal etched with mystical symbols. He also continued to pursue his interest in local cultures and religious practices, making the most of every opportunity to engage with people of all races and backgrounds. His personality and enthusiasm inspired friendship and confidence and he was invited to join an Indian secret religious and philosophical society in Ooty; 'this was the only secret society I was ever associated with. It helped me to useful knowledge and native friendships.' The invitation to a serving British army officer less than a generation after the Indian

Insurrection indicated the extraordinary degree of trust Indians were prepared to place in this charismatic and inquisitive Welshman.

Evans's lifelong commitment to the cause of temperance soon became known and he was invited to join the Church of England Temperance Society. He had always refused to become a member because, as a Welsh Nonconformist, he had no wish to be associated with the Church of England. Furthermore, he disapproved strongly of the Society's willingness to compromise in offering a pledge for moderate drinkers as a first step to abstinence. However, the Society in Ooty showed him evidence that, once they were members, many 'moderate pledgers' listened to the arguments for total abstinence and signed up; Evans was persuaded and joined.

Both parents kept up a constant stream of letters to their daughters in Wales. These give a running account of the progress of their baby brother who was joined, in April 1884, by a fourth daughter. Fearful that Evans might be tempted to call her Ootacamunda, Katie insisted on the good, plain Welsh names, Mair Olwen. Katie's letters are sensitive and understanding. She appreciated that the girls were growing up and she attempted to relate her letters to their changing circumstances and interests. By 1884, it had been almost seven years since Evans had seen them and he found it difficult to adjust to the fact that they were developing fast. Not surprisingly, his letters were full of stories and sentiments suitable for younger children. Both took a keen interest in the children's progress at school and in reports of their behaviour but Evans's letters often lapse into exhortation and moralising[8] where Katie's are sympathetic and encouraging.[9]

On 2 June 1883, Evans had a lucky escape. He and Katie were out in their pony trap when the horse bolted. The trap overturned and Katie was thrown clear but Evans was dragged along the road pinned under it. Shouting at the syce (groom) to hold the horse's head and calm it, Katie, who was unhurt, ran forward to find Evans pinned under a wheel and in great pain. Bracing herself against the wheel and with the strength that comes in an emergency, she managed to raise the wheel enough to allow Evans to free himself. Badly shaken, he describes the aftermath of the event in his diary: 'I could not stand and was in great agony for hours.

I certainly would have been killed if Katie had not had the presence of mind and coolness to make such an effort to release me.'

Sometime after this incident, Evans and Katie saw a European couple driving into Ooty in a tonga (a light carriage with open sides). They both noticed the woman's ethereal expression and soon learned that she was Madame Helena Petrovna Blavatsky, founder of the Theosophical Society in New York in 1875. She had come to Ooty with her American companion and co-founder of the Society, Colonel Henry Olcott,[10] to study the Todas, a local indigenous tribe. Intrigued, Katie and Evans invited the couple to lunch at Warley Lodge. With Evans's interest in philosophy and comparative religion, the conversation was lively and wide-ranging. The guests showed great interest in Evans's collection of artefacts, especially in the crystal prism engraved with mysterious symbols. Examining it, Madame Blavatsky expressed astonishment that its owner should have agreed to part with it. It was, she told Evans, a 'Solomon's Seal': anyone possessing it was absolved from having to seek the mediation of a priest in worship.[11] During their conversation, it transpired that Colonel Olcott had been serving in the US Army at the time Evans was in Virginia during the American Civil War and that they had several mutual acquaintances.

Mme Blavatsky went on to claim that she had been initiated into the mysteries of the most arcane forms of Buddhism by Tibetan spiritual teachers or 'Mahatmas' who had, she said, imparted to her supernatural powers. Evans was sceptical and told her so.[12] Increasingly uncomfortable at the confrontational turn the conversation was taking, Katie created a diversion by 'accidentally' knocking something over to defuse the situation. Referring to Madame Blavatsky's visit much later, Evans claimed that she had admitted that her 'powers' were no more than tricks and sleight of hand.

Meanwhile, there were indications of a reassessment of Evans's reputation in Kolkata as the frequency of calls for his advice on veterinary questions increased. In late 1884, his colleague, John Steel, was asked to investigate an outbreak of a fatal disease, possibly surra, affecting mules and horses in Myanmar. Still only twenty-nine, he was already a prominent figure in army veterinary circles and an obvious choice to investigate the outbreak. Steel had been impressed by Evans's work in Dera Ismail Khan and invited him to join him on the assignment. Evans readily accepted.

Steel's report on the investigation is exhaustive.[13] He and Evans soon established that the principal cause of the fatalities was a parasitic disease very similar, if not identical, to surra as characterised by Evans in Dera Ismail Khan. There were, however, differences in the symptoms which they attributed to the fact that they were dealing with mules rather than horses; a pony in Yangon (Rangoon) presented symptoms exactly comparable to those in Dera Ismail Khan. A notable achievement of their study was the demonstration of a clear association between the level of parasitaemia and the cycles of the relapsing fever. In supplementary experiments, Steel infected a dog and a monkey with the surra parasite and both developed relapsing fever, lost condition and eventually died. Efforts to transmit the disease to a goat and bullocks failed.

In spite of having Evans's expertise and experience of surra to hand, Steel was adamant that the parasite causing the disease in Myanmar was a spirochaete bacterium[14] and not the flagellate protozoan parasite Evans had described. Steel's obduracy on this point clearly frustrated Evans as he related many years later:

He persisted in stating that the parasite I discovered was a spirillum … he persisted in refusing to look at the parasite with my lens that magnified more and defined better than his own, a rather inferior quarter inch, 'because he was used to it'.

Although Steel had misidentified the surra parasite, he did give Evans full credit for its discovery and in a subsequent article in the *Veterinary Journal*, stated that his own contribution had been no more than to prove the pathological effects of the parasite and to have 'confirmed Dr Evans' important discoveries', an endorsement that helped restore Evans's reputation.[15]

Evans in turn valued Steel's confirmation of the parasite's pathogenicity and forgave his errors and limitations. He later provided a fulsome tribute to Steel's work and recommended the award of an honorarium in recognition of his contribution to veterinary science in India. Sadly, Steel did not live to claim it, dying in Mumbai in 1890 just before his thirty-sixth birthday. After his death, friends and colleagues, including Evans, contributed to a fund to establish the John Henry Steel Memorial Medal to be awarded by the Royal College of Veterinary Surgeons for scientific or literary work of merit connected with the profession; Evans himself was to receive the award many years later.

As usual, Evans seized the opportunity of his first visit to Myanmar to visit sites of interest as time allowed, among them the Kyaiktiyo or Golden Rock Pagoda in Mon State. His Burma scrap book contains photographs of the sites and of people he encountered including a family with the genetic disorder of hirsutism and young Burmese women smoking cheroots, all carefully described and annotated.[16] Pursuing his interest in comparative religion, he arranged an interview with a senior figure in the Buddhist hierarchy in Yangon. During their discussion, he mentioned Madame Blavatsky's claims to have been instructed by 'Mahatmas' in Tibet. He describes the exchange later in a letter to Erie:

> [He] told me ... he did not believe Madame Blavatsky's declaration about her Mahatma in Thibet, and was indignant at the suggestion of any place in Thibet being compared in Buddhistic sacredness with the great memorials at Rangoon and at Pegu.[17]

Evans probably returned to Ooty in February or March 1885 only to be asked to travel to Bengal to handle a crisis caused by an ineffective vaccine against anthrax. Completing this mission, he returned once again to Ooty for the final few months of his tour in India.

Early in November, he received a letter from Lieutenant-General Sir Frederick Roberts, Commander-in-Chief, Madras, congratulating him on the diligent work of the Veterinary Department in the Presidency during his term as Senior Inspecting Veterinary Surgeon and informing him of his new posting to Woolwich.

In Mumbai on 18 November 1885, Evans and Katie embarked for home. He had been in India for seven years and Katie for five.

13

RETURN TO BRITAIN –
UNHAPPY YEARS

Evans and Katie disembarked at Portsmouth on 16 December 1885. They lost no time in travelling to Wales where, three days later, they were reunited with their three elder daughters at Tywyn station.

The reunion and Christmas were not the happy occasions Evans and Katie had been anticipating with such impatience. The three little girls he had left in Wales in 1877 were now fourteen, twelve and nine years old. Only Wynona had any clear memory of him as a loving father and the girls were now confronted with a forbidding, gaunt stranger with a gruff, impatient manner. His frequently admonitory and moralistic letters had not helped. It was also difficult for the girls to relate to their two younger siblings: Goronwy, now four, spoke only Welsh and nursery Hindustani with no English at all and Mair was still an eighteen-month-old baby. It would be surprising, too, if the girls had not felt some jealousy towards the newcomers who had never been deprived of the presence of their parents.

Evans did not hide his disappointment that the girls had picked up little or no Welsh during their summers in Borth-y-Gest. Worse was his contempt for the fire-and-brimstone Methodism, bordering on Calvinism, which they had absorbed at school in Woolwich. He insisted that the girls had been indoctrinated and demanded peremptorily that they immediately abandon any literal belief in heaven, hell and pre-destination, forsake the Old Testament and base their faith on the precepts of the Sermon on the Mount. This was unreasonably harsh: the religious instruction they had received was common to all private schools at the time and little different to what they would have encountered in chapel in Wales. Evans's uncompromising stance confused Wynona and Towena without upsetting them unduly but the devout and intense Erie was deeply shocked at this assault on her passionately held beliefs and recoiled from her forbidding father.

Religious indoctrination was not the only shortcoming of the school to which Evans and Katie had entrusted their daughters. Like many other boarding establishments catering for children of expatriates, the regime was harsh with poor, often inadequate food and minimal care and individual attention so that the growing children's welfare and emotional needs were neglected. The three girls had come to rely increasingly on their holidays with Aunt Eliza Dedwydd in Borth-y-Gest as an escape from school life but Gwenddydd's marriage earlier in the year was making it difficult for her to escort them to and from school. So Evans and Katie's return from India had been timely and the girls were immediately removed from the school.

Evans had taken a comfortable house, 208 Burrage Road, Plumstead, from the 1 February 1886. The house, home to the family for the next five years, was just over a mile from the Royal Artillery Barracks at Woolwich where Evans reported for duty early in the New Year of 1886. The three girls were enrolled in a day school close enough for them to return home for meals. However, the tensions within the family did not subside. At their new school and the Congregational Sunday School, the girls were subjected to the same narrow Victorian religious instruction to which Evans objected so strongly, compounding their confusion. The emotional strain between them and the younger children was exacerbated by Evans's insistence that Welsh should continue to be Goronwy's and Mair's first language so his hope that his children would be 'united like a bundle of sticks' was becoming further from realisation than ever.

Evans and Katie realised that they would have to address this problem. The solution they decided upon was to try to involve the older three more directly in the care of the little ones. They asked Towena to share a bedroom with and to take a special interest in Goronwy and Erie to share her bedroom with and care for the baby, Mair. Wynona was to have a bedroom of her own and was asked to take an overall interest in the welfare of all her siblings. Instead of drawing the children together, the plan created new divisions between them. Towena took her role in relation to Goronwy to an extreme, indulging him and taking his side unconditionally. This unhealthy attachment persisted into adulthood. The close bond that developed between Erie and Mair also lasted the rest of their lives. Both Towena and Erie and later the two youngest, came to resent the domineering interference of the bossy Wynona. As Jean Ware wrote, '[this] seemed a sensible plan, but in practice it proved disastrous, merely converting the horizontal split into a vertical one.' However, Evans and Katie remained as devoted to each other and to their children as ever.

As well as tensions at home, Evans found himself in a difficult position in his new posting. As Inspecting Veterinary Surgeon with the Royal Artillery, he reported directly to the now Principal Veterinary Surgeon to the Army, George Fleming, who had succeeded James Collins on his retirement in 1883. This was the same George Fleming to whom, as Editor of the *Veterinary Journal*, Evans had sent the manuscript of his 'Report on Surra' in 1880. After Fleming's editorial decisions on its publication, the working relationship between the two men was never going to be easy.

The personalities of the two men aggravated their mutual mistrust.

[George Fleming] suffered under the disadvantage of not having served in India.

He was about the middle height, slight in build with good features and a bright, attractive manner … He wrote well and clearly, but his writings are frequently marred by an intolerance of opposition … He was the victim of hero-worship by the civil profession in this country … [which] did much to spoil a character that needed restraint rather than undue encouragement. His weaknesses were an incurable optimism, extraordinary impetuosity, a love of popularity and insatiable ambition.[1]

FIGURE 16 George Fleming. (Wellcome Collection)

Evans was also unwilling to compromise. Although interested in the views of others and ready to make every effort to understand them, he was unshakeable when he believed himself to be in the right and when challenged, could be wilful and confrontational. As Evans later wrote: 'Fleming … was not friendly towards me, because I would not say "ditto" to all he said when I was certain he was wrong and [acting] against the interest of the service'. The combination was incendiary and the relationship lurched between suspicion and open hostility.

Evans was still only fifty-one and the scepticism with which his discoveries had been greeted, still irked. Once established in his new life in Woolwich, he began to look for an institution that might offer him the opportunity to prove conclusively that his conclusions from his studies in Dera Ismail Khan had been correct.

By a particular stroke of luck, King's College Hospital in London had, in 1885, appointed Edgar Crookshank as its first Professor of Bacteriology and Comparative Pathology with a remit to found a new Laboratory for Human and Veterinary Pathology. Crookshank was only twenty-six and rapidly establishing a reputation.[2] He had read Evans's work on surra as published in the *Veterinary Journal* and was one of the few in Britain who had understood its significance. The two men had exchanged letters and Evans had sent him some specimens of surra-infected blood from India. Crookshank also knew of Lewis's work and of the disagreement between the two men regarding the pathogenic-ity of blood parasites. Evans wrote to Crookshank outlining his pro-posals for research and in early spring 1886, visited him. Crookshank was enthusiastic; with its implications for both human and animal health, the project was entirely consistent with the objectives of his new laboratory.

Woolwich was perfect for his purposes. The fast train took only thirty-five to forty-five minutes to Charing Cross with King's College Hospital in Portugal Street within easy walking distance of the sta-tion. Evans began to plan his research in earnest. His principal aim was to demonstrate, once and for all, that trypanosomes in the blood of mammals, including Lewis's *Trypanosoma lewisi*, were pathogenic and often lethal to their hosts, including humans. To achieve this, he needed a primate model and decided to conduct his infection experi-ments on monkeys. He and Crookshank hoped the project might shed light on the cause of the trypanosomiases which had so hampered and continued to obstruct, development and economic progress in Africa.[3] David Livingstone's observation in 1852 that cattle succumbed to the wasting disease, *nagana*, following bites from tsetse flies and similarities with the symptoms of surra suggested to both men that a blood parasite might be involved.[4] If this could be established, parallels between surra, *nagana* and human sleeping sickness would be proof of a similar cause.

Scientists intending to undertake animal experiments now had to contend with the recent advance of the anti-vivisection movement. The National Anti-Vivisection Society had been founded in 1875 by Frances Power Cobbe, a vigorous campaigner against animal cruelty who had won the support of many powerful individuals including Queen Victoria and the prominent politician, social reformer and philanthropist, Lord Shaftesbury.[5] The Society had achieved sufficient political clout to induce the Government to appoint the First Royal

Commission on Vivisection in July the same year. Its report led to the enactment in 1876 of the Cruelty to Animals Act which among other provisions, regulated animal experiments. Under the Act, procedures which might involve the infliction of pain on vertebrate animals would only be permitted if the experiment was performed 'with a view to the advancement ... of physiological knowledge or of knowledge which will be useful for saving or prolonging life or alleviating suffering'.[6] Experiments were only to be carried out by 'a person holding [a] license from one of Her Majesty's Principal Secretaries of State' at a registered location which would be subject to inspection. Applications to the Secretary of State had to be signed by the President of the Royal Society, the Royal College of Surgeons, the Royal College of Physicians, the Royal College of Veterinary Surgeons or the Royal Veterinary College, London.

Evans considered this interference nonsense arguing that no scientist would inflict cruelty on animals in frivolous experiments and that, in any case, the legislation would not prevent them if they chose to. He believed that, on the contrary, the anti-vivisectionist movement perpetuated animal suffering by refusing to recognise that procedures on a few individuals could alleviate suffering generally. Nevertheless, he and Crookshank submitted their application signed by the Presidents of the Royal College of Surgeons and the Royal College of Physicians, a license was duly granted and the new laboratory registered. With all obstacles overcome, Evans prepared to commence his experiments.

In May, Evans received the news that Timothy Lewis had died of pneumonia at only forty-five, shortly after being proposed for election to the Royal Society. Although Lewis's reception of his Report on Surra had damaged his career prospects, Evans always claimed that the two had remained firm friends and his tributes to Lewis were fulsome. His death was a blow also because an element of Evans's motivation had been the prospect of correcting Lewis's misconceptions. He was not, however, distracted for long and pressed ahead with his plans.

Some weeks later, a sombre Evans arrived in the laboratory to announce that he had decided to abort the whole project. Crookshank and his associates were shocked and astounded; Evans's enthusiasm for his programme had been infectious and his change of heart seemed incomprehensible. But try as they might, no-one could persuade him to explain his volte-face and he maintained his public silence on his reasons until his death. The answer only came to light in the papers of the veterinary historian Sir Frederick Smith after his death in 1929. Preparing his *History of the Royal Army Veterinary Corps*, Smith had written to Evans, then ninety, asking for an explanation. Insisting that Smith treat his reply in strict confidence, Evans disclosed that he had abandoned the research after the personal intervention of Queen Victoria. When she had heard of his proposal to experiment on live monkeys, she had asked the relevant Secretary of State to revoke his license. She had then dispatched an official to see Evans and tell him of her wish that he abandon his plans. In his reply to Smith, Evans said that he had 'insisted on not publishing the "why-not" while [he] lived' because 'it involved the direct interference of the Queen which was given and explained to [him] privately'.[7] As a serving officer and loyal subject, Evans felt he had no alternative but to comply but it was a terminal blow to his hopes.

The outcome of his research might have hastened the recognition of parasites as an important factor in the causation of human and animal disease.[8] Definitive proof of that link would have to await the discovery by David Bruce in Zululand in 1894 that a blood parasite was the cause of *nagana* and that the parasite was transmitted by tsetse flies, *Glossina* spp.[9] Bruce suggested that this 'haematozoan' would be shown to be 'identical with the haematozoan causing surra, which is called Trypanosoma Evansi or at least a species belonging to that genus'. The principal parasites causing *nagana* are now known to be *Trypanosoma congolense*, *T. vivax* and *T. brucei*, the latter regarded by some authorities as synonymous with *T. evansi*.[10]

It is interesting to speculate how Queen Victoria could have got wind of the research proposals of a then unknown Army veterinary surgeon. Very few people were aware of Evans's plans and the enthusiasm for them at King's College Hospital makes it unlikely that anyone there or involved in the licensing procedure could have been responsible. However, one man may have had a motive for obstructing Evans: his superior George Fleming who, as Principal Veterinary Surgeon, would have had the necessary contacts among the Queen's advisors. As well as their mutual animosity, there seems little doubt that Fleming was jealous of Evans: he was never in India, regarded as most demanding posting for an Army veterinarian, where, despite the official repudiation of his conclusions on surra, Evans was deemed to have distinguished himself. The obvious respect in which Evans was held by senior members of Flemings's staff must also have rankled.

Another cause for resentment on Fleming's part may have been that Evans had not told him of his plans. Evans's view was that, as the research would be undertaken in his spare time and would not interfere with his duties, he had no obligation to inform his superior and he had only done so after the license had been granted. When he heard the details of Evans's proposal, Fleming may well have feared that he intended to resume his public quarrel with his recently deceased colleague, Lewis, with consequent damage to his reputation and potentially, that of the Army Veterinary Service. The evidence that Fleming was the source of the Queen's awareness of Evans's plans is circumstantial but whoever informed her, her personal request was enough for Evans. Bitterly disappointed, he abandoned hope of proving definitively that blood parasites were pathogenic. However, despite the blow, he continued to visit Crookshank's laboratory taking courses in advanced bacteriology and becoming directly involved in research.

Meanwhile, Evans did his best to manage his troubled relationship with Fleming. On official and ceremonial occasions, the two men were forced to hide their animosity. On St David's Day in 1887, together in full uniform they represented the Army Veterinary Service at the Jubilee Levée in St James Palace where Fleming was required to present Evans to the Prince of Wales.[11] Next to the Prince in the uniform of a Field Marshal stood the Duke of Cambridge, still Commander-in-Chief of the British Army. Evans had a brief exchange with him about his service in India, wisely refraining from reminding the Duke of their encounter twenty-seven years earlier (p. 25). On 21 June, Fleming and Evans sat together in Westminster Abbey at the service to mark the Jubilee. In the Jubilee Honours list Fleming received the Companionship of the Bath, Civil Division but there was no award, civil or military, for Evans.

This uneasy truce was to prove impossible to sustain. In 1889, a bitter dispute between the two men erupted into open hostility. Its cause was a difference of opinion on the treatment of 'roaring' in horses.[12] Fleming favoured surgical intervention but early operations in Aldershot in 1888 often caused a growth which could reach serious proportions together with ossification of the laryngeal cartilage.[13] Although Fleming was shown the evidence for these negative outcomes, he supervised large numbers of these operations at Woolwich under what appeared to be an unusual degree of secrecy. During the discussion following a paper that Fleming gave at a meeting of the Aldershot Military Society, 'an officer' criticised Fleming for his failure to take account of the indications against surgical intervention. Such a public attack on the senior veterinary officer was unprecedented and an acrimonious discussion ensued.[14] Evans who does not appear to have been present, made no secret of his opposition to and disapproval of Fleming's actions. It would have been difficult to re-establish a working relationship after such an open quarrel with his superior so it was fortunate that the usual practice was for the Senior Inspecting Veterinary Officer to be posted to the Curragh Camp in Kildare for the final year of service. Accordingly, Evans left Woolwich and his diary records that on 6 September 1889, he 'took over the duties of Inspecting Veterinary Officer Ireland from my old friend Meyrick, who retires from the Army today'. Katie meanwhile left Burrage Road and took the two youngest children, Goronwy and Mair, to Tywyn.

Evans's final tour in Ireland was uneventful professionally but not personally. On 5 December 1889, he suffered a bad attack of bronchitis. Katie was worried enough to cross to Dublin to nurse him. Then, in January 1990, Mair became seriously ill with a perforated tympanum and meningitis. The doctor warned Katie to prepare for the worst and Evans was summoned from Dublin. Confident that he could save the child, Evans nursed her day and night until, in early March, she was out of danger. This was the second time he had successfully nursed one of his children back to health after serious illness: the three-year-old Goronwy had almost died of a severe fever in India.

Back in Dublin, Evans spent his spare time in the study of Roman Catholicism which he had begun in Canada. His other preoccupation was Home Rule for Ireland which he believed to be the only just means of meeting Irish aspirations. In a letter to Katie, he wrote that he was appalled at the deterioration in relations between Westminster and Ireland since he was last there. Irish demands and resentment, he believed, would only escalate as Westminster persisted in thwarting them.

In July 1890, Evans returned to Woolwich and on his fifty-fifth birthday, he retired from the Army with the rank of full Colonel. He had served for thirty years.

14

NORTH WALES AND RETIREMENT

Hopes for his research project thwarted by the Queen and his relationship with George Fleming becoming more and more strained, Evans's thoughts had turned increasingly to his forthcoming retirement. He and Katie had always planned to return to their beloved north Wales and in the summer of 1887, he suggested that they should holiday there to consider where to settle down. Mindful of his strained relationship with Erie and seeing an opportunity for father and daughter to establish a better understanding, Katie wisely suggested that he should take her as his companion instead. Evans agreed and the ploy was successful. They left London in August and spent two weeks together in Eryri walking and climbing and most importantly, talking. Erie was immediately seduced by the dramatic landscape and was to turn to the mountains for relaxation and solace for the rest of her life.[1] Before returning to Woolwich, they spent a few days with Eliza in Borth-y-Gest. Then a pretty fifteen-year-old, Erie was a serious and intelligent girl. During their week together, father and daughter explored their many common interests, foremost among them religion about which they argued fiercely as she grew up. A close and lasting bond was established and the respect and love she came to feel for her father on this holiday shaped her life and was a major influence in her decision to make her career in medicine.

As the date of his retirement approached, Evans and Katie arranged to meet in north Wales to search for a suitable house. Granted three days leave, Evans crossed from Dublin to meet her in Bangor on 1 October 1889. They had always hoped to settle in Tywyn but that evening they changed their minds and decided in favour of Bangor. A decisive factor was the presence of the new University College of North Wales founded in 1884. Apart from the educational opportunities it offered their older daughters, Evans must have thought of the social and intellectual benefits for the family of living in a university town.

Among the houses they saw the next day, Katie preferred a Victorian family house, Brynkynallt, on the northern flank of Bangor Mountain overlooking the town. The house was halfway up Lôn Pobty (literally, Oven Lane), a steep lane that climbed from the upper end of the High Street. This was not a 'genteel' location, the neighbouring cottages being no more than hovels, but Katie and Evans liked it. Warned that the house saw very little sun (it disappeared behind Bangor Mountain before noon), Evans retorted 'I've had enough sun in India to last me until I am a hundred!' They bought Brynkynallt for £1,200, deciding to add a porch and an indoor lavatory for a further £400.

The cost of the house and improvements was more than Evans believed he could afford and the worry preyed on him: 'I feel very sore and disquieted in mind for having to pay so much more for Brynkynallt than I think is its market value. I have so little to leave my wife and children.' When he became ill back in Ireland in early December, Katie believed this worry was the underlying cause. As he recovered,

FIGURE 17 Brynkynallt, Bangor. (Wellcome Collection)

he rationalised the expenditure on the grounds that living in Bangor rather than Tywyn would 'save hundreds of pounds in the long run'.

The work on the house complete, the furniture arrived from Woolwich on 23 July 1890, the family following a few days later. Evans's entry in his diary for his birthday, the 7 August, reads 'Retired. Settling in at Brynkynallt.' The house was to be his home for the remaining forty-five years of his life.

Evans had always set great store by his Welsh origins and his roots in Tywyn. In a letter to Katie from India he had written: 'I would rather be less wise and poorer than be without Towyn and its associations'. The emotion of 'hiraeth'[2] was a constant feature of his state of mind during his long absence from Wales and he nurtured his links with home, maintaining regular contact with his family in Tywyn and Porthmadog. As he wrote to a friend: 'I have been knocking about the world with all sorts and conditions of men since I left home as a lad of eighteen. So I am more out of touch with my native country than I would wish to be.' As his Welsh roots were so central to his sense of identity, it is perhaps surprising that there is no evidence that he ever joined or attended meetings of the various Welsh societies in London[3] while he was at Woolwich. Nor is there any indication that he ever participated in the National Eisteddfod of Wales[4] before or after he retired although he served on a committee to invite the 1912 National Eisteddfod to Bangor.[5] He took pride in his British nationality and in his own contribution in British India although this did not preclude him from being openly and often vehemently critical of the conduct of individuals and government both at home and in India. In every aspect of life, he disliked extreme positions and prided himself in being able to appreciate the points of view of others.

Evans had always endeavoured to retain his Welsh, reading and speaking the language at every opportunity. Although they wrote to each other in English, Katie and he spoke Welsh at home and he had insisted that it should be the first language of their two youngest children. His written Welsh included mistakes in grammar and spelling but it was remarkably good for someone who had received little formal schooling in the language and who had spent most of his life far from Wales.

The new occupants of Brynkynallt aroused great interest in what was still a small community. Evans was an imposing figure with his loud voice (a consequence of his deafness) and military bearing as he strode vigorously about Bangor in his Welsh tweeds. He had no intention of slowing down in retirement and with much still to offer, he set about looking for outlets for his dynamism.

Soon after settling in, he joined the Menai Society of Natural History and Literature and the University's Scientific and Antiquarian Societies, contributing to meetings on subjects including science, literature, climate and history and frequently taking the chair. These contributions over the years of his retirement and a short article he published on exorcism practices in Wales in the journal *Folklore* in 1892[6] illustrate the breadth of his interests.

The University must soon have become aware of Evans's arrival in Bangor and it was no surprise that the young institution was as anxious to make use of his talents and experience as he was to become involved in its affairs. The Department of Agriculture took the initiative, inviting him to deliver a course of lectures in Veterinary Hygiene during the forthcoming academic year, 1890–1. He accepted and the course was so popular that he was prevailed upon to repeat it and in June 1891, he was given official standing as Instructor in Veterinary Hygiene.[7] He was to hold this post for twenty years, only withdrawing when, in 1912, cataracts began seriously to impair his eyesight. Evans enjoyed his interaction with students. On one occasion when he had brought his own microscope into the Department for their use, he noticed one of them handling the instrument roughly. Remonstrating with the culprit, he told him to be gentle: 'You should handle a microscope as you would a lady!' A student in whom he took a special interest was William Roberts, a farmer's son from Anglesey. Roberts later became a wealthy cotton grower in the Punjab and in his retirement, was a generous friend to the College and its Vice President.[8]

In 1892, Evans took up the case of an older student, Violet Osborn, a friend of Erie's, who had become involved in a dispute with the Lady Principal responsible for the women's hall of residence, Frances Hughes. The dispute culminated in a court case for libel against the *London*

FIGURE 18 Griffith Evans (far right with his Welsh terrier) with women students and tutors outside the original buildings (the old Penrhyn Arms) of the University College of North Wales in the 1890s. (Tony Craven Walker).

Weekly Dispatch brought by Miss Hughes in which Evans gave evidence for the defence. However, the jury found for Miss Hughes who was awarded exemplary damages. The dispute and consequent upheaval in the provision of accommodation for women students at Bangor attracted the attention of the local and national press.[9] Following the case, the company then owning the Women's Hostel was replaced by the Bangor Women's Hostel Company with Evans as vice-chairman and a new hostel was opened by Miss Helen Gladstone, daughter of William Gladstone and Principal of Newnham College, Cambridge, in October 1897. As well as his interest in individual students, in 1892 Evans was elected one of the Honorary Vice-Presidents of the new Bangor Welsh Students Union established to discuss Welsh educational, literary, social and political matters.

By the turn of the century, it was apparent that the University had outgrown its original accommodation at the Penrhyn Arms Hotel for which the lease from Lord Penrhyn, landowner and proprietor of the Bethesda slate quarries, terminated in 1905. In January 1900, the University Court decided unanimously to seek a site for new, permanent buildings.[10] After much discussion, a decision was made in favour of part of the Bishop's Palace Park in Bangor and the Penrallt site on the bluff overlooking the city and Evans participated in the long negotiations that led to their acquisition, building commencing in 1907.[11] He also chaired the Local Committee charged with canvassing for subscriptions to the College's Permanent Buildings Fund.

In December 1908, Evans was nominated by Aberdovey Urban Council as its representative on the University's Court of Governors, providing him with a formal role in the governance of the College and he was reappointed for five-year terms in 1910 and 1915. The Court's half-yearly meeting in April 1914 at Barmouth discussed the implications for the University of the Welsh Church Act 1914, then passing through Parliament. Evans intervened vigorously for the Nonconformist view that proceeds from the proposed disestablishment of the Church in Wales that might be offered to the University should be accepted, contrary to the 'Churchmen's' view that they should not.

The University also benefitted from Evans's generosity. In October 1890 he donated the sum of £15 towards the acquisition of natural history specimens and over the years, gave many books to the library. Other libraries that profited from his generosity included the Bangor City Free Library in 1908 and the National Library of Wales in 1909.

Evans took a close interest in the Bangor Normal College founded in 1858 to train teachers for the British School Movement in Wales; he himself had been among the first pupils at the British School in Bryncrug near Tywyn in 1846. As well as government grants and student fees, the Normal College relied on subscriptions from its many supporters, Evans among them. Finally, in 1908, he served briefly on the Organisational Committee of the Congregational Memorial College in Brecon.

The family joined the Pendref Congregational Chapel in the High Street immediately below Brynkynallt where Evans could be seen every Sunday in the front pew in his characteristic pose with his ear cupped in his hand. He listened to every sermon with close attention often pursuing the preacher into the vestry after the service to question him on points of disagreement or to demand clarification. His independent views often surfaced at chapel meetings. At a missionary meeting, he accused the missionaries of creating 'curry and rice Christians by bribing good Hindus with gifts of food to renounce their excellent faith'. His suggestion that girls who had illegitimate children should not be penalised but supported did not go down well in the chapel community; they were, he claimed, not wicked but simply too kind to men. Notwithstanding these unconventional notions, he was asked to lead a group of university students at the Pendref chapel on Sundays where it can be assumed the discussion was wide-ranging and challenging. The meetings were popular and he was invited to become superintendent of the Chapel's Sunday school.

Evans's long-standing and apparently sincere commitment to Nonconformist Christianity obscured a more complex and enigmatic interest in religion. He claimed throughout his adult life that he was agnostic and he adhered firmly to this doctrine until his death.[12] In a long letter to Katie in 1879,[13] he had given a comprehensive account of his interpretation of Christianity but the essence of his beliefs is perhaps best expressed in a long letter to his close friend, Henry Jones, in April 1905 which included the following forthright résumé:[14]

I am an agnostic in line with Herbert Spencer and Huxley ...
Last summer I was publicly labelled a materialist ... I did not
and do not object to that label if it means only my disagreement
with metaphysical idealism. Therefore I am not expected to be in
sympathy with extreme emotional demonstrations of a religious
revival ...

A. I believe it is good for people to be religious.

B. No religion can be good, effectively, unless it is emotional ...
A profession of religion is either sincere, with some degree of
enthusiasm, or else it is a sham. Of all shams, a sham religion
is the worst ...

C. Every man's religion ought to be his own.

D. Full freedom should be allowed everyone to express his religion
in his own way ... so long as he does not interfere with the
freedom of others.

Like Huxley, he believed that there are no rational or scientific grounds
to accept or refute the existence of God.[15] His membership of the
Rationalist Press Association[16] supports the conclusion that, despite
his enduring engagement with Nonconformist Christianity in general
and Congregationalism in particular, he was unable to subscribe to the
central tenets of Christianity.

Evans's allegiance to Nonconformist Christianity as an expression
of his fundamentally liberal beliefs is well expressed in his essay 'Un
Eglwys i Gymru' (One Church for Wales) published in *Y Genhinen* in
1909.[17] In it, he attacks the idea of a single church for Wales arising
from the assimilation of Nonconformist churches by the Established
Church and celebrates the proliferation of 'free' churches to cater for
diverse spiritual needs in society. This commitment to liberalism in worship is evident in Evans's active participation in Nonconformist organisations in north Wales. Between 1902 and 1907, he was involved with
the North Wales Summer School of Theology, speaking, chairing sessions and serving on the Executive Committee and as Treasurer. At the
inaugural meeting in 1902, he participated in the discussion following

Professor Henry Jones's lectures on 'The Attitude of Recent Thought towards Religion' and 'Agnosticism or Positivism'. At the third Summer School held in Trefriw, Evans from the Chair, revealed something of his beliefs in a 'warm' exchange with a Reverend David Davies following lectures which touched on Evolution. Davies, a convinced creationist, had deplored a remark by 'their materialistic chairman' that all spiritual entities were 'Bunkum'. The newspaper account has Evans denying an intention to cause offence and claiming that the use of the term was merely 'shorthand ... for what he meant ... his faith began where his knowledge ended, but he did not think it right to make use of his faith as if it were knowledge.' The implication here that he had 'faith' is interesting in light of his letter to Henry Jones the following year and suggests that he may have been reluctant to reveal his true convictions in the setting of the Summer School of Theology.

In September 1902, the Bangor Free Church Council convened a conference in Bangor to protest against the Conservative Education Bill then going through Parliament at which the Caernarfonshire MPs, David Lloyd George and J Bryn Roberts, were the principal speakers. The Education Act of 1902, the Balfour Act, became law in December. It abolished the independent, elected School Boards funded by a precept on the rates[18] that had run schools under the 1870 Elementary Education Act, transferring control to county council education authorities and for the first time, channelling taxpayer's money to voluntary Church of England and Catholic schools. The extreme hostility of Nonconformists provoked the formation of a National Passive Resistance Committee in London which campaigned against this extension of the influence of central government and the established church in education. The annual meeting of the North Wales Federation of Free Church Councils in Caernarfon in April 1904 supported the campaign and Evans contributed to the impassioned discussion, seconding a resolution 'demanding the repeal of the Education Act, or its amendment in such a way as to redress Nonconformist grievances and remove religious tests'. He attended the Federation's meetings until at least March 1915 representing the Bangor Free Church Council of which he was elected Chairman in February 1907.

With his life-long commitment to the cause of abstinence from alcohol, Evans lost no time in becoming actively engaged in the North Wales Temperance Association (NWTA); he was already contributing actively at its Annual Meeting in Bangor in October 1891. At this meeting, a new local organisation, the Arvon and Vale of Conway Temperance Association (AVCTA), was formed and he attended its meetings until at least 1909, serving on the Executive Committee and as Treasurer. Among the many concerns they addressed were the progress of Temperance legislation in Parliament, the 'Drink Traffic', the abolition of drinking clubs, the availability of alcohol on pleasure steamers and at agricultural shows and alcohol in the Labour Movement. He frequently represented the AVCTA at Licencing Sessions at Police Courts, leading objections to license renewals, criticising magistrates where they had made inappropriate decisions and urging the Bench to consider the needs of local neighbourhoods in assessing cases. When, in 1909, there was anxiety that Lloyd George, then Chancellor of the Exchequer, might be persuaded to contest a seat in Cardiff, Evans suggested the Association remind him of their support; '[The Association] knew no politics, but they looked upon Lloyd George as their temperance representative.'

Evans attended NWTA annual meetings and conferences until 1910 usually as a delegate of the AVCTA and by 1903, was on the Executive Committee. These meetings received reports from the local temperance associations, promoted temperance work in schools, supported temperance candidates in local and national elections and pressed for the strengthening of existing and the passage of new temperance legislation in Parliament including, over this period, the Local Veto (Wales) and Sunday Closing, and Licencing Bills.[19] The failure of these Bills for a variety of reasons led the NWTA Executive to conclude in 1910 'that the main work for temperance within the [following] ten to twenty years would be done in the midst of the people rather than in Parliament'.

In politics, Evans had maintained a moderate, liberal stance throughout his adult life. He disapproved of both Marxism and Imperialism and in a letter to Erie, outlined his position:

Liberalism involves liberty for each individual to better himself as much as he can so long as by doing so he does not prevent others doing so. Fair play for each and all. That is the meaning of 'individualism' for which the Socialists oppose Liberals. Socialism means not freedom but strict government by bureaucracy.[20]

Imperialism may be compared to cancer in the human body … Ancient and modern imperialism has always destroyed itself by its own growth.

The fact that the Evanses attended the marriage of T. E. Ellis, the leading Welsh Liberal MP, in June 1898 suggests that Evans was already active in Liberal politics in north Wales.

On 2 March 1900, the Bangor Liberal Association considered a letter from Lloyd George in which he proposed a public meeting in Bangor to discuss his controversial opposition to the current war in South Africa.[21] Evans supported the proposal but it met with strong opposition and after some discussion and a split vote, it was decided to leave the matter in the MP's hands. Evans had probably met David Lloyd George through their mutual friend, Henry Jones. The two men soon became friends and Lloyd George often stayed at Brynkynallt on his visits to Bangor. Aged twenty-seven in 1900 and a rising figure in the Liberal Party, his radical views with which Evans sympathised, were regarded with hostility by the local establishment. Despite the opposition and attempted obstruction by the Trustees of the Penrhyn Hall, the venue for the proposed meeting, Lloyd George went ahead.

The meeting with admission by ticket only was held on 11 April 1900. Lloyd George stayed at Brynkynallt and Evans and Katie accompanied him to the packed Hall through a hostile crowd. The audience was already rowdy during the Chairman's introductory remarks and when Lloyd George commenced his address, his pro-Boer views infuriated his listeners. The platform where Katie and Evans were sitting was pelted with rotten eggs and tomatoes and in the melee, Katie's bonnet was dislodged. When a degree of order had been restored, Lloyd George was able to continue although he was repeatedly interrupted by 'the discordant tones of a brass instrument'. At the end of the meeting, Lloyd

George and his supporters, including Evans and Katie, left by the front door to be greeted by jeers from the crowd which became increasingly threatening as it followed them up Waterloo Street. Stones were thrown and Lloyd George was struck on the head with a heavy stick. Fearing for their safety, the party took refuge in the Central Café until police were able to escort them back to Brynkynallt.[22]

Later in 1900, the British Union for the Abolition of Vivisection arranged a meeting in Bangor following the granting of a license to vivisect to the University College in Cardiff and the prospect of an application from the University College in Bangor. Unsurprisingly, Evans attended and reminded those present that license holders were obliged to carry out all vivisection procedures under anaesthetic and pointing out that it was through vivisection that the circulation of the blood had been discovered.

By March 1901, he was representing the West Ward of the town on the Executive Committee of the Bangor Liberal Association and he served as President from 1902–4. As well as mobilising Liberal support during local and national elections and fostering the links between the town and Lloyd George as MP, the Association campaigned on local and national issues. Over the three years following the passage of the 1902 Education Act, the Association campaigned for 'a universal system of undenominational and national education'. In 1906, Campbell-Bannerman's Liberal Government introduced an Education Bill which aimed to satisfy these demands, proposing to bring all public elementary schools under the control of Local Authorities. The Bill received a majority in the House of Commons but was vigorously opposed in the House of Lords which passed wrecking amendments leading the Government to withdraw it.

The second half of the nineteenth century saw the emergence of the urban working class as a political force leading to the formation of the Independent Labour Party in 1893 and in 1900, of the Labour Representative Committee, later the Labour Party. The Liberal and Conservative Parties responded by seeking themselves to garner support from this growing constituency. Following precedents in many other towns and cities, the Bangor Labour Organisation was inaugurated in

August 1906. With both Liberal and Conservative members, it sought to promote working class representation on the Town Council and invited the well-known Labour MP, Philip Snowden, to speak in the town. Evans played a prominent role in the new organisation and was on the platform at the inaugural meeting and at the very successful Labour Demonstration addressed by Snowden in October 1906.

On a national level, he was a Bangor delegate at the Welsh Liberal National Convention in Rhyl in November 1907 where he objected to a resolution on Licencing Reform as a surrender and in 1914, he represented the Carnarvon (Caernarfon) Boroughs on the Executive Committee of the Welsh Liberal Council in Cardiff.

In June 1917 at a joint meeting of the Arvon and Conway Boroughs Liberal Associations, Evans seconded a resolution inviting Lloyd George to stand again for the Carnarvon Boroughs constituency in the forthcoming General Election. He was then almost eighty-two and although he continued to attend meetings of the local organisations that interested him, his active involvement appears to have been on the wane.

During these years, Evans and Katie led a full social and family life at Brynkynallt. Soon after they arrived, they met Henry Jones, a brilliant young philosopher at the College.[23] Jones's explosive but charismatic personality, his humanitarian views and his sense of humour struck a chord with Evans. The two of them enjoyed many long conversations in the year before Jones left Bangor in 1891, first to a Chair at St Andrews and then, in 1894, to Glasgow as Professor of Moral Philosophy where he became one of the leading philosophers of the day. Although it was said that they could never agree on anything except that Welsh Terriers were the best breed of dog, Evans and Henry Jones remained lifelong friends and corresponded and met regularly.

Other family friends included the Bruce Whites. Jacob Bruce White had been the first lecturer in Zoology at the College and Evans appears to have had a particular influence on his young son, Philip, while he was at Friars School and then the University College. Philip, later a leading bacteriologist who was elected to the Royal Society for his work on *Salmonella*, credits Evans with encouraging him in the experimental approach to science.[24]

Katie quickly embraced settled domestic life after her years as an army wife. She soon acquired a circle of friends and her regular tea parties became important events in their social calendar. Now a comfortable, middle-aged matron, she enjoyed presiding at these affable gatherings which were a hub for the exchange of local news and gossip. As politeness demanded, Evans would make an appearance to welcome the guests but would soon retreat to his study, probably to the relief of the ladies who could then resume their conversations free of his overbearing presence.

As well as pursuing his interests in microbiology, Evans kept pace with scientific advance in other fields, devouring the latest journals and books as they were published. In an appreciation shortly before his one-hundredth birthday, R. F. Montgomerie wrote of this period of his life: 'No advancement of science escaped his notice. He kept abreast of the times.'[25] A particular interest was heredity and the developing field of evolution. In later life, he recalled being captivated by *Vestiges of the Natural History of Creation* by Robert Chambers (1844) which he read before the publication of *On The Origin of Species* in 1859. Other books he identifies as especially influential were Herbert Spencer's *First Principles* (1867) which, he said, 'made me sit at his feet ever after', Charles Lyell's *The Geological Evidence of the Antiquity of Man* (1863) and his *Principles of Geology or the Modern Changes of the Earth and its Inhabitants* (1830–3), Edward Tylor's *Primitive Cultures* (1871) and James Frazer's *The Golden Bough* (1890). Psychology was another interest and he read all the leading literature available in English. 'All such spiritual pabulum I devoured in a hungry state of mind, so I was lifted and carried on the crest of the greatest scientific wave in history.'[26] He also read voraciously in other subjects, foremost among them history, religion and political and moral philosophy, as well as finding time for fiction. He considered Tolstoy the greatest novelist and *Anna Karenina* the greatest novel. The margins of his worn copy were filled with comments in pencil; when Levin soliloquises on reason and faith, Evans observes, 'Faith begins where true knowledge ends; it leads to evil as often as good.'

Both Evans and Katie took full advantage of the proximity of Eryri. Soon after arriving at Brynkynallt, they organised an expedition

up Yr Wyddfa (Snowdon) for the whole family. Similar family outings became a regular occurrence and both Katie and Evans continued their mountain walks after the children had left home. Sometimes
Evans would walk in the hills with friends. The botanist Dr John Lloyd
Williams, twenty years his junior, wrote a vivid account of an expedition
they made together to Cwmglas on Yr Wyddfa when Evans was in his
late seventies.[27] Although still 'cyn sythed â brwynen a chyn sionced â
hogyn' (upright as a rush and as agile as a lad), Evans was by then too
short of breath to make the demanding ascent so they took the train
to the summit before descending to the cwm (coomb or glen). In his
account of this happy summer's day – the varied colours of the wild-
flowers, ring ouzels whistling among the rocks and the bright sunshine
– Lloyd Williams recalled their wide-ranging conversation in which
Evans recounted his experiences in North America and India, his discovery of *Trypanosoma evansi*, his ideas on religion, his commitment to
liberalism and his lively interest in every aspect of society and culture. As
they made their descent, Evans turned to gaze up to the ridge of Crib
Goch: 'Fantastic, fantastic, here we are having just climbed through lava
fields which once flowed red hot, through beds of volcanic dust which
descended in showers of fire and now we are trudging through terrain
ploughed by a great sheet of ice! What a fantastic variety of "artists"
have carved Eryri so sublimely!'

Between these excursions, Evans walked his Welsh Terriers on
Bangor Mountain in defiance of the landowner, Lord Penrhyn, who
disputed public right of way on the ridge. Undaunted, Evans set
off every day along the paths, casting aside the obstacles erected on
Lord Penrhyn's orders. Later, when Eryri was beyond his physical cap-
abilities, these shorter excursions became a central element of his daily
routine. Throughout his busy retirement, Evans found time to maintain
his wide correspondence with friends and influential figures on the local
and national stage. A regular correspondent was James Meyrick, with
whom one vigorous exchange of letters early in his retirement dealt
with the issue of Free Trade and Tariff Reform. Meyrick with his wife
were also among the earliest visitors at Brynkynallt where they stayed
for a few days in August 1891 and two years later, Evans with Erie paid

them a return visit in Devon. Another regular correspondent was Owen Prys, a theological college Principal in mid-Wales; their long letters covered all aspects of religion and faith. At the end of one in which they discussed their disagreements, Prys concluded 'your letter convinces me that though unknown to me you are an honourable man'.[28]

Meanwhile, the Evans's children were growing up. Wynona found academic life difficult and tedious and she seized her first opportunity to escape. This came in the form of an invitation to live with her maternal uncle, Owen Jones, a prosperous farmer in Montgomeryshire, as housekeeper and companion. His wife had died recently and he had shocked the local community by insisting she be buried under apple trees in the farmhouse garden. Wynona and her uncle got on well and she was soon happily settled as mistress of his farmhouse; in time, it became understood that she would inherit his estate. When, at forty, she married a Sheffield businessman, Charles Garfitt, she showed her commitment to her uncle by stipulating that she would remain with him till he died. They had two daughters, the second dying in childhood.

Erie was very different. In 1894, she left Bangor where she had read sciences to train at the London School of Medicine for Women. After graduating, she moved to Cardiff (Caerdydd) where she embarked on a varied and distinguished medical career to which she devoted her life; she never married. Her father's daughter, she was active in a variety of associations and organisations, medical and non-medical. She retired in 1931 to look after her father.

Towena was impetuous, passionate and emotionally unstable but the only daughter to complete her course at Bangor. In her final year, she became engaged to a fellow student, Herbert Greaves, who was destined for a career in teaching. Evans's response to the engagement was to send her to a domestic science college to, as he put it, 'learn to become a poor man's wife'. Greaves's first teaching post was in Pwllheli where the young couple lived after their marriage, moving later to Denbighshire (Sir Ddinbych). They had two daughters.

Goronwy was not academic but was an excellent draughtsman. After training as a naval architect in Glasgow, he established a normal architectural practice in Tywyn. Proud of his Welsh heritage and descent from a sixth century Welsh king, he changed his name to Goronwy ap Gruffudd. Regarded by some in the family as having delusions of grandeur, he appears to have been something of a disappointment to Evans who was apparently scornful of his obsession with his noble lineage. However, he was entrusted with writing Evans's biography in the Dictionary of Welsh Biography.[29] He married an Irish girl, Clara Tucker and having no children, referred to himself as 'the last of the line' despite his nine nephews and nieces. Their children remember 'Uncle Gron' with affection as 'great fun'.[30]

The youngest daughter, Mair was, like her mother, gentle, empathetic and charming, qualities that especially endeared her to Evans. After school in Bangor, she enrolled at the College but her career there was cut short by a serious injury sustained in the gymnasium. In 1907 during her convalescence, Evans took her with him to Stockholm to the Eleventh International Conference against the Abuse of Alcohol.[31] While there, Mair, encouraged by Evans, decided on a career practicing Swedish massage and stayed on in Sweden to train. On her return to Bangor she set up in practice, a bold decision for a woman at the time. Evans was delighted when she became engaged to Henry Jones's eldest son, Elias Henry, known as Harry, who was in the Indian Civil Service. As Evans said, she would have servants in her married life and so no need for domestic science. Instead, he provided her with a trousseau from Liberty's of London to equip her for the tropics. The couple had two daughters and three sons.

Soon after their marriage in 1913, Mair and Harry Jones were to leave for Myanmar where Harry had been posted. Evans feared that at his age, he might never see his daughter again. He need not have worried.

'I KNEW I SHOULD BE PROVED RIGHT'

Although Evans was well known in north Wales, few, if any, outside his immediate circle knew anything of his scientific discoveries and their importance in understanding the causes of human and animal diseases. However in 1907, a resourceful journalist came across the name Dr Griffith Evans, with a portrait, in the *Journal of Tropical Veterinary Science* published in Kolkata.[1] Surprised by what he read, he arranged for the whole article to be published in the *North Wales Express* on 31 May 1907 adding the following commentary:[2]

> With this issue a portrait and biography of Dr Griffith Evans, Brynkynallt, will appear. Dr Evans is well-known in Bangor as a stalwart Free Churchman and Liberal, always ready to express his opinions without fear or favour, and never truckling to public opinion if his own opinion is opposed to it.
>
> But many in Bangor may not be aware that in the outside world Dr Evans is known as a scientist of great ability and originality. He is a man who has done good work in India and in Canada, and he was one of the first to make good use of what we laymen call the microbe theory. His name is well known as that of a keen experimental scientist, and his connections with politics and other public movements are only secondary aspects of his work.

There followed the full text of the article in which Evans was referred to in the past tense as if he were dead:

> Griffith Evans received no worldly recognition for his valuable work, but the names *Trypanosoma evansi* and *Filaria evansi* will always remain to the honour of a man, who, at a period when ignorance and prejudice were more marked and universal, brought into play faculties and powers of observation that would do credit to any man today ... it can be readily understood how great were the difficulties to recognize that a minute organism, such as the one he had found, was the causal agent of disease.

The article goes on to describe *Trypanosoma evansi* as:

> not only a scourge in India, but [it] has within recent years been found to have a field of action extending from the Philippines to the east to Algeria in the west. In ... British India it probably accounts for more deaths in horses and camels than all other diseases combined.

When Evans had read it, he showed the paper to Katie remarking that, past his allotted span at seventy-two, he should be dead as the article implied, 'Os mynni glod, bid farw, Katie fach' (If you want glory, you must die first, Katie dear). The *North Wales Express* story was not taken up and in Britain, Evans's scientific repute remained largely confined to north Wales.

It was in continental Europe in the laboratories of Robert Koch in Berlin and Louis Pasteur in Paris, that the full significance of his discovery of the pathogenicity of *Trypanosoma evansi* was first recognised. In the first years of the new century, scientists in these laboratories were exploiting his findings in their research on the more serious challenge posed by the African trypanosomiases of man and domestic animals. In Britain, only James Meyrick, a small number of fellow veterinarians and notably, William Osler had acknowledged the potential impact of Evans's work. In 1886, Osler had given a paper on malaria in

FIGURE 19 William Osler in 1888. (Courtesy of the Osler
Library of the History of Medicine, McGill University)

Philadelphia in which he discussed the nature of the malarial parasite.
Referring to Evans's and Steel's work on surra and the evidence for the
association of the parasitaemia with the cycles of relapsing fever characteristic of both diseases, he concluded somewhat tentatively that the
parasites are pathogenic and advocated additional studies.[3] However,
Evans would have to wait another thirty years for there to be any general acknowledgement of the importance of his discovery although he
received some recognition from the War Office in the form of the award
of a Distinguished Service Pension in 1913.

On 26 June 1916, Evans attended the annual meeting of the North
Wales Branch of the British Medical Association in Bangor.[4] After the
formal meeting, William Osler then Regius Professor of Medicine at
Oxford, gave an address on the proposed National Medical School for
Wales and Evans was deputed to give the vote of thanks. After he sat

down, Osler rose to his feet again to tell the meeting of his long friendship with Evans dating from when they had worked together in Toronto
in 1868. He pointed out that the medical profession owed a great debt
to Evans for his discovery in India that blood parasites, specifically
trypanosomes, were pathogenic. The importance of the discovery, he
went on, lay in the fact that other trypanosomes had been found to cause
the critically important African trypanosomiases. Evans thanked Osler
adding that they had not met since 1870 apart from once when Osler
had visited Woolwich forty-two years earlier. Osler had, nonetheless,
taken a keen interest in Evans's scientific work just as Evans had followed Osler's distinguished medical career.

The encounter in Bangor rekindled their friendship. A few months
later, the eighty-one-year-old Evans accompanied by Erie visited Osler
in Oxford. The two exchanged reminiscences from their time in Canada
and Osler remarked to Erie that it was 'most extraordinary that your
father can remember all these people'. Later, Erie remembered the
occasion:

> In seeing them together I felt as if they were affectionate
> brothers ... I heard Father tell Osler ... that he had observed
> leucocytosis in the first stage of anthrax at Sialkot before bacilli
> were visible. [Examining the blood every hour, he] saw leucocytes
> increasing in number and later saw the bacilli 'glued to them'...
> Father failed to fathom the significance of the phenomenon. It
> tantalised him to think how near he had been to making the dis-
> covery which was later made by Metchnikoff. 'I was very near it',
> Father said ... and Osler agreed.

When the time came for them to leave, a concerned Osler took Erie
aside at Oxford station and asked her to take good care of his oldest
friend.

The two men continued to correspond and early in 1918, Evans
sent Osler a copy of his Report on Surra, some letters, a book and a
scrapbook containing photographs of victims of the Mysore famine of
1877–88 as well as some of tiger hunting in India.[5] Osler wrote:

You are most kind to send those valuable contributions for my
McGill collection ... the Surra paper will ... go on the shelf with
Manson, Ronald Ross, Bruce and Cunningham ... 'Tis a fine bit of
work and will carry the name of Griffith Evans a long way down
the track of fame.[6]

Sadly, Osler died in Oxford on 29 December 1919; Evans was to survive
him by sixteen years.[7]

Osler's tribute to Evans in Bangor at last brought Evans to national
attention. First to honour him formally was the Liverpool School of
Tropical Medicine (LSTM) with the award of the Mary Kingsley Medal,
the highest honour conferred by the School and awarded annually to
'distinguished scientists who have assisted the cause of tropical medi-
cine by original research'.[8] On 14 December 1917, the British Medical
Association's North Wales Branch held a luncheon in his honour at the
Imperial Hotel in Llandudno. Afterwards, J. W. W. Stephens, Alfred Jones
Professor of Tropical Medicine, presented Evans with the Medal. Evans
was joining a distinguished company: earlier recipients had included
David Bruce, Robert Koch, Charles Laveran, Sir Patrick Manson, Camillo
Golgi and Joseph Lister.[9] In his address, Stephens declared:

We, the undersigned members of the Professional Committee of
the Liverpool School of Tropical Medicine, desire to offer you our
hearty congratulations on the presentation of the Mary Kingsley
Medal to you in recognition of your distinguished scientific work.
We recall that you were the first to associate trypanosomes with
the production of disease, and the specific name of the trypanosome of surra which you discovered will perpetuate your name in
connection with that discovery. All the more honour is due to you
also for maintaining the correctness of your view that the trypanosomes caused the disease surra, in the face of official opinion
to the contrary.

The Chairman, Dr Drinkwater, added that almost forty years had had
to pass before Evans was acknowledged to be right. A report of the

meeting appeared in the Welsh language newspaper, *Y Brython*, followed by an appreciation of Evans's scientific contribution in a letter to the paper from Edward Morgan in Venezuela.[10]

Hard on the heels of the LSTM was the Royal College of Veterinary Surgeons (RCVS) which awarded him its highest honour, the John Henry Steele Memorial Medal, the following year. The irony of this award was not lost on Evans. He confided his amusement in a letter to Erie in October 1918:

> The Medal was instituted to commemorate young Steel, who investigated surra in Burma ... He died after a short illness. His loss was felt by many good friends, who devoted themselves to collect contributions to commemorate him by instituting a medal called by his name ... I am amused and surprised by the honour of it being given to me.[11]

Evans had, himself, subscribed to the fund.

Soon afterwards, Evans received a letter from the Principal of the University College of North Wales, Henry Reichel, offering him the degree of Doctor in Scientia *honoris causa* in the University of Wales for his pioneering research in Parasitology.[12] Pleased at this recognition by the College, he travelled to Aberystwyth with Erie in the summer of 1919 to receive his degree at the Convocation of the University of Wales. On the way, they made a detour to Tywyn to visit the graves of Evan and Mary Evans.

The War Office had already acknowledged Evans's service in India with the award of his Distinguished Service Pension in 1913 and when news of the public acknowledgement of his scientific distinction reached the military, some effort was made to find additional means of recognising it. However, in 1919 the War Office was preoccupied with the aftermath of the World War and nothing came of it.

Evans's unwavering confidence in the conclusions he had reached in Dera Ismail Khan had been vindicated at last. His national and international reputation as a pioneer in parasitology, tropical medicine and veterinary science was now widely acknowledged.

'ENJOYING A LONG SUNSET'[1]

The Evanses continued to lead full lives in retirement in the first decades of the twentieth century. Evans maintained his wide-ranging correspondence and his active interest in local and national affairs.

After his involvement in the procurement of the site for the new University Building, he must have watched its construction across the valley, visible through the trees from Brynkynallt. It seems probable that he was present at the laying of the foundation stone by Edward VII on 11 July 1907 and at the opening of the new buildings by George V almost exactly four years later. He did not, however, approve of all aspects of the finished buildings which came to be known as Top College, joining in the criticism of the acoustics of the main, Prichard Jones Hall: 'the Hall, he thought would do admirably for banquets or as the nave of a cathedral where people do not preach to be heard.'[2]

Just before Mair and Harry Jones returned to Myanmar in September 1913, they invited Katie and Evans to a performance of the comedy 'Charley's Aunt'. His deafness made following dialogue difficult and his rational outlook made him impatient with the illusions of the stage. Straining to hear with his hand cupping his good ear, his patience was soon exhausted. With the rest of the audience convulsed with laughter, Evans bellowed 'I cannot see anything funny in this play at all!'

Mair and Harry were not to be in Myanmar for long. Following the outbreak of the Great War the following year, Mair returned to Wales in April 1915. Harry joined the Indian Army and was posted to the Middle East. Captured at the siege of Kut-al-Amara which surrendered to an Ottoman Army in April 1916, he and the other, mostly Indian, prisoners were taken more than 2,000 miles north and west to camps in Anatolia, being forced to march much of the distance. There Harry led a bizarre but successful escape in which he made use of his fluency in Welsh to confound his Turkish captors[3]. On 3 January 1916, while Harry was in Kut, Mair gave birth to a son at Brynkynallt. The boy, Harri Bevan, was the second of their five children; the first, Jean Bevan, had been born in Myanmar in 1915. He was the Evanses' first grandson.

After the flurry of recognition, life at Brynkynallt returned to normal. Paying close attention to the issues of the day as usual, in 1921 Evans heard tell of a new play, 'Abraham Lincoln' by John Drinkwater,[4] in which General Ulysses S. Grant was portrayed as a drunkard. Evans reacted with a firm letter to Drinkwater explaining that he had spent a week as the General's guest and could vouch for the fact that although he had once been a heavy drinker, he had given up some years earlier. Such distortion of the truth for dramatic effect was, in Evans's view, inexcusable and he asked that Drinkwater alter the text. Drinkwater responded affably but refused to do so. Evans was deluding himself in thinking Grant who waged a continuing battle with alcoholism, had succeeded in giving up drink; his passionate advocacy of abstinence was one of the few things that could cloud his judgement.

The Joneses had returned to Myanmar after the war but were back in Wales on leave in January 1922. They had decided that Mair and the children should not return and to the delight of Evans and Katie, the family bought a house in Bangor. But their happiness was short-lived. One night in July 1923, a month before his eighty-eighth birthday, Evans was woken by Katie grasping his hand. She had suffered a severe heart attack and died in his arms. Evans was inconsolable.

Erie was the only person to whom he confided the depth of his grief and distress. In a letter to her three months later he wrote: 'She always helped me, helped me much in many troubles, official and other, always in her quiet way of strength ... My greatest comfort is in recollecting her presence with me, enjoyment was always multiplied when she shared it. Sometimes I am overpowered, failing to find her.'[5] Katie had no scientific background but had supported him always: 'Griff, if

FIGURE 20 The Evans family at Brynkynallt. Back row (from left to right): Towena Greaves (née Evans) with Dorothy, Enid Jones (Harry Jones's sister), Clara and Goronwy Evans, Mair Jones (née Evans), Harry Jones (seated); Middle row (seated from left to right): Griffith Evans with Olwen Greaves, Katie Evans, Wynona Garfitt (née Evans), Charles Garfitt; Front seated on the rug: Erie Evans, Nona Garfitt. (Tony Craven Walker)

you think it right you must do it'. She took great satisfaction in the recognition Evans eventually received for his achievements and was particularly delighted at the award of his DSc by the University of Wales.[6]

Evans now entered the darkest phase of his long life. That autumn and through his eighty-ninth year, he stuck steadfastly to his long-established daily routine: rising at 6.30 a.m., he breakfasted at 7.15, checked his barometers and thermometers, read the newspapers and took the dogs for their morning walk. This ended with a brisk run through the gorse down Bangor Mountain which, Evans insisted, kept his knee joints supple. The rest of the day was spent at meetings, maintaining his correspondence and reading. He found the meetings tiring but his interest in what was going on in the world was undiminished; he wrote to Erie: 'I was exhausted after attending 2 meetings of [the] Temperance Conference last week and the meeting of Governors [of the] University College last Wednesday, but I am glad I went'[7].

On 1 April the following year, the fifty-fifth anniversary of their betrothal, Evans wrote to Erie that he wished he were in Montgomeryshire 'to wander alone by the banks of the River Banwy where we two walked together that day'. He then quoted Coleridge:

> A grief without a pang — void, dark, and drear;
> A stifling, drowsy, unimpassioned grief
> That finds no natural outlet, no relief
> In word, or sigh, or tear[8]

Erie returned to Bangor to be with her father whenever her Cardiff practice allowed. They would take a cab up Nant Ffrancon to Llyn Ogwen and set off on the mountain walks that Evans had shared with Katie.

Between these visits Evans struggled with depression and ill health but not all was gloom and despondency. Every year on his birthday, he arranged a treat for his grandchildren, usually an expedition to somewhere of their choosing. In 1924 on his eighty-ninth birthday, he took his Garfitt and Jones grandchildren to the Marquis of Anglesey's Column.[9] He led the children up the 115 steps of the spiral staircase and when they reached the viewing platform at the top, hardly out of breath but badly out of tune, he burst into the first verse of the Welsh National Anthem. That he could do that at eighty-nine was, he told the children, a consequence of steering clear of cigarettes and alcohol. Evans loved his grandchildren, as Jean Ware said, 'as he loved his Welsh Terriers, with a continued practical concern for our welfare'.

Towards the end of 1924, there was discussion in the Royal College of Veterinary Surgeons on how they should mark the seventieth anniversary of the graduation of Evans and his contemporary, James Meyrick. Sir Frederick Smith wrote to the Secretary of the College, Dr Fred Bullock: 'Both are too old to dine out. How would an illuminated address do?' The discussion was interrupted by Meyrick's death in February 1925. Bullock wrote to Evans to inform him adding, 'The honour [of Father of the Veterinary Profession] now falls upon you, who were his junior, as a graduate, by only a week.'[10] The College's congratulations were little consolation for the death of the friend with whom he had shared so much and did nothing to ease his sombre mood. Reporters who came to interview him about his new status in the profession were given short shrift: 'I wish they would leave me alone. I do not like being flattered in public.'

Soon afterwards, he received two letters from Bullock asking for his memories of the Royal Veterinary School in the 1850s and of John Wilkinson, the Queen's Principal Veterinary Surgeon, to whom Meyrick and Evans had reported at Woolwich in 1860. The second letter also asked for an autobiographical sketch which Sir Frederick Smith had requested for his history of the Royal Army Veterinary Corps.[11] Evans made several attempts to respond but his heart was not in the task and Bullock's request remained largely unanswered.[12] Smith then wrote to Bullock:

> I have been in touch with him … lately in order to get his biography correct.[13] I have written his obituary which I hope will not be required for some time. He has to pass one day and I should like the *Times*, *Morning Post*, and perhaps *Nature* as well as our own periodicals to know correctly the great service he rendered to

science … Our men have been greatly neglected, they disappear and no one takes the trouble to record the fact, or if they do, it is blemished by error or misprint.

In May, Evans received a formal letter from Sydney H. Slocock, President of the RCVS, congratulating him on the seventieth anniversary of his graduation as MRCVS.[14]

In mid-June, four months after Meyrick's death, Evans met with a serious setback. Running down Bangor Mountain at the end of his usual walk, he tripped over a root and fell heavily, fracturing his left femur. An ambulance was called and the attendants offered him brandy to ease the pain. Evans's reaction was predictable: 'Alcohol is poison', he boomed and emptied the glass on the ground before being carried home. In bed and in great pain, he realised that his walks were at an end and that he would no longer be able to exercise his beloved Welsh Terriers, Tango and Dell. With a heavy heart, he summoned the vet and asked that they be put down. After they had been taken away, he was offered some consolation: Erie came to his bedside to tell him that Mair had given birth to a boy, to be named Griffith Bevan after him. The news raised his spirits and he vowed that he would walk again and take 'little Griffith on my good knee'.

It was now clear that Evans would need more support than the Brynkynallt housemaids could provide and Erie began to look for a suitable carer. Her choice, Ellen Williams, a young housemaid from a village in the hills above Bethesda, was inspired. Ellen was a spirited twenty-year-old with auburn hair, a winning smile and brown, intelligent eyes. She was used to hard work and appeared undaunted by the prospect of caring for Evans although, as Erie took her upstairs to meet him, she confided that she had never spoken to anyone so old.

Entirely untrained, Ellen was a born nurse and attended to Evans's every need without demur. A strong bond developed between them and when at last he achieved his first step from his bed after the accident, she was as delighted as he was. With patience and her encouragement, Evans was soon able to walk around upstairs with his stick. As the pain receded, he required less nursing and Ellen's primary role gradually became that of personal assistant: she would run up and down stairs to supply him with books and papers from his study, run errands in the town and make and receive telephone calls.

During this period of confinement, Evans especially valued his stream of regular visitors who included Dr Edward Greenly, a well-known geologist; Mr W. R. Owen, the Borough Librarian; a Bangor plumber with whom he discussed politics; staff and students from the University College and pupils from local schools. Occasional visitors included friends and acquaintances visiting Bangor and increasingly, now his scientific distinction was recognised, journalists from home and abroad. Evans particularly looked forward to visits from his family. Every Sunday, Mair and Harry's children and any others of his grandchildren who happened to be in Bangor, trooped up the hill for tea. Although no longer able to take them on outings on his birthday, the institution survived with Evans paying for them to go without him.

Evans continued to work hard to regain his mobility and before long, with his stick and very carefully, he was able to negotiate the stairs. Regaining the freedom to move around the house was an important fillip to his morale and in the spring of 1927, he was finally able to reach the seat in the courtyard in front of the house to sit in the sun. There, on his ninety-second birthday, he fulfilled his promise to take his little grandson, Griffith Bevan Jones, on his knee.

One morning another challenge presented itself: Evans found himself unable to hear what Ellen said to him. Calling for his amplifier,[15] he asked her to count into the receiver while he watched her lips intently. When she reached 'chwech' (six) and he could hear nothing, he pushed the instrument aside exclaiming that he was now stone deaf. Ever resourceful, Ellen responded with a consoling message written on his bedside notepad. Written messages now replaced his hearing and Evans ordered a stock of notepads and pencils and abandoned his lifelong habit of cupping his ear in his hand.

The same year, 1927, saw the publication of Sir Frederick Smith's *A History of the Royal Army Veterinary Corps 1796–1919* which contained a brief account of Evans's discovery of the trypanosome causing surra and a biographical note.[16] Smith described Evans as 'of medium height, and on medical grounds for some years [he] wore a beard, one of the few officers in the Service so permitted'. On a facing page is a striking photograph of a bewhiskered but not bearded Evans in the formal uniform of an Inspecting Veterinary Surgeon in the Indian Army (Figure 10, p. 104). That summer, Evans received a visit from Dr Fred Bullock who reported back to Smith. Smith replied:

I was most interested to learn that you had called on Evans. Does he bear any resemblance to the portrait of him in the 'History' which is a striking likeness of the man as I knew him? His voice was always strong, his delivery jerky, abrupt, decisive, final. What a pity he does not write a paper dealing with Grant and Lincoln. The number of men alive who saw these builders of the modern USA must be fast dwindling.

Smith wrote to Bullock again in November 1928:

The old rarely have the quality of enthusiasm. You and I have seen it recently in the case of Evans. He could have been of immense service to me in the preparation of the 'History of the RAVC'. He politely said, 'Pray do not bother me, I am carefully nursing what is left of my life and have no desire to expend energy unduly', or words to that effect.

Evans was now experiencing some deterioration in his health and suffered from recurrent attacks of inflammation of the bladder. More seriously, he would occasionally suffer spells of dizziness, a symptom of bradycardia[17] or heart block. When this happened, he would ask Ellen to sit with him, reassuring her that it would soon pass.

In the autumn of 1929, disaster struck again when he fell heavily getting out of bed in the night, this time causing an impacted fracture near the neck of his right femur. His shouts for help failed to wake Ellen but he managed to heave himself onto the bed where she found him in the morning, exhausted. She was distraught that she had not heard him but he reassured her that he would walk again, contradicting the doctor who told him he would never again leave his bed. Ellen replied on the pad that they had done it once and would do it again. He was now in his ninety-fifth year but they were right; after eighteen months he had recovered enough to hobble around the first floor. With prodigious effort, he was able once or twice to get downstairs but an attack of bradycardia as he climbed upstairs on the last occasion persuaded him not to repeat the experiment. A daily excursion round the bedrooms with Ellen was now his only exercise. All meals had to be taken in bed which meant occasional spillages were inevitable. These distressed Evans greatly; his pride made it difficult for him to become reconciled to his dependence on others. During the periodic downwards swings in his mood, Katie was never far from his thoughts. One particularly dreary winter's day, he covered his face with his hands and said to Ellen: 'I am so lonely. My dear, dear wife is not here.'

The pain from his second fracture gradually subsided and he began to come to terms with his new situation. Soon, his positive outlook and intellectual impetus were sufficiently restored for him to embark on a study of psychology. He acquired the latest textbooks and was soon deeply immersed in this new field of interest. Some of his notes showed a characteristic prescience:

> Animals have a great capacity for acclimatising themselves to changing circumstances. But a whole species can perish if the change is too sudden or too severe. It is probable that man's scientific development is outpacing his psychological evolution, and I doubt if human psychology can adapt itself with sufficient speed to survive the rapidly-changing conditions of this century. This may mean that in the next few decades there will be a serious increase in the incidence of mental diseases.

At the annual meeting of the British Association for the Advancement of Science[18] in Bristol in September 1930, Dr P.J. du Toit gave his Presidential Address to the Agricultural Section on 'The Role which Veterinary Science plays in the Development of a Country' with particular reference to South Africa. In a section on Trypanosomiasis, du Toit described how the African trypanosomiases had thwarted economic and social development in the most potentially productive regions of the continent. He went on to refer to surra and to Evans's role in identifying the cause of the disease:

> Only a few words need be added about those trypanosome infections which are carried mechanically by ordinary biting flies. The most important of these is 'Surra' in India and other countries. Great advance has been made since September 1880, exactly 50 years ago, when Evans ... was sent to the Punjab to investigate this disease, and when he succeeded, in a remarkably short time, in discovering its cause ...
>
> It is with great satisfaction that the fact can be recorded that this veteran of science, Griffith Evans, the discoverer of the first pathogenic trypanosoma, is still alive today ... and is able to watch, from his home in Bangor, the progress which has been made in this field

His remarks attracted the attention of the national press. The *Daily Herald* ran a story headlined 'Great Scientist Forgotten'[19] and stories about the 'forgotten man' of British science appeared in newspapers all over England and Wales and even in India.[20] From this point to the end of his life, Evans was pestered by journalists: 'I do not like to be lionized ... I have long ago been sufficiently honoured by those best able to judge my professional work. Others do not count in my mind.'

The publicity alerted the city fathers of Bangor to Evans's distinction and the Municipal Corporation voted to offer him the Freedom of the City. The casket containing the scroll was received first by Wynona representing him at a council meeting in early January 1931. The citation outlined the significance of his discovery and mentioned the appalling conditions under which he had worked in Dera Ismail Khan. A few days later, he received the honour in person in his bedroom where he was attended by a small delegation comprising the Mayor, Alderman W. R. Jones J. P., the Town Clerk Mr Pentir Williams, two other aldermen and two councillors. One reporter and a photographer

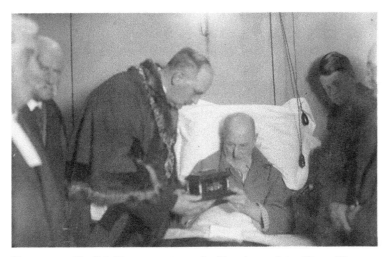

FIGURE 21 Griffith Evans receiving the Freedom of the City of Bangor

witnessed the ceremony while the rest of the press and the general public gathered in the courtyard and in the road outside. After the presentation, Evans spoke: 'Now you gentlemen, sit down, and I will talk to you.' He then 'in clear, fluent tones which would have filled a large-sized hall, and without the aid of notes, delivered a speech of gratitude'. His strong voice carried through the open window and his audience inside and out heard him disclose for the first time the part he had played in the University's acquisition of the site for Top College.[21]

The ceremony was widely reported with many papers carrying the photograph of Evans receiving the casket: 'Freedom for bedridden scientist – Dr Griffith Evans bedridden and deaf at the age of ninety-six, receiving the Freedom of Bangor from the Mayor'; 'Scientist whom England Forgot'; 'Honour from fellow citizens comes when he is ninety-five and deaf'. Wynona Garfitt was quoted in the *Western Mail*: 'He is five years off his century, and a national recognition now, not to mention local recognition, would be dust and ashes in his mouth.'[22] She was wrong. When the delegation left, Evans remarked that he valued this honour 'from my own people' more than any other.

The previous November, Evans had received a letter from Thomas Ridley Currie MD of Philadelphia asking for a photograph for a paper on 'The Discoverer of the Trypanosome' to be given to the Medical History Section of the College of Physicians of Philadelphia and to be published in *Medical Life*.[23] Evans responded and the article in Currie's florid style, appeared in May 1931:

> The last forty years of his life have been spent in the quaint sea-port town of Wales, known as Bangor. He has never made any secret of his religious opinions, he being a frank, outspoken sceptic ...
>
> Time seems powerless to stiffen his mind, and today, at the ripe old age of 95, one of his favourite amusements is to tackle some new book on Philosophy or Psychology.
>
> All honour then, to this veterinary physician and also Doctor of Medicine, who sixty-six years ago suspected the infectious nature of tuberculosis, and urged rest, fresh air and sunlight in its treatment. All honour to the man who 50 years ago discovered the cause of Pernicious Anaemia in horses, mules and camels, and thereby started tropical medicine on its fruitful way.
>
> It is very gratifying to know, that his work was known, and appreciated, by Pasteur and Koch, and our own beloved Osler. A man who, in a short interview, won the trust and esteem of our noble Abraham Lincoln.[24]

In August 1932, Nona Garfitt, Evans's third granddaughter, was killed in a riding accident at the age of twenty-two. He was deeply distressed and soon afterwards, he received another unexpected blow. Sensing that Ellen was uneasy one day, he asked her what was wrong. Ellen wrote that Jack Williams had asked her to marry him. Evans was shocked: the prospect of losing her support seemed devastating and struggling to control his emotion, he asked what answer she had given. She replied that she had accepted and when Evans asked if he were a good man and would treat her kindly, Ellen nodded and burst into tears. A new arrangement was now needed to care for Evans. Erie, then fifty-nine, had recently retired and rather than employ anyone new, she decided to return to north Wales to look after her father. They had been close since their holiday together in Eryri in 1887 and he had shared his thoughts and concerns with her throughout her adult life. Now the relationship was put on a new footing as Erie took over Ellen's nursing duties as well as acting as his doctor and companion.

After this upheaval, Evans resumed his routine of reading, maintaining his correspondence and receiving visitors, including journalists whom he now treated with consideration. He continued his studies in psychology and philosophy marking passages of interest and those which he wished to discuss with his correspondents and visitors. The long letters he wrote in his tenth decade covered a multitude of topics and are full of interest and insight. There were no signs of any diminution in his mental powers or memory, a consequence, he insisted, of his life-long abstinence from tobacco and alcohol.

As time passed, Evans's thoughts began to turn to questions of mortality and beyond and he expressed these in his letters. In August 1934, his niece, Eliza's daughter Gwenddydd, who had chaperoned his daughters to and from school when he and Katie were in India, died. In his letter of condolence to her son, he quoted a verse from T. H. Huxley's tomb:

> And if there be no meeting past the grave,
> If all is darkness, silence, yet 'tis rest.
> Be not afraid ye waiting hearts that weep
> For God still giveth his beloved sleep
> And if an endless sleep he wills – so best.[25]

He had underlined the last line three times. Gwenddydd's death affected him deeply. He began to feel isolated and left behind as those dear to him died and he turned more and more to his Bible which he kept by his bedside; noticing this, one of his visitors wondered if 'the man of science was giving way to the mystic'. Although he spent an increasing amount of time in silent contemplation, his grasp of what was going on around him and in the wider world did not diminish. Nor did his agnosticism waver. On New Year's Day 1934, he wrote to his cousin, Adelaide Cox:

> I sometimes compare myself to one with others in the anteroom of a physician, watching for the inner door to open, and a call to enter for examination or judgment. I have not any fear of that. I have not the slightest knowledge of any life other than the present … I think it is my duty not to pry beyond the limit given, it would distract me from my duties here and now … Religiously I am an agnostic rationalist.

In another letter written at about the same time, he wrote:

> I have no fear of what may be in another possible state of being. My duty is here: take what comes and make the best of it, for self and others … If I am asked what I wish for post-mortem, my reply is, to meet all my old friends in some kind of purgatory for betterment. Nevertheless I am quite content to abide by order assigned to humanity by the good Director General of living beings. My ignorance is profound.

These conjectures were reflected in his views on what should happen following his death. During one of his daily sessions with Erie, he gave her strict and precise instructions. There was to be no funeral service or ceremony of any kind. His body was to be taken from the house before dawn on the day following his death, transported directly to Anfield Crematorium in Liverpool – then the nearest to Bangor – and cremated.

The year of Evans's centenary duly arrived and it was clear from a surge in visits from journalists that his birthday was to be the focus of public interest, local, national and international. Letters arrived asking for his photograph and for his views on a wide range of topics and each received an answer in his robust, legible hand. An example of his remarkable calligraphy was his contribution to the album produced by the Royal Veterinary College to mark their appeal for their Giant Nosebag 250,000,000 Farthing Endowment Fund.[26] The album comprised contributions from royalty and leading figures from every aspect of national life and Evans was invited to participate as Father of the Veterinary Profession. His hand-written contribution, dated 1 June 1935, reviews his time at the Royal Veterinary College. He recalls[27]

> the long-ago pleasure I had as the youngest student at the R.V.C. with Professors Spooner, Simmonds, Varnel and Morton, all so kind and all so personally different in character and manners. I never missed a lecture and dissected all that Varnel advised me ... [I] passed the examination accordingly. The Professors congratulated me.

He goes on to describe his current situation:

> I have been confined to bed a number of years ... so deaf that I cannot hear any human voice. My sight continued good until last year ... I write slowly but I have not ceased to be a student ... With retrospect of over 95 years I recollect events happening on my fourth birthday clearly. I am glad to observe that progress has been on the whole for betterment.

Just over two months later, on 7 August, Evans reached the age of one hundred.

17

CENTENARIAN

Two weeks before Griffith Evans's one-hundredth birthday, Erie received a letter from the Librarian of the Osler Library at McGill University requesting a photograph of their famous alumnus. In her reply, she described her father's state of health and mind: 'His last years have demanded more courage than anything in his earlier life, in my opinion.'[1]

A few days later, an article by R. F. Montgomerie was published in the *Veterinary Record* reminding its readers of his achievement in discovering the pathogenicity of *Trypanosoma evansi*.[2] He wrote 'When Evans came to place on record the reasoning which brought him to regard his microbes as pathogenic ... his light shone with real brilliance ... The purest of pure thinking set out what, even today, seems an unanswerable case.'

On the eve of the birthday, Sir Frederick Hobday, Principal and Dean of the Royal Veterinary College, arrived in Bangor by train. He was met by Captain W. H. Savage, the local veterinary surgeon, who took him to Brynkynallt for an informal evening meeting with Evans. Sir Frederick later described their conversation:

> The interview was of such mutual interest that the midnight hour struck before the lapse of time was noticed. It was difficult to find a veterinary subject on which Dr Evans was not *au fait* ... whilst the accurate recollections of men and things sixty and even eighty years ago were astonishing ... his mental faculties are almost perfect; so much so that there was not the slightest difficulty in

maintaining an interchange of ideas and questions by means of writing pad and pencil ... He is indeed a wonderful man for (next day) he was literally as fresh as a daisy ... and when ... we bade him goodbye it was with a feeling of wonderment at the vitality of this superman.

Responsibility for the preparations for the occasion fell to Erie. Such was the public interest that meticulous planning was required and by the time the day arrived, she was tired and nervous. The first visitor on the morning of 7 August was Evans's twenty-year-old granddaughter, Jean or Sian as Evans called her, who arrived at 7 a.m. to help her aunt. When Erie told her of Sir Frederick's visit, Jean asked if Evans was exhausted: 'Not a bit of it, but I'm sure Sir Frederick was!' 'Oh dear', Erie continued with a sigh, 'I shall be glad when today is over. Anything could happen.'

Jean went upstairs and into Evans's bedroom: 'Taid was propped up with pillows, his long Viking head bent slightly forward, like a resting warrior. The bones of his face had strength and dignity.' On top of the pile of papers and journals at his bedside, she noticed the new issue of the *Veterinary Record* in which he had been reading the editorial tribute:

> No account of Griffith Evans's life and work could be written without evoking that almost breathless interest so frequently associated with fiction. Had there been no Evans the scientist, Evans the man must have made his name. Else how could he in person have persuaded Abraham Lincoln himself to make an exception in his favour when authority in Washington point-blank refused access to the American Civil War front to Commanders of the Guards, medical and other officers, heaven knows how high? And the encounter with General 'Beast' Butler, too. How would a less amazing personality have dealt with him?
>
> Human tuberculosis and tetanus, anthrax and surra in India – he left the mark of his brilliant, virile brain upon them all ... [His] character and achievement in his chosen ways may well stand as an example to veterinarians for all time.[3]

When Evans saw Jean, he beckoned her to him taking her hand as she wished him Happy Birthday. Telling her to go down to the kitchen for some breakfast, he lay back to gather strength for the afternoon's proceedings.

Telegrams began to pour in from relatives and friends, scientists, dignitaries and institutions, over eighty in total, including one from the Prince of Wales offering Evans his 'sincere congratulations' and another from his old friend, David Lloyd George:[4]

> The Principality feels great pride in one of her sons whose remarkable researches have brought so much relief of human suffering and whose discoveries in veterinary surgery have had such far-reaching results in the preventing of disease among our dumb friends.
>
> It is an added joy to me to-day to send greetings to one of my constituents who actually had personal contact with Abraham Lincoln, of whom I have always been a great admirer.

As the greetings were handed to him, Evans asked if the telegraph boy had been offered a glass of lemonade to refresh him after his repeated ascents of Lôn Pobty. Erie nodded at Evans but in an aside to Jean, said: 'He refused it – said he never drinks anything except beer, and he well knows he won't get *that* in this house!'

Soon after 2 p.m., the visitors assembled in front of the house while onlookers crowded onto Lôn Pobty outside the gate. The select few who could be accommodated in Evans's bedroom were ushered into the hall, sidling past the dresser, sideboard and ostler cupboard from Tŷ Mawr and a clutter of souvenirs and memorabilia of his travels, to reach the stairs.

The scene in Evans's bedroom was described by Jean:

> My eldest brother and I had been placed in the open dressing room door behind the bed, from which we could see the faces ranged in a respectful arc round Taid (Grandfather) …
>
> Sir Frederick Hobday stood at Taid's left hand. Next to him was our Bangor vet, Mr Savage, known locally as 'Savage the Animals'. Beside him loomed the dark aloof figure of Uncle Goronwy, Taid's

only son. Completing the semi-circle were my father, and, next to him, the Mayor, the Town Clerk and the Press: Mr MacDermid, the reporter, and a photographer ... On chairs at the foot of the bed sat Taid's daughters: Wynona, Erie, Towena and my mother, Mair, the youngest and gentlest of the four.

At exactly 2.30 p.m., Sir Frederick opened the proceedings with a short speech, handing a copy to Evans who read it with his magnifying glass as it was delivered.[5] Sir Frederick explained that the purpose of the gathering was to honour the Father of the Royal Veterinary College and of the whole veterinary profession. He then took up a framed parchment scroll and presented it to Evans. The scroll, signed by the President of the College, Prince Henry of Gloucester, and himself as Principal, recognised the great service Griffith Evans had rendered to veterinary and human medicine:[6]

**Tribute of the Royal Veterinary College to
Dr Griffith Evans, DSc Wales, MD, CM, MRCVS.
Qualified 1855.**

In recognition of the valuable research services to veterinary and human medicine by Dr Griffith Evans, rendered with a high courage over a phenomenally lengthy period, this illuminated scroll from his Alma Mater, is presented by the President, HRH the Duke of Gloucester, KG and Sir Frederick Hobday, CMG, FRCVS, FRSE (Hon. Veterinary Surgeon to His Majesty the King), Principal and Dean of the Royal Veterinary College.

Further, it is proposed to set up in the Common Room of the College a carved plaque to commemorate the consent of Dr Griffith Evans – the father of the veterinary profession – to lead the veterinarians of the Empire in support of the Royal Veterinary College Hospital Giant Nosebag 250,000,000 Farthing Endowment Fund, and in felicitation of his 100th birthday, August 7, 1935.

HENRY, President
FREDERICK F.E. HOBDAY, Principal and Dean
The Royal Veterinary College

Sir Frederick explained that its frame was made from wood taken from the original building where Evans had enrolled in 1853. As he handed it to Evans, he congratulated him as a great pioneer whose work had been of immense benefit to humanity and to veterinary science.

FIGURE 22 Griffith Evans receiving the scroll from Professor Frederick Hobday, Principal of the Royal Veterinary College, on his 100th birthday. (North Wales Chronicle)

Evans examined the scroll with his magnifying glass for a few moments in silence. Then he looked up and raised his hands 'as though he was about to address a vast audience'. The volume and steadiness of his voice must have surprised anyone unfamiliar with his normal speech and the resounding delivery of his address was clearly audible through the open window to those gathered outside. He spoke without notes for exactly half an hour.

Evans started by saying how overwhelmed he was by this special message from his old college where he had begun his scientific career. He continued fluently and eloquently, moving effortlessly from science to personal thoughts with occasional flashes of humour. Reminiscing about his time at the Royal Veterinary College, he remembered Professors Spooner, Simmonds and Morton and explained how their teaching and influence had shaped his approach to veterinary science. He recalled a lecture by Simmonds on the process of rumination in sheep, remarking that he had been ruminating ever since. He reflected on the importance to him of microscopy recalling that, as microtomes[7] to prepare tissue sections had not been invented, he had started to study fresh blood. Blood had become his lifelong preoccupation and had led ultimately to his discovery of the cause of surra in horses and camels in India. Evans concluded by speaking of his admiration for Professor Spooner who was never afraid to say he did not know the answer to a question or the solution to a problem, an example Evans had aspired to follow.

As he was nearing the end of his address, the acting Postmaster delivered a telegram from King George V and Queen Mary sent from the Royal Yacht at Cowes:

> The King and Queen are much interested to hear that today you are celebrating your hundredth birthday and desire me to convey to you their hearty congratulations. Their Majesties are aware of your distinguished services to veterinary science and send you their best wishes on this great anniversary.

The *North Wales Chronicle* reported that this 'took the breezy centenarian by surprise and he showed it' but Jean thought it had been the interruption that had surprised Evans, not the telegram. He read the telegram, looked up and concluded his address.

When he had finished, the Mayor of Bangor, Alderman Richard Thomas, and the Town Clerk conveyed the congratulations of the citizens of Bangor. The formalities completed, there followed a hiatus during which no one spoke or made a move. Then,

the white-haired Mayor and his Town Clerk drew closer to the bed and each clasped one of Taid's hands without speaking. The three old men had known each other for many, many years. These were Taid's own people, representing the town he had lived in for nearly half his life. For the first time he broke down and gave a queer little strangled sob. It was agonising to see him try not to weep.

Struggling to compose himself, he spoke:

I don't know what to say … I have just received … the congratulations of my college; then came the telegram from the King and Queen, but I have now received something from my own people, those among whom I have lived and among whom I have worked.

Evans paused, then his composure restored, continued

[n]o congratulations could be more acceptable than those from the people among whom I have lived … Whatever exultation I may feel as the result of what you have presented to me and said, is transcended by this message from the people of Bangor … I only wish my dear wife was with me this day. Whatever I did in Bangor was due to her help.

Referring to Evans as 'one of our respected Freemen', the Mayor spoke:

Our pleasure is all the more because the good feelings we extend are shared by the people of Bangor generally. We all join in wishing you in the remainder of your days, peace and happiness and, above all, that you will be spared the suffering of any pain.

With this, the visitors departed.

The family remained and later in the afternoon, gathered in Evans's bedroom. All seemed well as they offered their own congratulations but beneath the display of affection and goodwill, all but Evans and the grandchildren were aware of a tension which was to erupt later. After the brief gathering, they all left and Evans and Erie were alone. The old man had managed to withstand demands on his strength and concentration, let alone his emotions, which might well have overwhelmed someone many years his junior.

Of the congratulatory messages and telegrams that had flooded into Brynkynallt that day, he particularly valued those from the members of his profession at home and abroad. These included a message from the Quarter-Master General, India, on behalf of the Royal Army Veterinary Corps:

> Since the day when you … discovered the first pathological trypanosome, great strides have been made in diagnosis and treatment which have had a marked effect on animal transport in the Army … we owe you a great debt of gratitude and consider it a great honour and privilege to offer our congratulations.

Another was from the President of the National Veterinary Medical Association of Great Britain: 'The Association recognises that if it had not been for the high ideals which you carried out and instilled in others in the days of long ago, the profession would not now be holding the position that it does in the eyes of the world generally.' And one received from P. J. du Toit from South Africa: 'I still think that your discovery of *Trypanosoma evansi* and your elucidation of the cause of surra were masterpieces of scientific achievement, and laid the foundation for modern veterinary protozoology.'[8]

The centenary was reported in at least twenty newspapers in Wales and throughout England, Ireland and Scotland. It had also been anticipated by an article in the *Manchester Guardian*[9] and was celebrated in the scientific journal, *Nature*, which published a congratulatory notice and outline of his career.[10]

Evans resolved to respond himself to every one of the congratulatory messages. Although exhausted by the previous day's events, he began this daunting task the following morning. That day, he was interrupted by the arrival of an American reporter, Edgar de Witt Jones from the *Detroit News*, who hoped to interview the last living Briton who had met Abraham Lincoln. Evans agreed to see him and recounted his memories of Lincoln at their meeting in 1864. At the end of the interview, De Witt Jones observed 'that the great old man was tired. He looked pathetically frail.'[11]

It was becoming apparent to Erie that Evans's strength was flagging. His heart was giving cause for concern and cataracts were beginning seriously to impair his vision, the loss of which would have cut him off from all communication except by touch. A further irritation was a persistent tinnitus. Nevertheless, his resolution did not flag. In late September, he heard that the Senate of McGill University had passed a resolution congratulating him on his centenary at its meeting on 16 September 1935.[12] His short response dated 2 October 1935 was among his last as he neared the end of his undertaking: 'What I have been able to do in the development of Pathology, has been the result of what was put into me by my good teachers during my course of study at McGill [Medical School], where I spent some of the most happy years of the hundred.'[13]

However, the demands on him had not ended. In September, he received a request from the editor, Mr P. Srinivasa Rao, asking for a 1,000-word reminiscence of his time in India for publication in the *Indian Veterinary Journal*. Evans set about the task immediately and by 21 September his letter was ready to post. After mentioning his failing eyesight – 'It is with difficulty I see to write this slowly, but I shall do my best for you' – he went on to recount his 'happy recollections of India, and of the many different kinds of natives I had the delightful pleasure of being friendly with'. He concluded

I was, and am, in sincere sympathy with the people of India in working for their own salvation, in every direction, medical and others ... political, religious, etc. Of course there have been lamentable mistakes, such as the feuds between Mohammedans and Hindus, but the law of progress in this world has always been the law of the wheel – construction, destruction, and reconstruction, Vishnu and Shiva alternatively.

Rao was delighted to receive Evans's piece. His answer by return post was effusive:

I was so overjoyed that I ran to all my professional brothers in the city of Madras to show them your letter and express how deeply you feel even now for the Profession in India. May God bless you with cheerfulness and happiness till the end of your days. Your loving, P.S.R.

He went on to beg Evans for a short message, 'an old man's blessing', for the veterinary profession in India. Evans replied in November in what was to be his last letter and his 'blessing' was published in the same January 1936 issue of the Journal that carried his obituary:[14]

I cannot do better than in the prayer of the ancient Welsh bards standing in their mystic, symbolic circle, when opening their proceedings on great national occasions:

> 'May God give his Protection
> And in Protection, Strength,
> And in Strength, Understanding,
> And in Understanding, Knowledge,
> And in Knowledge, Knowledge of the Right,
> And in Knowledge of the Right, the Love of it,
> And from Love, the Love of every Being,
> And in every Being, the Love of God,
> God and every Good'.[15]

So likewise may the All Indian Veterinary Association be blessed
is my most sincere wish, hope and trust.
        Griffith Evans, MD, DSc, MRCVS

He had now achieved his self-imposed obligation to write personally to
everyone who had wished him well. Very frail, he was reconciled to the
approach of death but he was troubled by one further concern. Evans
had always wanted his children to be 'united like a bundle of sticks' and
he had hoped that his centenary would draw them together. Knowing
this, the family contrived to conceal their mutual animosities during the
celebrations but the atmosphere after the dignitaries had left was tense.

Goronwy had always caused Katie and Evans concern and among
other worries, they had little confidence in his prudence with money.
Consequently, in her will, Katie had decided that his inheritance should
be placed in trust so that he received only the income without access
to the capital until late in life, a restriction that was not applied to his
sisters. Towena, who had always championed her younger brother, was
aggrieved on his behalf and complained bitterly to Katie's executors, her
own husband Herbert Greaves and Mair's husband Harry Jones. The
tension was exacerbated by the fact that Towena had always been jealous
of Mair and suspected her and Harry of having had undue influence
on Katie. Her animosity was apparent to all except Evans but when
Towena sought legal advice, it was impossible to conceal matters from
him. He revealed his distress and impatience by writing a postcard. On
one side he wrote 'ER COF AWST' (Remembering August) in capitals
and on the other:

> Beware! It is remarkably common of emotional sympathetic kind-
> hearted people with very limited information to try rectifying what
> appears to them a wrong treatment and by interfering they actually
> do much greater wrong, injustice, which no one can remedy. Such
> people with little knowledge of facts involved in and related to
> the case in question, act as if they thought it not possible for them
> to be incompetent for judging it. Thus evil is wrought by want of
> thought as much as by want of heart.

He left the postcard in his wallet to be found after his death. It was directed at Towena, the 'emotional, sympathetic kind-hearted person' who, he believed, had misunderstood the motive behind the stipulation in Katie's will.

Evans's hold on life now waned and in late November and early December, he suffered a series of heart attacks. He had stopped reading anything except essential messages and Erie's summary of the evening news each day. On the 28 November, Erie wrote to Wynona:

> I am afraid Father will not be able to write to you. His breath is so short and it is such a labour for him to take his food. But he usually improves after his tea and his mind becomes active and clear.

Much weaker now, he said to Erie, 'Erie, I am a small boat rocking on a dark sea'. He slept most of the time and spoke less and less but liked to have Erie or Mair at his bedside.

Then, on 7 December as he was recovering from his last heart attack and seemed relatively calm and relaxed, he opened his eyes and said to Erie: 'I am very much with your Mother now'. A few moments later, he died.

Evans's explicit instructions for the disposal of his body were to frustrate the desire of the people of Bangor to say farewell to one of their most prominent citizens. As stipulated in his instructions, Evans's body was removed early the following morning and accompanied only by Goronwy, was taken straight to Anfield Cemetery and cremated without ceremony.

EPILOGUE

Evans's death was widely reported in local newspapers the length and breadth of Britain. *The Times*, *The Manchester Guardian* and *The Scotsman* published obituaries as did science journals including *Nature* and *The Veterinary Record*, the latter with an accompanying editorial.[1] All drew attention to the significance of his work in the study of parasitic diseases in humans and animals although the accuracy of the accounts was not always what it might have been.[2]

Notices of his death also appeared widely in the American and Canadian press and the Medical Faculty of McGill University at its meeting on 18 December 1935 adopted a resolution of condolence to be sent to his family.[3] However, emphasis in these press notices was generally on the fact that Evans was one of the last men alive to have met Abraham Lincoln. Typical was the notice in the *Cincinnati Enquirer* on 9 December 1935:[4]

SURGEON, 100, IS DEAD

Bangor, North Wales, December 8 – (AP) – Dr Griffith Evans, 100-year-old veterinary surgeon who knew both Abraham Lincoln and General Ulysses S. Grant is dead. During the American War Between the States Dr Evans, stationed with the Royal Artillery at Montreal, visited field hospitals of the Union Army.

Others were less accurate, for example the *Pittsburgh Press* also of 9 December:[5]

AGED WAR VETERAN IS DEAD IN WALES
Dr Griffith Evans, 100,
Fought for Union Army in Civil War

Bangor, Wales, Dec 9 – Dr Griffith Evans, 100 years and four months old, who served in the Federal Army during the American Civil War, died late Saturday. Mr Evans, an Englishman, known as the 'father of the British veterinary service', obtained special permission from the Union Army authorities to enlist.

Evans would not have appreciated being identified as an Englishman.

After the burst of interest following his death, his name and the significance of his work were less and less frequently acknowledged, even in his native north Wales. Histories of the University College in Bangor[6] refer to him as 'a firm friend of the College' briefly mentioning his involvement in its affairs and listing him as a member of the teaching staff from 1892 to 1912. They do scant justice to his standing as a scientist or to his long and constructive association with the institution.

There was one attempt to provide a tangible memorial.[7] A meeting of the School of Agriculture Committee on 16 December 1935, nine days after Evans's death, resolved that the planned new veterinary extension of the School of Agriculture building be named the 'Dr Griffith Evans Memorial Wing'. A subscription fund raised £1,400 and the Government promised a pound-for-pound grant up to £2,000 towards the cost of the wing.[8] The wing was built but the dedication was repeatedly postponed at successive meetings of the Committee until May 1937 when the reason given was 'changes in the Veterinary and Agricultural Zoology Section'. The proposal then appears to have been quietly dropped in spite of the fact that Evans's son-in-law, Harry Jones, had held the influential post of Registrar of the College since 1933. A factor may have been the departure from Bangor of the Veterinary Officer, R. F. Montgomerie, a champion of Evans, in 1937.[9]

An outline of Evans's Will was published in the *Liverpool Echo* and *Daily Herald*.[10] He left £19,648 and his bequests included a 'special gift' of £500 to his daughter, Erie, 'in recognition of her close and devoted services to me, medical and otherwise, which services have prolonged my life and enhanced my comfort since she has been residing with me'.

There appears to be no further mention of Evans in documents in the University College or in the local or national press until 1943 when a short article by 'Celt' appeared in the *Liverpool Daily Post* of 23 August 1943 entitled 'Notable Doctors'.[11] Celt remarked on the fact that although many Welshmen had had distinguished careers in medicine, he singled out Evans and Dr Timothy Lewis as examples, there were no biographies of Welsh doctors; a proposal for a biography or biographical essay on Evans by L. J. Kelly of Worthing in 1941 had come to nothing.[12] Also in 1943, a letter appeared in the *Western Mail*[13] making the case for a veterinary school in Wales and citing a number of distinguished Welsh veterinarians, including Evans, to support the case. The writer, Edward Morgan, pointed out that a past president of the Royal College of Veterinary Surgeons, Professor Share-Jones, was the first to propose the establishment of a college in Wales and that he and others had been promoting the cause for several years.[14] However, their appeals were ignored causing Morgan to write again to the *Western Mail* in January 1946 reiterating his arguments.[15] The campaign stuttered on until 1965 but to no avail. After this, Griffith Evans's name seems to have faded from the public consciousness.

Well before his death, Erie had begun to encourage Evans to reminisce on his life and times and had recorded his recollections. She added these records to a collection of his papers, letters, publications and other items which she collated and assembled into an archive after his death and donated to the National Library of Wales in 1942; additional papers were donated by other members of the family between 1943 and 1969, the whole comprising the Griffith Evans Papers. Drawing on her own recollections and this resource, Jean Ware wrote her thesis 'The Life and Letters of Griffith Evans, MD, DSc, MRCVS 1835–1935' for which she was awarded her MA in 1966. This was followed by the publication by Jean Ware and her husband Hugh Hunt of their memoir of Griffith Evans 'The Several Lives of a Victorian Vet' in 1979.

NOTES

The Griffith Evans Papers are held by the National Library of Wales in Aberystwyth. Throughout this book, the sources for those elements not specifically referenced are:

J. Ware, 'The Life and Letters of Griffith Evans' (unpublished MA thesis, University College of North Wales, Bangor, 1966).
Jean Ware and Hugh Hunt, *The Several Lives of a Victorian Vet* (London: Bachman and Turner, 1979).

Prologue

1. Ernest Cotchin, *The Royal Veterinary College London: A Bicentenary History* (Buckingham: Barracuda, 1990).
   G. Fleming, 'Veterinary Science – A Sketch', *Journal of Veterinary Science and Comparative Pathology*, 24 (1887), 247–53, 343–52.
   E. A. Gray, 'John Hunter and veterinary medicine', *Medical History*, 1/1 (1957), 38–50.
   Pamela Hunter, *Veterinary Medicine: A Guide to Historical Sources* (Abingdon: Routledge, 2004).
2. Robert Burton, *The Anatomy of Melancholy* (Oxford: Lichfield and Short, 1621).
3. He was also known as Charles Vial de Bel or de Bel (the family estates were at Saint-Bel, near Lyons). In some English publications, his name appears as de Sainbel.
4. *rcvsvethistory.org/st-bel-charles-vial-de-plan-for-establishing-an-institution-to-cultivate-and-teach-veterinary-medicine-19-mar-1790/.*
5. Sir Frederick Smith, *A History of the Royal Army Veterinary Corps 1796–1919* (London: Baillière, Tindall and Cox, 1927).

Chapter 1

1. The contemporary spelling, Towyn, was used consistently by Griffith Evans and his contemporaries in letters and other writings. I have used current place names or spellings throughout but have included, at their first mention, the names that would have been familiar to Evans. In the case of counties in Wales, I have used the English names with the Welsh names in parentheses.

2. Griffith Evans Papers 220; Bound vol. of typescripts, press cuttings, and photographs entitled 'Memories of Griffith Evans'.
J. Ware, 'The Life and Letters of Griffith Evans' (unpublished MA thesis, University College of North Wales, Bangor, 1966).
Jean Ware and Hugh Hunt, *The Several Lives of a Victorian Vet* (London: Bachman and Turner, 1979).
This account of Evans's childhood is based on his reminiscences in his nineties recorded by his daughter, Erie, and grand-daughter, Jean. These references provide a more comprehensive account of Evans's early years. He told Erie that he did not wish to give a consecutive account of his life because doing so would prevent him from maintaining his interest in present and future developments.

3. On her father's side, Catherine was descended from Baron Lewis Owen, Sheriff of Merioneth murdered in 1555 by the 'Red Bandits (Gwylliaid Cochion)' of Mawddwy, a band of political dissidents who terrorised the Mawddwy district.

4. The baptism dates of the sons of Griffith Evan in the Towyn Parish Register are Griffith, 6 October 1796; Evan, 15 April 1800; John, 9 December 1798 *and* 1 May 1803. There is no mention in family records of a fourth son so it seems likely that the first John died in infancy. John's descendants regarded him as older than Evan while Evan's descendants considered him the elder.

5. Griffith Evans Papers 27; Sheet of paper recording the marriage, 24 Sept. 1830, of Evan Evans and Mary Jones.

6. William Cobbett (1763–1835), pamphleteer, Member of Parliament and agrarian reformer.

7. British Schools were established throughout Britain in the nineteenth century by the British and Foreign School Society. They were based on non-sectarian principles unlike the more numerous National Schools founded by the National Society for the Promotion of Religious Education sponsored by the Church of England. Both operated a monitorial system in which paid teachers taught the senior pupils who in turn taught the junior classes. The Government assumed responsibility for elementary education with the Elementary Education Act of 1870.

8. The portrait is mentioned in *The Several Lives of a Victorian Vet* but none of Evans's descendants that I have been able to contact know its whereabouts.

9. Often referred to as the Welsh Robin Hood.
Margaret Isaac, *Thomas Jones of Tregaron: Alias Twm Siôn Cati* (Caerleon: Apecs Press, 2009).

10. Anon, 'Presentation of the Mary Kingsley Medal to Dr Griffith Evans', *Annals of Tropical Medicine and Parasitology*, 12 (1918), 1–16.
Asa Briggs, 'Cobden and Bright', *History Today*, 7/8 (1957), 496–503.

11. The Hungry Forties refers to the decade when economic depression and failures in food production, including the failure of potato crops due to blight and difficulties with distribution, caused misery and starvation in Britain and throughout northern Europe. Potato blight had a particularly severe impact in Ireland causing the Great Famine 1845–52.

12. John Pughe who was thirty-eight in 1852, became a prominent local figure. He was a JP and patron of many charitable and cultural organisations. His brother and four sons were also physicians.

13. The quotation of this *englyn* by Ware and Hunt, *The Several Lives of a Victorian Vet* contains typographical errors which have been corrected here. An *englyn* is a traditional Welsh and Cornish short poem form, usually a quatrain, conforming to strictly prescribed metric and rhyming structures.

Chapter 2

1. Griffith Evans Papers 220; Bound vol. of typescripts, press cuttings, and photographs entitled 'Memories of Griffith Evans'.

2. Ernest Cotchin, *The Royal Veterinary College London: A Bicentenary History* (Buckingham: Barracuda, 1990).

3. The first decades of the nineteenth century had seen significant advances in the optics of compound microscopes, in achromatic objective lenses and in the mechanical elements of the instruments. Several models were available on the market in 1854.

4. Although the term 'agnostic' was not coined by T. H. Huxley until 1869, it describes Meyrick's and later, Evans's religious doctrine.

5. *https://www.ncbi.nlm.nih.gov/pmc/articles/PMC7150208/*.
This outbreak was made famous by Dr John Snow's identification of its source in water contaminated by sewage from a street pump in London.

6. Anon, 'Examinations at the Royal College of Veterinary Surgeons', *The Veterinarian: A Monthly Journal of Veterinary Science*, 28 (1855), 370.

7. In October 1855, the Royal Veterinary College imposed a regulation that no student under the age of twenty could be presented for the final examination.

8. *www.atcherley.org.uk/wp/james-rennell-atcherley-a-life-and-death-with-horses-part-2/*.

9. Painful inflammation of the bursa at the nape of the neck caused by bacterial infection, particularly brucellosis, or trauma. *www.atcherley.org.uk/wp/james-rennell-atcherley-a-life-and-death-with-horses-part-1/*.

10. Griffith Evans Papers 304; Letter from [J.] J. M[eyrick], to Griffith Evans.

11. Griffith Evans Papers 220.

Chapter 3

1. Griffith Evans Papers 220; Bound vol. of typescripts, press cuttings, and photographs entitled 'Memories of Griffith Evans'.

2. The 'Camp at Aldershot' was established in 1854.
3. Griffith Evans Papers 88; Commission as Veterinary Surgeon in the Royal Regiment of Artillery.
4. Evan Evans and John Jones shared a great-grandfather, Robert Jones of Aberllyfni.

Chapter 4

1. C. P. Stacey, 'The Defense Problem and Canadian Confederation', *Revista de Historia de América*, 138 (2007), 169–75.
2. A battery of the Royal Artillery at the time comprised 100–50 men and 100 horses.
3. Osler Library Archival Collection, McGill University, extracts from journal of Griffith Evans, 1835–1935 [Partial content: body-snatching at McGill], Acc. 237.
4. George S. Emmerson, *The Greatest Iron Ship: S.S. Great Eastern* (Newton Abbot: David and Charles, 1981).
5. The accumulation of fluid in the pleural space.

Chapter 5

1. Osler Library Archival Collection, McGill University, extracts from journal of Griffith Evans, 1835–1935 [Partial content: body-snatching at McGill], Acc. 237.
The Old Cavalry Barracks were located just outside the city but an 1851 map of the Québec Gate Barracks on Dalhousie Square in the city (Montreal Archives, Québec Gate Barracks, VM66-S4P025) shows buildings, including stables, occupied by the Royal Artillery.
2. Osler Library Archival Collection, McGill University, Acc. 237.
D. G. Lawrence, '"Resurrection" and Legislation OR Body-snatching in relation to the Anatomy Act in the Province of Quebec', *Bulletin of the History of Medicine*, 32/5 (1958), 408–24.
3. Robert Vineberg, 'The British Garrison and Montreal Society, 1830–50', *Canadian Military History*, 21 (2012), 3–16.
4. Griffith Evans Papers 220; Bound vol. of typescripts, press cuttings, and photographs entitled 'Memories of Griffith Evans'.
5. The American Civil War had started in 1861.
6. Griffith Evans Papers 582; Letter from Griffith Evans, Montreal, to Evan Evans (his father).
7. Griffith Evans Papers 220.
8. Osler Library Archival Collection, McGill University, Acc. 237.
9. Mass evictions of rural populations in the 18th and 19th centuries, principally to make way for sheep farming.
10. Griffith Evans Papers 220.
11. Griffith Evans Papers 205; Press cuttings relating to the Sioux Indians, with a pencil note by Griffith Evans, together with cuttings from *The Chronicle*.
12. Griffith Evans Papers 220.

13. J. F. Murray, 'A Century of Tuberculosis', *American Journal of Respiratory and Critical Care Medicine*, 169/11 (2004), 1181–6.

14. E. Cambau and M. Drancourt, 'Steps towards the discovery of *Mycobacterium tuberculosis* by Robert Koch, 1882', *Clinical Microbiology and Infection*, 20/3 (2014), 196–201.

15. Griffith Evans Papers 89; Diploma of the degree of Medicinae Doctoris et Chirurgiae Magistri of McGill University, Montreal.
In Canada, the M.D. was an undergraduate degree awarded on graduation from medical school. Students then entered a residency phase of training followed by further examination for their license to practice. Evans never pursued this course. Jean Ware and Hugh Hunt, *The Several Lives of a Victorian Vet* (London: Bachman and Turner, 1979).

Chapter 6

1. The account in this chapter relies on the following sources
Griffith Evans Papers 600; Extracts from Griffith Evans's journal of his visit to North America from Canada.
Griffith Evans Papers 199; Notes made by Griffith Evans on his visit to the Northern Army. 21 ff.
Griffith Evans Papers 201; Letter from Griffith Evans to Erie, 25 July 1919, describing his visit to the Northern Army, and enclosing 202.
Griffith Evans Papers 205; Press cuttings relating to the Sioux Indians, with a pencil note by Griffith Evans, together with cuttings from *The Chronicle*.
Griffith Evans Papers 220; Bound vol. of typescripts, press cuttings, and photographs entitled 'Memories of Griffith Evans'.

2. John Keegan, *The American Civil War* (London: Vintage, 2010).

3. Confederate losses were 22,600 to the Union's 22,800.

4. Griffith Evans Papers 199.

5. Anon, 'Man who met Lincoln. The Civil War. Observer with Grant's Army. Centenarian's Memories', *Manchester Guardian*, 23 May 1935, p. 13.

6. Although Evans was never explicit in expressing an opinion on slavery in his journals, his generally liberal views and readiness to engage with people irrespective of race suggests he would have abhorred the institution. This is born out in a note by Erie contained in Griffith Evans Papers 220; Bound vol. of typescripts, press cuttings, and photographs.

7. Griffith Evans Papers 220.

Chapter 7

1. Griffith Evans Papers 600; Extracts from Griffith Evans's journal of his visit to North America from Canada.
Griffith Evans Papers 199; Notes made by Griffith Evans on his visit to the Northern Army. 21 ff.

Griffith Evans Papers 220; Bound vol. of typescripts, press cuttings, and photographs entitled 'Memories of Griffith Evans'.
Griffith Evans Papers 201; Letter from Griffith Evans to Erie, 25 July 1919, describing his visit to the Northern Army, and enclosing 202.

2. *www.battlefields.org/learn/biographies/benjamin-f-butler*.
3. Griffith Evans Papers 220.
4. A line of defence consisting of a barrier of felled or live trees with sharpened branches pointed toward the enemy.
5. The Army's senior law enforcement officer.
6. Possibly Dougherty.
7. Graduates of West Point Military Academy.
8. Griffith Evans Papers 198; Pass issued to Griffith Evans, 9 July 1864, to proceed from Army HQ to Washington D.C. by Government boat.
9. Griffith Evans Papers 292; John Drinkwater, Abraham Lincoln London, Sidgwick and Jackson Ltd., 1919, containing marginal notes made by Griffith Evans. Inserted at the front of the vol. are a note, a press cutting, a letter (1919) from Griffith Evans to Dr Erie Evans, and correspondence (1921) between Griffith Evans and John Drinkwater.
10. General Stephen Thomas.
11. Jennifer Hanna, *Arlington House, The Robert E. Lee Memorial* (Washington D.C.: U. S. Department of the Interior, 2001).
12. Griffith Evans Papers 220.
13. Griffith Evans Papers 199.

Chapter 8

1. Griffith Evans Papers 197; Griffith Evans's commonplace book when in Canada, 1863–4.
2. Griffith Evans Papers 220; Bound vol. of typescripts, press cuttings, and photographs entitled 'Memories of Griffith Evans'.
3. Griffith Evans Papers 90; Diploma awarded Griffith Evans by Dr George Washington Stone, certifying his being qualified to practise experiments in Electro-Biology and Mesmerism.
In retirement, he sent the diploma to his daughter, Erie, with a note: 'You may be amusingly surprised by my "diploma" which you may destroy as of no use.'
4. Osler Library of the History of Medicine, McGill University, Report on 'Surra' Disease, Griffith Evans, Microform Collection: Military Dept., Dec. 1880. No. 7 with MS note by author.
5. The Irish Republican Brotherhood active in Ireland and the United States in the mid to late nineteenth and early twentieth centuries. Fenian raids into Canada in 1866 and 1870 were easily repulsed.
6. *www.veterans.gc.ca/eng/remembrance/medals-decorations/details/1*.
7. Prince Arthur, Duke of Connaught, third son of Queen Victoria. He later served as Governor-General of Canada.

8. Osbourne House in East Cowes on the Isle of Wight was completed in 1851 as a summer residence for Queen Victoria and Prince Albert.

9. Osler Library Archival Collection, McGill University, extracts from journal of Griffith Evans, 1835–1935 [Partial content: body-snatching at McGill], Acc. 237.

10. Black Robin of Snowdon (Robyn Ddu Eryri), Dictionary of Welsh Biography, *biography.wales/article/s-PARR-ROB-1804*.

11. Griffith Evans Papers 118; Letter, 28 July 1935, from R. G. Owen, Bangor, enclosing a transcript of 'englynion' by 'Robyn Ddu Eryri' upon Griffith.

12. The 'up' and 'down' trains travelled in separate tubes so the couple cannot have entered the bridge as Evans recalled in old age (Griffith Evans Papers 220). The pair must have been between the lines just outside the entrances to the tubes.

13. Griffith Evans Papers 274; The Temperance Record, No. 817, 2 Dec. 1871, containing a speech delivered by Griffith Evans on 'Temperance in the Army'.

14. Anon, 'Presentation of the Mary Kingsley Medal to Dr Griffith Evans', *Annals of Tropical Medicine and Parasitology*, 12 (1918), 1–16.

15. Tetanus is caused by the bacillus, *Clostridium tetani*. The transmissibility of the disease was not proven until 1884 and the bacillus was not discovered until 1891 in Robert Koch's laboratory in Berlin.

16. Griffith Evans Papers 65; Diary kept by Griffith Evans and his wife in the name of their eldest daughter, Myfanwy Wynona, 1871–7.

17. Griffith Evans Papers 309; Letter from Griffith Evans, to Evan Evans ('Ap Ieuan').

18. Evans himself was no poet, making only one recorded attempt to write in verse when his only son was born later in India. However, in 1876, he wrote the forward to a volume of poetry by his father, Evan:
Evan Evans (Ap Ieuan), *Undeb yr Eglwys yn ngolwg ei Gwynfyd dyfodol gyda Myfyrion dyddanol ar destynau ymarferol eraill* (Dolgellau: D. H. Jones, 1876). Griffith Evans Papers 275.

19. Sir Frederick Smith, *A History of the Royal Army Veterinary Corps 1796–1919* (London: Baillière, Tindall and Cox, 1927).

Chapter 9

1. Her Majesty's Indian Troop Ship.

2. Griffith Evans Papers 311; Letter from Catherine Mary Evans (Katie), to Griffith Evans.

3. Griffith Evans Papers 312; Letter from Griffith Evans, Malta, to Katie.

4. Griffith Evans Papers 312.

5. James Frey, *The Indian Rebellion, 1857–1859: A Short History with Documents* (Indianapolis: Hackett Publishing Company, 2020). Known at the time as the Indian Mutiny.

6. Griffith Evans Papers 312.

7. Griffith Evans Papers 317; Letter from Griffith Evans, Bombay, to Katie.
Griffith Evans Papers 318; Letter from Griffith Evans, Bombay, to Katie.

8. Elephanta Island (Gharapuri) in Mumbai harbour, the site of the Elephanta cave temples dedicated to the Hindu God, Shiva.

9. The Parsis are Zoroastrians who fled Persia for India to escape persecution following the Muslim conquest in the sixth century.
10. Anon, 'Presentation of the Mary Kingsley Medal to Dr Griffith Evans', *Annals of Tropical Medicine and Parasitology*, 12 (1918), 1–16.
11. Griffith Evans Papers 316; Letter from Griffith Evans, Bombay, to Katie.
12. Griffith Evans Papers 319; Letter from Griffith Evans, Bombay, to Katie.
13. J. Cule, 'The postulates of Griffith Evans MD, MRCVS (1835–1935) and the Specificity of Disease', in A. H. M. Kerkhoff, A. M. Luyendijk-Elshout, M. J. D. Poulissen (eds), *De Novis Inventis: Essays in the History of Medicine in Honour of Daniel de Moulin on the Occasion of his 65th Birthday* (Amsterdam & Maarssen: APA – Holland University Press, 1984), pp. 81–93.
14. A. Kannadan, 'History of the Miasma Theory of Disease', *ESSAI*, 16 Article 18 (2018). dc.cod.edu/essai/vol16/iss1/18.
15. *www.encyclopedia.com/science/science-magazines/biomedicine-and-health-germ-theory-disease*.
16. *www.britannica.com/biography/Agostino-Bassi*.
www.britannica.com/biography/Friedrich-Gustav-Jacob-Henle.
T. H. Tulchinsky, 'John Snow, Cholera, the Broad Street Pump; Waterborne Diseases Then and Now', *Case Studies in Public Health*, 2018, 77–99.
17. *www.britannica.com/biography/Francesco-Redi*.
Louis Pasteur, *Sur les corpuscules organisés qui existent dans l'atmosphère: Examen de la doctrine des générations spontanées. Leçon Professée a la Société Chimique de Paris, le 19 Mai* (Paris: Imprimerie de Ch. Lahure et Cie, 1861).
www.pasteurbrewing.com/famous-louis-pasteur-experiment-spontaneous-generation/.
18. K. Codell Carter, 'The Koch-Pasteur dispute on establishing the cause of anthrax', *Bulletin of the History of Medicine*, 62/1 (1988), 42–57.
19. Transparent gelatinous tissue filling the eyeball behind the lens in mammals.
20. Griffith Evans, 'The "Loodiana Disease," or "Malignant Fever" of India', *The Veterinary Journal and Annals of Comparative Pathology*, 6 (1878), 320–34. *https://www.woah.org/en/disease/anthrax/*.
21. A. Javaeed, S. Qamar, S. Ali, M. A. T. Mustafa, A. Nusrat, S. K. Ghauri, 'Histological Stains in the Past, Present, and Future', *Cureus*, 13/10 (2021), e18486.
22. Anon, 'Presentation of the Mary Kingsley Medal to Dr Griffith Evans', *Annals of Tropical Medicine and Parasitology*, 12 (1918), 1–16.
23. Griffith Evans Papers 322; Letter from Griffith Evans, Sialkote, to Katie. Griffith Evans Papers 328; Letter from Griffith Evans, Sialkote, to Katie.
24. Griffith Evans Papers 332; Letter from Griffith Evans, Sialkote, to Katie.
25. Griffith Evans Papers 326; Letter from Griffith Evans, Sialkote, to Katie.
26. Griffith Evans Papers 330; Letter from Griffith Evans, Sialkote, to Katie.
27. A long, open carriage drawn by four horses with postillions.
28. Nautch dancers working alone, in pairs or in troops of ten or more, were itinerant entertainers who performed stylised nautch dances at all kinds of events or celebrations from durbars to private parties.
29. Griffith Evans Papers 340; Letter from Griffith Evans, Calcutta, to Katie.

30. Griffith Evans Papers 343; Letter from Griffith Evans, Calcutta, to Wynona, Erie and Towena.
31. Griffith Evans Papers 343.
32. A dak-gharry was a four-wheel, often springless carriage drawn by one or a pair of horses.
33. Griffith Evans Papers 340.
34. Griffith Evans Papers 350; Letter from Griffith Evans, Morar and Allahabad, to Katie.
35. Griffith Evans Papers 377; Letter from Griffith Evans, Simla, to Katie.
36. Griffith Evans Papers 351; Letter from Griffith Evans, Lucknow, to Katie.
37. Griffith Evans Papers 354; Letter from Griffith Evans, Futtehpore, to Katie.
38. Griffith Evans Papers 355; Letter from Griffith Evans, Futtehpore, to Katie.
39. Griffith Evans Papers 355.
40. Griffith Evans Papers 356; Letter from Griffith Evans, Kureli, to Katie.
41. Griffith Evans Papers 353; Letter from Griffith Evans, Lucknow, to Katie.
42. Griffith Evans Papers 355.
43. Griffith Evans Papers 354.
44. Griffith Evans Papers 363; Letter from Griffith Evans, Calcutta, to Katie.
45. Griffith Evans Papers 360; Letter from Griffith Evans, Calcutta, to Katie. Griffith Evans Papers 367; Letter from Griffith Evans, Calcutta, to Katie.
46. Griffith Evans Papers 365; Letter from Griffith Evans, Calcutta, to Katie.
47. Brian Robson, *The Road to Kabul: The Second Afghan War 1878–1881* (Cheltenham: The History Press, 2008).
48. Evans states that 'surra' was used locally to describe anything rotten and was also applied loosely to chronic debilitating ailments.
49. Griffith Evans Papers 371; Letter from Griffith Evans, Meerut, to Katie.
50. Griffith Evans Papers 379(a); Letter from Griffith Evans, Simla, to Katie.

Chapter 10

1. Griffith Evans Papers 362; Letter from Katie, Towyn, to Griffith Evans.
2. Harriet Martineau's autobiography was published posthumously in 1877. A prolific writer on society from political, religious, domestic and above all feminine perspectives, she has been described as the first woman sociologist. Her progressive views alarmed Nonconformist opinion.
3. Griffith Evans Papers 366; Letter from Griffith Evans, Calcutta, to Katie.
4. Griffith Evans Papers 370; Letter from Katie, Great Malvern, to Griffith Evans.
5. Griffith Evans Papers 381; Letter from Griffith Evans, Calcutta, to Katie.
6. Griffith Evans Papers 382; Letter from Griffith Evans, Calcutta, to Katie.
7. Griffith Evans Papers 389; Letter from Griffith Evans, Simla, to [Katie].

Chapter 11

1. Anon, 'Presentation of the Mary Kingsley Medal to Dr Griffith Evans', *Annals of Tropical Medicine and Parasitology*, 12 (1918), 1–16.

James L. Hevia, *Animal Labor and Colonial Warfare* (Chicago and London: University of Chicago Press, 2018).

2. M. Desquesnes, P. Holzmuller, D-H. Lai, A. Dargantes, Z-R. Lun, S. Jittapalapong, '*Trypanosoma evansi* and Surra: A Review and Perspectives on Origin, History, Distribution, Taxonomy, Morphology, Hosts, and Pathogenic Effects', *BioMed Research International Review Article*, (2013), 194176.

3. T. R. Lewis, 'Flagellated Organisms in the Blood of Healthy Rats', *Quarterly Journal of Microscopical Science*, s2/19 (1879), 109–14.
T. R. Lewis, *The Microscopic Organisms found in the Blood of Man and Animals, and their Relation to Disease* (Calcutta: Office of the Superintendent of Government Printing, 1879).

4. Griffith Evans Papers 399; Letter from Griffith Evans, Dera Ismael Khan, to Erie.

5. Griffith Evans Papers 399.

6. 28 °C.

7. Liquid immersion in microscopy increases the resolution of the image by increasing the effective aperture of the objective lens. It seems probable that Evans used water rather than oil immersion.

8. A. Javaeed, S. Qamar, S. Ali M. A. T. Mustafa, A. Nusrat, S. K. Ghauri, 'Histological Stains in the Past, Present, and Future', *Cureus*, 2021 Oct 4, 13(10): e18486.

9. Report by the Inspecting Veterinary Surgeon Griffith Evans M.D. on Surra, published by the Punjab Government Military Department, No. 439–44–67. Included in Griffith Evans Papers 111, Bound vol. of papers and correspondence brought together by Dr Erie Evans.

10. A whip or lash-like appendage whose primary function is in locomotion.

11. In 1885, the parasite was initially identified incorrectly by a young army veterinary surgeon, J. H. Steel, as a spirochaete bacterium and named *Spirochaeti evansi*. In 1886, Edgar Crookshank recognised the organism's similarity to a fish parasite and renamed the species *Haematomonas evansi*, later revising this to *Trichomonas evansi*. Three years later, the parasite was correctly classified as belonging to the genus *Trypanosoma* and renamed *Trypanosoma evansi* by Balbiani in 1888. Its full designation is *Trypanosoma evansi* (Steel, 1885) Balbiani, 1888.

12. Mirza Nuryady et al., 'Characterization and phylogenetic analysis of multidrug-resistant protein-encoding genes in *Trypanosoma evansi* isolated from buffaloes in Ngawi district, Indonesia', *Veterinary World*, 12/10 (2019).

13. The numbers of parasites present in the blood.

14. J. H. Steel, *Report of Veterinary Surgeon J. H. Steel, A.V.D., on his investigation into an obscure and fatal disease among transport mules in British Burma, which he found to be a fever of relapsing type, and probably identical with the disorder first described by Dr Griffith Evans under the name "Surra", in a report (herewith printed) published by the Punjab Government, Military Department, No. 439–4467, of 3rd December 1880 – vide the Veterinary Journal (London), 1881–1882* (Calcutta: Government of India, 1886).

15. The process whereby one allele or version of a gene is expressed while all others are silenced.

16. 'A Brief Introduction to Antigenic Variation in African Trypanosomes', The Rockefeller University. *http://tryps.rockefeller.edu/trypsru2_avariation_intro. html#emlowpower.*

17. T. R. Lewis, *On a Haematozoon Inhabiting Human Blood: its relation to Chyluria and other Diseases* (Calcutta: Office of the Superintendent of Government Printing, 1872). T. R. Lewis, *The Pathological Significance of Nematode Haematozoa* (Calcutta: Office of the Superintendent of Government Printing, 1874).

18. Now *Dipetalonema evansi*.
T. R. Lewis, 'Remarks on a Nematoid Haematozoon discovered by Dr Griffith Evans in a Camel', *Proceedings of the Asiatic Society of Bengal* (1882), 63–4.

19. L. D. Foil, 'Tabanids as vectors of disease agents', *Parasitology Today*, 5/3 (1989), 88–96.

20. 'Mechanical' transmission contrasts with 'biological' transmission in which the parasite undergoes developmental stages within the body of the vector as happens with malaria in the mosquito or with African trypanosomiasis within the tsetse fly. No parasitic diseases transmitted by Tabanid flies are known to undergo biological transmission.

21. This probably accounts for Evans's finding that some camels can carry significant levels of parasitaemia without apparent symptoms.

22. M. Desquesnes, P. Holzmuller, D-H. Lai, A. Dargantes, Z-R. Lun, S. Jittapalapong, '*Trypanosoma evansi* and Surra: A Review and Perspectives on Origin, History, Distribution, Taxonomy, Morphology, Hosts, and Pathogenic Effects', *BioMed Research International Review Article*, (2013), 194176.
M. Desquesnes, A. Dargantes, D-H. Lai, Z.-R. Lun, P. Holzmuller, S. Jittapalapong, '*Trypanosoma evansi* and Surra: A Review and Perspectives on Transmission, Epidemiology and Control, Impact, and Zoonotic Aspects', *BioMed Research International Review Article*, (2013), 321237.

23. V. Singh and H. R. Parsani, Animal trypanosomosis: '*Trypanosoma evansi* – an emerging threat to humans', in V. Tandon, A. K. Yadav and B. Roy (eds), *Current Trends in Parasitology, Proceedings of the 20th National Congress of Parasitology, Shillong, India* (New Delhi: Pamina, 2008), pp. 61–4.

24. Griffith Evans Papers 401; Letter from Griffith Evans, Dera Ismail Khan, to Erie.

25. The Second Afghan War.

26. T. R. Lewis, 'Flagellated Organisms in the Blood of Healthy Rats', *Quarterly Journal of Microscopical Science*, s2/19 (1879), 109–14.

27. T. R. Lewis, 'Further Observations on Flagellated Organisms in the Blood of Animals', *Quarterly Journal of Microscopical Science*, 2/24 (1884), 357–69.

28. L. Pasteur et J. F. Joubert, 'Charbon et septicémie', *Comptes rendus hebdomadaires des séances de l'Académie des sciences*, 85 (1887), 101–15.

29. T. R. Lewis, 'Flagellated Organisms in the Blood of Healthy Rats', *Quarterly Journal of Microscopical Science*, s2/19 (1879), 109–14.
T. R. Lewis, *The Microscopic Organisms found in the Blood of Man and Animals, and their Relation to Disease* (Calcutta: Office of the Superintendent of Government Printing, 1879).

30. E. Metchnikoff, 'Untersuchungen über die mesodermalen Phagocyten einiger Wirbeltiere', *Biologisches Centralblatt*, 3 (1883), 560–5.

   E. Metchnikoff, *Immunity in infective diseases* translated from the French (Cambridge: Cambridge University Press, 1905).

31. Griffith Evans (*Report by the Inspecting Veterinary Surgeon Griffith Evans MD on Surra*, Punjab Government Military Department, No. 439–44–67, 1881).

32. Griffith Evans Papers 402; Letter from Griffith Evans, Silchar, to Erie.

33. D. Steverding, 'The development of drugs for treatment of sleeping sickness: a historical review', *Parasites and Vectors*, 3 (2010), 15.

34. Anon, 'Presentation of the Mary Kingsley Medal to Dr Griffith Evans', *Annals of Tropical Medicine and Parasitology*, 12 (1918), 1–16.

35. R. Koch, 'An Address on Bacteriological Research', *The British Medical Journal*, 2/1546 (1890), 380–3.

   L. S. King, 'Dr Koch's Postulates', *Journal of the History of Medicine and Allied Sciences*, 7/4 (1952), 350–61.

Koch's postulates provide four criteria to establish a causal relationship between an invasive micro-organism and disease:

- *The micro-organism must be found in abundance in all organisms suffering from the disease but should not be found in healthy organisms.*
- *The micro-organism must be isolated from a diseased organism and grown in pure culture.*
- *The cultured micro-organism should cause disease when introduced into a healthy organism.*
- *The micro-organism must be re-isolated from the inoculated, diseased experimental host and identified as being identical to the original specific causative agent.*

Not all diseases conform to all four postulates but they nonetheless provided an invaluable basis for identifying the causative organisms at the time. The results of Evans's surra experiments conformed to Postulates 1, 3 and 4, sufficient to establish *T. evansi* as the causative agent of the disease.

36. Sir Frederick Smith, *A History of the Royal Army Veterinary Corps 1796–1919* (London: Baillière, Tindall and Cox, 1927).

37. Anon, 'Presentation of the Mary Kingsley Medal to Dr Griffith Evans', *Annals of Tropical Medicine and Parasitology*, 12 (1918), 1–16.

38. Griffith Evans, 'On a horse disease in India known as "surra", probably due to a haematozoon', *The Veterinary Journal and Annals of Comparative Pathology*, 13 (1881), 1–10, 82–8, 180–200, 326–33; 14 (1882), 97–110, 181–7.

39. S. Mishra, 'Beasts, Murrains, and the British Raj: Reassessing Colonial Medicine in India from the Veterinary Perspective, 1860–1900', *Bulletin of the History of Medicine*, 85/4 (2011), 587–619.

40. Griffith Evans Papers 111; Bound vol. of papers and correspondence brought together by Dr Erie Evans.

Chapter 12

1. The Zion Chapel, built in the 1850s, remained the only Nonconformist chapel in Ooty until the foundation of the Union Chapel in 1896. It was attended by all Nonconformist denominations.
2. Sir Frederick Smith, *A History of the Royal Army Veterinary Corps 1796–1919* (London: Baillière, Tindall and Cox, 1927).
3. Anon, 'Reviews. A Veterinary Manual for the Use of Salootries and Native Horse-Owners in India. By J. J. Meyrick, MRCVS, Army Veterinary Inspector', *The Veterinary Journal and Annals of Comparative Physiology*, 13 (October 1881), 285–6.
4. J. J. Meyrick, 'Correspondence, etc. The Army Veterinary Department', *The Veterinary Journal and Annals of Comparative Physiology*, 14 (1882), 226–9.
5. Anon, 'Editorial. The Army Veterinary Department', *The Veterinary Journal and Annals of Comparative Physiology*, 14 (1882), 334–6.
6. Smith, *A History of the Royal Army Veterinary Corps 1796–1919*.
7. Griffith Evans Papers 37; Obituary notice of Evan Evans.
8. Griffith Evans Papers 404; Letter from Griffith Evans, Silchar, to Myfanwy, Erie and Towena.
   Griffith Evans Papers 410; Letter from Griffith Evans, Ootacamund, to Wynona, Erie and Towena.
9. Griffith Evans Papers 405; Letter from Katie, Gauhati, to Erie.
10. *www.britannica.com/topic/theosophy#ref99400; www.britannica.com/biography/Helena-Blavatsky.*
    www.britannica.com/biography/Henry-Steel-Olcott.
11. Griffith Evans Papers 592; Letter from Griffith Evans, to Erie.
12. Griffith Evans Papers 603; Notes on Griffith Evans's meeting with Madam Blavatsky, and of Balu Chunder Sen's accounts of the motives of some Indians.
13. J. H. Steel, *Report of Veterinary Surgeon J. H. Steel, A.V.D., on his investigation into an obscure and fatal disease among transport mules in British Burma, which he found to be a fever of relapsing type, and probably identical with the disorder first described by Dr Griffith Evans under the name "Surra", in a report (herewith printed) published by the Punjab Government, Military Department, No. 439–4467, of 3rd December 1880 – vide the Veterinary Journal (London), 1881–1882* (Calcutta: Government of India, 1886).
14. Spiral or helicoid shaped bacteria of the order Spirochaetales.
15. J. H. Steel, 'On Relapsing Fever of Equines', *The Veterinary Journal and Annals of Comparative Physiology*, 22 (1886), 166–74.
16. Griffith Evans, scrap book in the family archive.
    During his career, Evans produced several similar scrap books of photographs, postcards, newspaper cuttings, etc., all extensively annotated.
17. Griffith Evans Papers 220; Bound vol. of typescripts, press cuttings, and photographs entitled 'Memories of Griffith Evans'.

Chapter 13

1. Sir Frederick Smith, *A History of the Royal Army Veterinary Corps 1796–1919* (London: Baillière, Tindall and Cox, 1927).
2. Anon, Edgar March Crookshank M.B., *British Medical Journal*, 2 (1928), 79.
3. D. Stevending, 'The History of African Trypanosomiasis', *Parasite Vectors*, 1/1 (2008), 1–8.
4. David Livingstone, *Missionary Travels and Researches in South Africa* (London: John Murray, 1857).
5. A. W. H. Bates, *Anti-Vivisection and the Profession of Medicine in Britain: A Social History* (London: Springer Nature Ltd, 2017).
6. The Cruelty to Animals Act (15 August 1876).
7. Griffith Evans Papers 596; Letter from Griffith Evans, to [n.d.] Sir Frederick [Smith, (1857–1929), Major-Gen., Army Veterinary Service].
8. J. Cule, 'The postulates of Griffith Evans MD, MRCVS (1835–1935) and the Specificity of Disease', in A. H. M. Kerkhoff, A. M. Luyendijk-Elshout and M. J. D. Poulissen (eds), *De Novis Inventis Essays in the History of Medicine in Honour of Daniel de Moulin on the Occasion of his 65th Birthday* (Amsterdam & Maarssen: APA – Holland University Press, 1984), pp. 81–93.
9. D. Bruce, *Preliminary report on the tsetse fly disease or nagana in Zululand* (Durban: Bennett and Davis, 1895).
10. J. Molinari and S. A. Moreno, 'Trypanosoma brucei Plimmer & Bradford, 1899 is a synonym of T. evansi (Steel, 1885) according to current knowledge and by application of nomenclature rules', *Systematic Parasitology*, 95/2–3 (2018), 249–56. The authors propose that, on the basis of the Principle of Priority in zoological nomenclature, *Trypanosoma brucei* and *T. equiperdum* should be known as *T. evansi* and that the subspecies currently termed *T. brucei brucei*, *T. brucei rhodesiense* and *T. brucei gambiense* (the causative agents of human sleeping sickness in Africa) should now be referred to as *T. evansi evansi*, *T. e. rhodesiense* and *T. e. gambiense*.
11. Griffith Evans Papers 103; Two presentation cards for a levée. Griffith Evans Papers 104; Page from *The Times*, 2 March 1887, containing a list of presentations at a levée, and including that of Griffith Evans.
12. The condition results from weakness of the muscles associated with the arytenoid cartilages which act as valves to prevent food entering the larynx. The cartilage then vibrates when the horse breathes heavily during exercise resulting in a wheezing or roaring sound.
13. F. Smith, 'Preliminary note on the surgical cure for roaring due to laryngeal paralysis', *Veterinary Journal and Annals of Comparative Pathology*, 27, 1–10.
14. Smith, *A History of the Royal Army Veterinary Corps 1796–1919*.

Chapter 14

1. Griffith Evans Papers 413; Letter from Griffith Evans, Portmadoc, to Katie.
2. 'Hiraeth' is not directly translatable. It expresses the sense of longing felt by exiles for home, Wales and Welsh culture and landscape.

3. The dominant Welsh society in London is the Honourable Society of the Cymmrodorion, a learned society founded in 1751 to encourage engagement with the Welsh language, literature, arts, science and Welsh affairs. *www.cymmrodorion.org/*.
4. *www.eisteddfod.cymru/eisteddfod-genedlaethol-cymru*.
5. Evidence of Evans's involvement with organisations in Wales and of his attendance at meetings and events during the years of his retirement between 1890 and 1919 comes from over 60 reports and articles in the newspapers listed below. All of these can be accessed online in the newspaper archives at the National Library of Wales and the British Library using the appropriate search terms and will not be individually referenced here.

   The Aberystwyth Observer, The Cambrian News and Merionethshire Standard, Cardiff Times, The Cardigan Bay Visitor, Carnarvon and Denbigh Herald and North and South Wales Independent, Denbighshire Free Press, Y Genedl Gymreig, Liverpool Mercury, Llandudno Advertiser and List of Visitors, North Wales Chronicle and Advertiser for the Principality, The North Wales Express, The North Wales Times, Rhyl Journal, Y Tyst, The Weekly News and Visitors' Chronicle for Colwyn Bay, The Welsh Coast Pioneer and Review for North Cambria, Western Mail.
6. G. Evans, 'Miscellanea', *Folklore*, 3/2 (1892), 274–7.
7. Anon, 'College News', *Magazine of the University College of North Wales*, 1/1 (1891), 34.
8. J. Gwynn Williams, *The University College of North Wales: Foundations 1884–1927* (Cardiff: University of Wales Press, 1985), p. 171.
9. Anon, 'Action for Libel', *Manchester Guardian*, 28 July 1893, p. 8.
   Anon, 'Verdict for Miss Hughes', *Manchester Guardian*, 31 July 1893, p. 8.
10. Williams, *The University College of North Wales.*
11. Williams, *The University College of North Wales.*
12. Griffith Evans Papers 220; Bound vol. of typescripts, press cuttings, and photographs entitled 'Memories of Griffith Evans'.
13. Griffith Evans Papers 366; Letter from Griffith Evans, Calcutta, to Katie.
14. Griffith Evans Papers 442; Letter from Griffith Evans, Brynkynallt, to [Prof.] Henry Jones.
15. Van A. Harvey, 'Huxley's Agnosticism', *Philosophy Now*, 99 (2013), 10–12.
    T. H. Huxley, *Agnosticism and Christianity and other Essays* (New York: Prometheus Books, 1992).
16. Griffith Evans Papers 220.
    Bill Cooke, *The Gathering of Infidels: A Hundred Years of the Rationalist Press Association* (New York: Prometheus Books, 2004).
17. Griffith Evans, 'Un Eglwys i Gymru', *Y Geninen*, 27(4) (1909), 183–6.
18. The Rates were a tax on property in the United Kingdom raised to fund local government (they are still collected in Northern Ireland).
19. David M. Fahey, 'The Politics of Drink: Pressure Groups and the British Liberal Party, 1883–1908', *Social Science*, 54(2) (1979), 76–85.
20. Griffith Evans Papers 457; Letter from Griffith Evans, Brynkynallt, to Erie.

21. The Second Boer War 1899–1902.

22. The account of the meeting in the *Liverpool Mercury* reports the hostility of the crowd but makes no mention of missiles being thrown at the platform as Ware and Hunt describe in *The Several Lives of a Victorian Vet*. It ends by stating that Lloyd George was staying at Belmont in Bangor while Ware and Hunt have him staying at Brynkynallt.

23. Daniel Davies, JONES, Sir HENRY (1852–1922), philosopher. Dictionary of Welsh Biography, *biography.wales/article/s-JONE-HEN-1852*.

24. Wilson Smith, 'Philip Bruce White', *Obituary Notices of Fellows of the Royal Society*, 7–19 (1950), 278–92.

25. R. F. Montgomerie, 'Dr Griffith Evans. The Profession's Centenarian. A Great Veterinary Scientist', *The Veterinary Record*, 15/31 (1935), 890–4.

26. Anon, 'Presentation of the Mary Kingsley Medal to Dr Griffith Evans', *Annals of Tropical Medicine and Parasitology*, 12 (1918), 1–16.

27. J. Lloyd Williams, 'Ar yr Wyddfa gyda Dr Griffith Evans', *Western Mail*, 19 December 1935.

28. Griffith Evans Papers 421; Letter from [Rev. Principal], to Owen Prys, Trevecca College, Talgarth.

29. Ywain Goronwy ap Griffith, EVANS, GRIFFITH (1835–1935), microscopist, bacteriologist, and pioneer of protozoon pathology. Dictionary of Welsh Biography, *biography.wales/article/s-EVAN-GRI-1835*.

30. Gail Kincaid, personal communication.

31. Griffith Evans Papers 449; Letter from Griffith Evans, Stockholm, to Erie.

Chapter 15

1. Anon, 'Editorial. Griffith Evans, MRCVS, MD, C M', *The Journal of Tropical Veterinary Science*, 2/1 (1907), 1–3.

2. Anon, 'A Pioneer of Science. Remarkable Tribute', *The North Wales Express*, 31 May 1907.

3. William Osler, 'The haematozoa of malaria', *Transactions of the Pathological Society of Philadelphia*, 13 (1887), 255–76.

4. Anon, 'North Wales Medical Association. Proposed Welsh Medical School', *The North Wales Chronicle and Advertiser for the Principality*, 30 June 1916.

5. The collection is now in the Osler Library at McGill University in Montreal.

6. Griffith Evans Papers 111; Bound vol. of papers and correspondence brought together by Dr Erie Evans.

7. Anon, 'Sir William Osler Bt., MD, FRS, FRCP', *British Medical Journal*, 1/3079 (1920), 30–3.

8. Named after the nineteenth century writer and traveller in Africa. Griffith Evans Papers 107; Letter … informing Griffith Evans that the Committee had agreed to offer the medal to him.

9. *www.lstmed.ac.uk/about/history/mary-kingsley-medal*.

10. Anon, 'Siaced Fraith, Tro Griffith Evans', *Y Brython*, 20 Rhagfyr 1917, p. 3.

Griffith Evans

Edward Morgan, 'Ffetan y Gol, Arloesydd Bryn Cinallt', *Y Brython*, 29 Awst 1918, p. 3.
11. Griffith Evans Papers 474; Letter from Griffith Evans, Brynkynallt, to Erie.
12. Griffith Evans Papers 478; Letter from Sir Harry R. Reichel, U. C. Bangor, to Griffith Evans.

Chapter 16

1. The Reverend R. G. Owen, Minister of Pendref Chapel in Bangor told Jean Ware that, many years before, he had asked Dr Griffith Evans how he was. Evans had chuckled and replied, 'Enjoying a long sunset'.
2. J. Gwynn Williams, *The University College of North Wales: Foundations 1884–1927* (Cardiff: University of Wales Press, 1985).
3. The escape is described in the first published prisoner-of-war escape story: E. H. Jones, *The Road to Endor: A True Story of Cunning Wartime Escape* (London: Hesperus, 2014, first published by Bodley Head, London, 1919).
4. Griffith Evans Papers 292; John Drinkwater, Abraham Lincoln London, Sidgwick and Jackson Ltd., 1919, containing marginal notes made by Griffith Evans.
5. Griffith Evans Papers 592; Letter from Griffith Evans, to Erie.
6. Griffith Evans Papers 220; Bound vol. of typescripts, press cuttings, and photographs entitled 'Memories of Griffith Evans'.
7. Griffith Evans Papers 592.
8. Samuel Taylor Coleridge, *Dejection: an Ode* (1802).
9. The monument overlooking the Menai Straits was erected in memory of the first Marquis, Henry William Paget, who lost a leg at the battle of Waterloo.
10. Griffith Evans Papers 493; Letter from Fred Bullock, Secretary, RCVS, to Griffith Evans.
11. Griffith Evans Papers 494; Letter from Fred Bullock, Secretary, RCVS, to Griffith Evans.
   Griffith Evans Papers 496; Letter from Fred Bullock, Secretary, RCVS, to Griffith Evans.
12. Griffith Evans Papers 495; Letter from Griffith Evans, Brynkynallt, to [Fred] Bullock.
13. Griffith Evans Papers 596; Letter from Griffith Evans, to [n.d.] Sir Frederick [Smith, (1857–1929), Major-Gen., Army Veterinary Service].
14. Griffith Evans Papers 499; Letter from Sydney H. Slocock, President, RCVS, to Griffith Evans.
15. Ware and Hunt in *The Several Lives of a Victorian Vet* describe Evans as ordering 'fortiphones', early electronic hearing aids manufactured by Siemens.
16. Sir Frederick Smith, *A History of the Royal Army Veterinary Corps 1796–1919* (London: Baillière, Tindall and Cox, 1927).
17. Slower than normal heart rate.
18. Founded in 1831 for the promotion and development of science.

227

19. Anon, 'Great Scientist Forgotten. Nearly 100, and Bedridden', *Daily Herald*, 9 September 1930, p. 3.
20. Anon. 'One of the Greatest Living Scientists. Dr Evans' Researches in Punjab Recalled', *Civil and Military Gazette (Lahore)*, 12 September 1930, p. 6.
21. Griffith Evans Papers 112–15; Press cuttings relating to the presentation of the casket containing the Freedom of the city of Bangor to Griffith Evans.
22. Anon, 'Welsh Doctor's Life Work. Bitter Regret of Daughter. "Oblivion has been his lot"', *Western Mail*, 15 January 1931, p. 8.
23. Griffith Evans Papers 519; Letter from [Dr] Thomas R. Currie, Philadelphia, to Griffith Evans.
    Griffith Evans Papers 522; Letter from [Dr] Thomas R. Currie, Philadelphia, to Griffith Evans.
24. T. R. Currie M.D., 'The Discoverer of the Trypanosome', *Medical Life*, New Series No. 128 (1931), 311–4.
25. Griffith Evans Papers 220.
26. The Giant Nosebag Appeal was launched by the Royal Veterinary College to raise funds for the rebuilding of its Camden Campus. Centred on war horses and a dog that had survived the First World War, the appeal was phenomenally successful.
27. Griffith Evans Papers 111; Bound vol. of papers and correspondence brought together by Dr Erie Evans.

Chapter 17

1. Osler Library Archival Collection, McGill University, extracts from the journal of Griffith Evans, 1835–1935 [Partial content: body-snatching at McGill], Acc. 237.
2. R. F. Montgomerie, 'Dr Griffith Evans. The Profession's Centenarian. A Great Veterinary Scientist', *The Veterinary Record*, 15/31 (1935), 890–4.
3. Anon, 'Editorial. To Whom Honour is Due', *The Veterinary Record*, 15/31 (1935), 894–5.
4. *North Wales Chronicle* published a comprehensive account of the day's proceedings on 9 August 1935 and in a special supplement.
   Griffith Evans Papers 111; Bound vol. of papers and correspondence brought together by Dr Erie Evans.
5. Sir Frederick Hobday, 'Dr Griffith Evans, Centenarian, "At Home"', *The Veterinary Record*, 1/34 (1935), 1044–7.
6. Anon, 'Congratulations for Dr Evans. Welsh Centenarian, Veterinary College Tribute', *Manchester Guardian*, 8 August 1935, p. 2.
   In his account, Hobday describes the presentation as taking place at 11 a.m. rather than at 2.30 p.m. as claimed in Jean Ware and Hugh Hunt's *The Several Lives of a Victorian Vet*.
   Anon, 'Centenarian Veterinary Surgeon. Presentation of Illuminated Scroll', *The Times*, 8 August 1935, p. 6.
   Anon, 'Notes and News. Dr Griffith Evans. Centenary Message from their Majesties', *The Veterinary Record*, 15/32 (1935), 938.

7. An instrument for cutting thin sections of tissue for examination under the microscope.
8. Griffith Evans Papers 111.
9. Anon, 'Man who met Lincoln. The Civil War Observer with Grant's Army. Centenarian's Memories', *Manchester Guardian*, 23 March 1935, p. 13.
10. Anon, 'News and Views. Dr Griffith Evans', *Nature*, 136 (1935), 173.
11. Griffith Evans Papers 152; Edgar Dewitt Jones, DD, Detroit, Michigan, USA (to Dr Erie Evans); together with a copy made by Dr Erie Evans.
12. Anon, 'McGill University's Tribute to Dr Griffith Evans', *The Veterinary Record*, 15/43 (1935), 1287.
13. Griffith Evans Papers 146; Senate of McGill University (with Griffith Evans's draft reply).
14. Griffith Evans, 'Communications. Letter to Dr Srinivas Rao', *Indian Veterinary Journal*, 12(3) (1936), 281–4
    Griffith Evans, 'A Centenarian's Blessings', *Indian Veterinary Journal*, 12(3), (1936), 193–4.
    Anon, 'Obituary. Dr Griffith Evans, DSc (Wales), MD, CM, MRCVS. A Great Pioneer Veterinary Scientist', *Indian Veterinary Journal*, 12(3), (1936), 290–4.
    All included in Griffith Evans Papers 111.
15. *The Druids' Prayer* by Iolo Morganwg (Edward Williams, 1747–1826) sung at the Orsedd ceremonies at the National Eisteddfod of Wales.

Epilogue

1. Anon, 'Dr Griffith Evans. Pioneer work in Pathology', *The Times*, 9 December 1935, p. 19.
   Anon, 'Dr Griffith Evans Dead. One-hundred-year-old Vet', *Manchester Guardian*, 9 December 1935, p. 7.
   Anon, 'Noted Scientist. Death of Dr Griffith Evans. Britain's oldest V.S.', *The Scotsman*, 9 December 1935, p. 11.
   Anon, 'Dr Griffith Evans', *Nature*, 136 (1935), 251.
   Anon, 'Obituary. Dr Griffith Evans. A Great Pioneer Veterinary Scientist', *The Veterinary Record*, 15/50 (1935), 1514–16.
   Anon, 'Editorial. Years and Honour', *The Veterinary Record*, 15/50 (1935), 1516–17.
2. Anon, 'Noted Scientist. Death of Dr Griffith Evans. Britain's oldest V.S.', *The Scotsman*, 9 December 1935, p. 11.
3. Griffith Evans Papers 137; Medical Faculty of McGill University.
4. Anon, 'Surgeon, 100, is Dead', *Cincinnati Enquirer*, 9 December 1935, p. 4.
5. Anon, 'Aged War Veteran is Dead in Wales Dr Griffith Evans, 100, Fought for Union Army in Civil War', *Pittsburgh Press*, 9 December 1935, p. 31.
6. J. Gwynn Williams, *The University College of North Wales – Foundations 1884–1927* (Cardiff: University of Wales Press, 1985).
   David Roberts, *Bangor University 1884–2009* (Cardiff: University of Wales Press, 2009).

7. David Roberts, Personal communication.
   Anon, 'Bangor College Extension', *Western Mail*, 6 February 1936, p. 8.
8. Anon, '£1,400 for Memorial Wing', *Western Mail*, 11 May 1936, p. 7.
9. R. F. Montgomerie, 'Dr Griffith Evans. The Profession's Centenarian. A Great Veterinary Scientist', *The Veterinary Record*, 15/31 (1935), 890–4. Included in Griffith Evans Papers 111.
10. Anon, 'Bangor Scientist's £19,648.', *Liverpool Echo*, 26 February 1936, p. 16.
    Anon, 'Veterinary Pioneer's £19,648. Centenarian who made Big Discoveries', *Daily Herald*, 26 February 1936, p. 9.
11. Celt, 'Notable Doctors', *Liverpool Daily Post*, 23 August 1943.
12. Griffith Evans Papers 543; Letter from L. J. Kelly, Worthing, to Dr [Erie] Evans.
13. Edward Morgan, 'Readers' Views. Veterinary College for Wales', *Western Mail*, 3 August 1943, p. 3.
14. Edward Morgan, 'Our Readers' Views. Veterinary School needed in Wales. Question for the Livestock Commission. Faculty of Animal Husbandry. In connection with University College, Cardiff.', *Western Mail*, 15 October 1937, p. 11.
15. Edward Morgan, 'Readers' Views. Veterinary College for Wales.', *Western Mail*, 30 January 1946, p. 3.

BIBLIOGRAPHY

Anon, 'Examinations at the Royal College of Veterinary Surgeons', *The Veterinarian: A Monthly Journal of Veterinary Science*, 28 (1855), 370.

Anon, 'Reviews. A Veterinary Manual for the Use of Salootries and Native Horse-Owners in India. By J. J. Meyrick, MRCVS, Army Veterinary Inspector', *The Veterinary Journal and Annals of Comparative Physiology*, 13 (1881), 285–6.

Anon, 'Editorial. The Army Veterinary Department', *The Veterinary Journal and Annals of Comparative Physiology*, 14 (1882), 334–6.

Anon, 'Discussion of the operation for "roaring" in horses carried out at Woolwich', *Veterinary Journal*, 29 (1889), 115.

Anon, 'College News', *Magazine of the University College of North Wales*, 1/1 (1891), 34.

Anon, 'Action for Libel', *Manchester Guardian*, 28 July 1893, p. 8.

Anon, 'Verdict for Miss Hughes', *Manchester Guardian*, 31 July 1893, p. 8.

Anon, 'Editorial. Griffith Evans, MRCVS, MD, CM', *The Journal of Tropical Veterinary Science*, 2/1 (1907), 1–3.

Anon, 'A Pioneer of Science. Remarkable Tribute', *The North Wales Express*, 31 May 1907.

Anon, 'North Wales Medical Association. Proposed Welsh Medical School', *The North Wales Chronicle and Advertiser for the Principality*, 30 June 1916.

Anon, 'Presentation of the Mary Kingsley Medal to Griffith Evans', *Annals of Tropical Medicine and Parasitology*, 12 (1918), 1–16.

Anon, 'Sir William Osler Bt., MD, FRS, FRCP', *British Medical Journal*, 1/3079 (1920), 30–3.

Anon, 'Edgar March Crookshank MB', *British Medical Journal*, 2 (1928), 79.

Anon, 'Great Scientist Forgotten. Nearly 100, and Bedridden', *Daily Herald*, 9 September 1930, p. 3.

Anon, 'One of the Greatest Living Scientists. Dr Evans' Researches in Punjab Recalled', *Civil and Military Gazette (Lahore)*, 12 September 1930, p. 6.

Anon, 'Welsh Doctor's Life Work. Bitter Regret of Daughter. "Oblivion has been his lot"', *Western Mail*, 15 January 1931, p. 8.

Anon, 'Man who met Lincoln. The Civil War. Observer with Grant's Army. Centenarian's Memories', *Manchester Guardian*, 23 May 1935, p. 13.

Anon, 'Congratulations for Dr Evans. Welsh Centenarian, Veterinary College Tribute', *Manchester Guardian*, 8 August 1935, p. 2.

Anon, 'Centenarian Veterinary Surgeon. Presentation of Illuminated Scroll', *The Times*, 8 August 1935, p. 6.

Anon, 'Notes and News. Dr Griffith Evans. Centenary Message from their Majesties', *The Veterinary Record*, 15/32 (1935), 938.

Anon, 'News and Views. Dr Griffith Evans', *Nature*, 136 (1935), 173.

Anon, 'Dr Griffith Evans. Pioneer work in Pathology', *The Times*, 9 December 1935, p. 19.

Anon, 'Dr Griffith Evans Dead. One-hundred-year-old Vet', *Manchester Guardian*, 9 December 1935, p. 7.

Anon, 'Noted Scientist. Death of Dr Griffith Evans. Britain's oldest VS', *The Scotsman*, 9 December 1935, p. 11.

Anon, 'Obituary. Dr Griffith Evans. A Great Pioneer Veterinary Scientist', *The Veterinary Record*, 15/50 (1935), 1514–16.

Anon, 'Editorial. To Whom Honour is Due', *The Veterinary Record*, 15/31 (1935), 894–5.

Anon, 'Editorial. Years and Honour', *The Veterinary Record*, 15/50 (1935), 1516–17.

Anon, 'Surgeon, 100, is Dead', *Cincinnati Enquirer*, 9 December 1935, p. 4.

Anon, 'Aged War Veteran is Dead in Wales Dr Griffith Evans, 100, Fought for Union Army in Civil War', *Pittsburgh Press*, 9 December 1935, p. 31.

Anon, 'Dr Griffith Evans', *Nature*, 136 (1935), 251.

Anon, 'McGill University's Tribute to Dr Griffith Evans', *The Veterinary Record*, 15/43 (1935), 1287.

Anon, 'Bangor Scientist's £19,648', *Liverpool Echo*, 26 February 1936, p. 16.

Anon, 'Veterinary Pioneer's £19,648. Centenarian who made Big Discoveries', *Daily Herald*, 26 February 1936, p. 9.

Bates, A. W. H., *Anti-Vivisection and the Profession of Medicine in Britain: A Social History* (London: Springer Nature Ltd., 2017).

Briggs, A., 'Cobden and Bright', *History Today*, 7/8 (1957), 496–503.

Bruce, D., *Preliminary Report on the tsetse fly disease or nagana in Zululand* (Durban: Bennett and Davis, 1895).

Burton, R., *Anatomy of Melancholy* (Oxford: Lichfield and Short, 1621).

Cambau, E. and Drancourt, M., 'Steps towards the discovery of Mycobacterium tuberculosis by Robert Koch', *Clinical Microbiology and Infection*, 20/3 (2014), 196–201.

Codell Carter, K., 'The Koch-Pasteur dispute on establishing the cause of anthrax', *Bulletin of the History of Medicine*, 62/1 (1988), 42–57.

Cooke, B., *The Gathering of Infidels: A Hundred Years of the Rationalist Press Association* (New York: Prometheus, 2004).

Cotchin, E., *The Royal Veterinary College London: A Bicentenary History* (Buckingham: Barracuda, 1990).

Currie, T. R., 'The Discoverer of the Trypanosome', *Medical Life, New Series*, 128 (1931), 311–14.

Cule, J., 'The postulates of Griffith Evans MD, MRCVS (1835–1935) and the Specificity of Disease', in A. H. M. Kerkhoff, A. M. Luyendijk-Elshout and M. J. D. Poulissen (eds), *De Novis Inventis Essays in the History of Medicine in Honour of Daniel de Moulin on the Occasion of his 65th Birthday* (Amsterdam & Maarssen: APA – Holland University Press, 1984), pp. 81–93.

Desquesnes, M., Holzmuller, P., Lai, D-H., Dargantes, A., Lun, Z-R., Jittapalapong, S., 'Trypanosoma evansi and Surra: A Review and Perspectives on Origin, History, Distribution, Taxonomy, Morphology, Hosts and Pathogenic Effects', *Biomedical Research International*, (2013), 194176 published online.

Desquesnes, M., Dargantes, A., Lai, D-H., Lun, Z-R., Holzmuller, P., Jittapalapong, S., 'Trypanosoma evansi and Surra: A Review and Perspectives on Transmission, Epidemiology and Control, Impact and Zoonotic Aspects', *Biomedical Research International*, (2013), 321237 published online.

Drinkwater, J., *Abraham Lincoln* (Ann Arbor: University of Michigan, 2009).

Emmerson, G. S., *The Greatest Iron Ship: S.S. Great Eastern* (Newton Abbot: David and Charles, 1981).

Evans, G., 'The "Loodiana Disease," or "Malignant Fever" of India', *The Veterinary Journal and Annals of Comparative Pathology*, 6 (1878), 320–34.

Evans, G., 'On a horse disease in India known as "surra", probably due to a haematozoon', *The Veterinary Journal and Annals of Comparative Pathology*, 13 (1881–2), 1–10, 82–8, 180–200, 326–33.

Evans G., *Report by the Inspecting Veterinary Surgeon Griffith Evans MD on Surra, published by the Punjab Government Military Department, No. 439–44–67* (Calcutta: Punjab Government Military Department, 1881).

Evans, G., 'Miscellanea', *Folklore*, 3/2 (1892), 274–7.

Evans, G., 'Un Eglwys i Gymru', *Y Geninen*, 27(4) (1909), 183–6

Evans, G., 'A Centenarian's Blessings. A letter from Dr Griffith Evans to Dr Srinivasa Rao dated Brynkynallt 11 November 1935', *Indian Veterinary Journal*, 12/3 (1936), 193–4.

Fahey, D. M., 1979. 'The Politics of Drink: Pressure Groups and the British Liberal Party', *Social Science*, 54(2) (1979), 76–85.

Fleming, G., 'Veterinary Science – A Sketch', *Journal of Veterinary Science and Comparative Pathology*, 24 (1887), 247–53, 343–52.

Fleming, G., 'Physical Condition of Horses for Military Purposes', *Veterinary Journal*, 29 (1889), 42.

Foil, L. D., 'Tabanids as vectors of disease', *Parasitology Today*, 5/3 (1989), 88–96.

Frey, J., *The Indian Rebellion, 1857–1859: A Short History with Documents* (Indianapolis: Hackett Publishing Company, 2020).

Gray, E. A., 'John Hunter and veterinary medicine', *Medical History*, 1/1 (1957), 38–50.

Hanna, Jennifer, *Arlington House, The Robert E. Lee Memorial* (Washington DC: US Department of the Interior, 2001).

Harvey, Van A., 'Huxley's Agnosticism', *Philosophy Now*, 99 (2013), 10–2.

Hevia, James L., *Animal Labor and Colonial Warfare* (Chicago and London: University of Chicago Press, 2018).

Hobday, Sir Frederick, 'Dr Griffith Evans, Centenarian, "At Home"', *The Veterinary Record* 1/34 (1935), 1044–7.

Hunter, Pamela, *Veterinary Medicine: A Guide to Historical Sources* (Abingdon: Routledge, 2016).

Huxley, T. H., *Agnosticism and Christianity and other Essays* (New York: Prometheus Books, 1992).

Isaac, M., *Thomas Jones of Tregaron: Alias Twm Siôn Cati* (Caerleon: Apecs Press, 2009).

Javaeed, A., Qamar, S., Ali, S., Mustafa, M. A. T., Nusrat, A., Ghauri, S. K., 'Histological Stains in the past, present and future', *Cureus*, 13/10 (2021), e18486.

Jones, E. H., *The Road to Endor: A True Story of Cunning Wartime Escape* (London: Hesperus, 2014).

Kannadan, A., 'A history of the Miasma Theory of Disease', *ESSAI*, 16 (2018), Article 18.

Keegan, John, *The American Civil War* (London: Vintage, 2010).

King, L. S., 'Dr Koch's postulates', *Journal of the History of Medicine and Allied Sciences*, 7/4 (1952), 350–61.

Koch, R., 'An Address on Bacteriological Research', *British Medical Journal*, 2/1546 (1890), 380–3.

Lawrence, D. G., '"Resurrection" and Legislation or Body-snatching in relation to the Anatomy Act in the Province of Quebec', *Bulletin of the History of Medicine*, 32/5 (1958), 408–24.

Lewis, T. R., *On a Haematozoon Inhabiting Human Blood: its relation to Chyluria and other Diseases* (Calcutta: Office of the Superintendent of Government Printing, 1872).

Lewis, T. R., *The Pathological Significance of Nematode Haematozoa* (Calcutta: Office of the Superintendent of Government Printing, 1874).

Lewis, T. R., *The Microscopic Organisms found in the Blood of Man and Animals, and their Relation to Disease* (Calcutta: Office of the Superintendent of Government Printing, 1879).

Lewis, T. R., 'Flagellated Organisms in the Blood of Healthy Rats', *Quarterly Journal of Microscopical Science*, s2/19 (1879), 109–14.

Lewis, T. R., 'Remarks on a Nematoid Haematozoon discovered by Dr Griffith Evans in a Camel', *Proceedings of the Asiatic Society of Bengal*, (March 1882), 63–4.

Lewis, T. R., 'Further Observations on Flagellated Organisms in the Blood of Animals', *Quarterly Journal of Microscopical Science*, 2/24 (1884), 357–69.

Livingstone, David, *Missionary Travels and Researches in South Africa* (London: John Murray, 1857).

Lloyd Williams, J., 'Ar yr Wyddfa gyda Dr Griffith Evans', *Western Mail*, 19 December 1835.

Marlow, Joyce (ed.), *Suffragettes: The Fight for Votes for Women* (London: Virago, 2015).

Metchnikoff, E., 'Untersuchungen über die mesodermalen Phagocyten einiger Wirbeltiere', *Biologisches Centralblatt*, 3 (1883), 560–5.

Metchnikoff, E., *Immunity in infective Diseases, Binnie, F.G. (transl.)* (Cambridge: Cambridge University Press, 1905).

Meyrick, J. J., 'Correspondence, etc. The Army Veterinary Department', *The Veterinary Journal and Annals of Comparative Physiology*, 14 (March 1882), 226–9.

Mishra, S., 'Beasts, Murrains, and the British Raj: Reassessing Colonial Medicine in India from a Veterinary Perspective, 1860–1900', *Bulletin of the History of Medicine*, 85/4 (2011), 587–619.

Molinari, J. and Moreno, S. A., 'Trypanosoma brucei (Plimmer and Bradford, 1899) is a synonym of T. evansi (Steel, 1885)', *Systemmatic Parasitology*, 95/2–3 (2018), 249–56.

Morgan, E., 'Our Readers' Views. Veterinary School needed in Wales. Question for the Livestock Commission. Faculty of Animal Husbandry. In connection with University College, Cardiff', *Western Mail*, 15 October 1937, p. 11.

Morgan, E., 'Readers' Views. Veterinary College for Wales', *Western Mail*, 3 August 1943, p. 3.

Morgan, E., 'Readers' Views. Veterinary College for Wales', *Western Mail*, 30 January 1946, p. 3.

Montgomerie, R. F., 'Dr Griffith Evans. The Profession's Centenarian. A Great Veterinary Scientist', *The Veterinary Record*, 15/31 (1935), 890–4.

Murray, J. F., 'A Century of Tuberculosis', *American Journal of Respiratory and Critical Care Medicine*, 169/11 (2004), 1181–6.

Osler, W., 'The haematozoa of malaria', *Transactions of the Pathological Society of Philadelphia*, 13 (1887), 255–76.

Pasteur, Louis, *Sur les corpuscules organisés qui existent dans l'atmosphère: Examen de la doctrine des générations spontanées. Leçon Professée a la Société Chimique de Paris, le 19 Mai* (Paris: Imprimerie de Ch. Lahure et Cie., 1861).

Pasteur, L. et Joubert, J. F., 'Charbon et septicemie', *Comptes rendus hebdomadaires des séances de l'Académie des sciences*, 85 (1887), 101–15.

Rao, P. S., 'Obituary. Dr Griffith Evans, D.Sc (Wales), MD, CM, MRCVS. A Great Pioneer Veterinary Scientist', *Indian Veterinary Journal*, 12/3 (1936), 290–4.

Roberts, David, *Bangor University 1884–2009* (Cardiff: University of Wales Press, 2009).

Robson, Brian, *The Road to Kabul: The Second Afghan War 1878–1881* (Cheltenham: The History Press, 2008).

Singh, V. and Parsani, H. R., 'Trypanosomas evansi – an emerging threat to humans', in V. Tandon, A. K. Yadav and B. Roy (eds), *Current Trends in Parasitology, Proceedings of the 20th International Congress of Parasitology, Shillong, India* (New Dehli: Panina Publishing Corporation, 2008), 61–4.

Smith, F., 'Preliminary note on the surgical cure for roaring due to laryngeal paralysis', *Veterinary Journal and Annals of Comparative Pathology*, 27, 1–10.

Smith, Sir F., *A History of the Royal Army Veterinary Corps 1796–1919* (London: Baillière, Tindall and Cox, 1927).

Smith, W., 'Philip Bruce White', *Obituaries of Fellows of the Royal Society*, 7/19 (1950), 278–92.

Stacey, C. P., 'The Defense Problem and Canadian Confederation', *Revista de Historia de América*, 138 (2007), 169–75.

Steel, J. H., *Report of Veterinary Surgeon J. H. Steel, A.V.D., on his investigation into an obscure and fatal disease among transport mules in British Burma, which he found to be a fever of relapsing type, and probably identical with the disorder first described by Dr Griffith Evans under the name "Surra", in a report (herewith printed) published by the Punjab Government, Military Department, No. 439–4467, of 3rd December 1880 – vide the Veterinary Journal (London), 1881–1882* (Calcutta: Government of India, 1886).

Steel, J. H., 'On Relapsing Fever of Equines', *The Veterinary Journal and Annals of Comparative Physiology*, 22 (1886), 166–74.

Steverding, D., 'The History of African Trypanosomiasis', *Parasite Vectors*, 1/1 (2008), 1–8.

Steverding, D., 'The development of drugs for the treatment of sleeping sickness: a historical review', *Parasites and Vectors*, 3/1 (2010), 15.

Tulchinsky, T. H., 'John Snow, Cholera, the Broad Street Pump: Waterborne Diseases Then and Now', *Case Studies in Public Health*, (2018), 77–99 (published online).

Vineberg, R., 'The British Garrison and Montreal Society, 1830–1850', *Canadian Military History*, 21 (2012), 3–16.

Ware, J., 'The Life and Letters of Griffith Evans' (unpublished MA thesis University College of North Wales, 1966).

Ware, J. and Hunt, H., *The Several Lives of a Victorian Vet* (London: Bachman and Turner, 1979).

Williams, J. G., 1985. *The University College of North Wales: Foundations 1884–1927* (Cardiff: University of Wales, 1985).

INDEX

Illustrations are indicated by page numbers in bold.

poverty, 11, 18
preventative medicine, 38
Prichard Jones Hall, 179
Primitive Cultures (Tylor), 168
Principles of Geology (Lyell), 168
Pritchard, William, 16
Prys, Owen, 170
psychology, 168, 187, 191
Pugh, Mair, 10
Pughe, John, 11–12, 76
Punjab Frontier Force, 115
Pwllheli, 170

Q
Québec, 33, 79; *see also* Montreal

R
Ramsay, George, 57
Rao, P. Srinivasa, 203–4
rationalism, 7, 9, 11, 162, 179
Rationalist Press Association, 162
rats, 127–8, 129, 133–4
Rayer, Pierre François, 92
Reading, 30
red corpuscles, 119
Redi, Francesco, 92
Rees, Mary, 78, 86, 112
Rees, William, 78, 86, 109–10
Regents Park Zoological Gardens, 18
Reiuchel, Henry, 178
revolutions of 1848, 11
Richmond, 61, 62–3, 64, 68
roaring, 153
Roberts, Frederick, 144
Roberts, John, 6
Roberts, J. Bryn, 163
Roberts, William, 134, 158

Robyn Ddu Eryri, 80
Rogers, Leonard, 125–6
Royal Artillery, 23–6, **24**, 29–33, 35–50, 76, 79–80, 86, 146–53
Royal College of Physicians, 150
Royal College of Surgeons, 150
Royal College of Veterinary Surgeons, 144, 150, 178, 183–4, 209
Royal Commission on Vivisection, 149–50
Royal Horse Artillery Infirmary, 23, 30
Royal Irish Dragoon Guards, 30–1
Royal London Ophthalmic Hospital, 84
Royal Society, 150, 167
Royal Veterinary College, 2–4, 12–13, 15–19, 150, 183, 192–3, 195, 198–200

S
Sagar Island, 100, 101–2
St James Palace, 152
St James River, 57, 61, 63, 70
St Lawrence River, 33, 41, 42, 43, 45, 53
Ste Marie, M. 43–4, 45
St Paul Island, 33
St Stephen's Church, Ooty, 137
Saratoga, 73
Savage, W. H., 195
scientific advances, 18, 92, 168
Scotland, 40–1, 202
Scotsman, 207
Scott, Edward, 7
Second Afghan War, 106–7, 115
Sen, Keshub Chandra, 106
Sewell, William, 3